Lecture Notes
in Business Information Processing   334

More information about this series at http://www.springer.com/series/7911

David Aveiro · Giancarlo Guizzardi
Sérgio Guerreiro · Wided Guédria (Eds.)

Advances in Enterprise Engineering XII

8th Enterprise Engineering Working Conference, EEWC 2018
Luxembourg, Luxembourg, May 28 – June 1, 2018
Proceedings

 Springer

Editors
David Aveiro 🄳
University of Madeira and Madeira
Interactive Technologies Institute
Funchal, Portugal

Sérgio Guerreiro 🄳
Instituto Superior Técnico,
Universidade de Lisboa
Lisbon, Portugal

Giancarlo Guizzardi
Free University of Bozen-Bolzano
Bolzano, Brazil

Wided Guédria
Luxembourg Institute of Science
and Technology
Esch-sur-Alzette, Luxembourg

ISSN 1865-1348   ISSN 1865-1356 (electronic)
Lecture Notes in Business Information Processing
ISBN 978-3-030-06096-1   ISBN 978-3-030-06097-8   (eBook)
https://doi.org/10.1007/978-3-030-06097-8

Library of Congress Control Number: 2018964608

This Springer imprint is published by the registered company Springer Nature Switzerland AG
The registered company address is: Gewerbestrasse 11, 6330 Cham, Switzerland

Preface

The CIAO! Enterprise Engineering Network (CEEN) is a community of academics and practitioners who strive to contribute to the development of the discipline of enterprise engineering (EE) and to apply it in practice. The aim is to develop a holistic and general systems theory-based understanding on how to (re)design and run enterprises effectively. The ambition is to develop a consistent and coherent set of theories, models, and associated methods that: enable enterprises to reflect, in a systematic way, on how to realize improvements; and assist them, in practice, in achieving their aspirations.

In doing so, sound empirical and scientific foundations should underlie all efforts and all organizational aspects that are relevant should be considered, while combining already existing knowledge from the scientific fields of information systems, software engineering, management, as well as philosophy, semiotics, and sociology, among others. In other words, the (re)design of an enterprise and the subsequent implementation of changes should be the consequence of rationalized decisions that: take into account the nature and reality of the enterprise and its environment; and respect relevant empirical and scientific principles.

Enterprises are systems whose reality has a dual nature by being simultaneously, on one hand, centrally and purposefully (re)designed, and, on the other hand, emergent in a distributed way, given the fact that its main agents, the humans that are the pearls of the organization, act with free will in a creative and in a responsible (or sometimes not) way. We acknowledge that, in practice, the development of enterprises is not always a purely rational/evidence-based process. As such, we believe the field of EE aims to provide evidence-based insights into the design and evolution of enterprises and the consequences of different choices irrespective of the way decisions are made.

The origin of the scientific foundations of our present body of knowledge is the CIAO! Paradigm (Communication, Information, Action, Organization) as expressed in our Enterprise Engineering Manifesto and the paper "The Discipline of Enterprise Engineering." In this paradigm, organization is considered to emerge in human communication, through the intermediate roles of information and action. Based on the CIAO! Paradigm, several theories have been developed and are still being proposed. They are published as technical reports.

The CEEN welcomes proposals of improvements to our current body of knowledge, as well as the inclusion of compliant and alternative views, always keeping in mind the need to maintain global systemic coherence, consistency, and scientific rigor of the entire EE body of knowledge as a prerequisite for the consolidation of this new engineering discipline. Yearly events like the Enterprise Engineering Working Conference and associated Doctoral Consortium are organized to promote the presentation of EE research and application in practice, as well as discussions on the contents and current state of our body of theories and methods.

Since 2005, the CEEN has organized the CIAO! Workshop and, since 2008, its proceedings have been published as *Advances in Enterprise Engineering* in the

Springer LNBIP series. From 2011 on, this workshop was replaced by the Enterprise Engineering Working Conference (EEWC). This volume contains the proceedings of the 8th EEWC, held in Luxembourg. There were 24 submissions. Each submission was reviewed (double blind) by three Program Committee members and the decision was to accept nine full papers and three short papers, which were carefully reviewed and selected for inclusion in this volume.

The EEWC aims at addressing the challenges that modern and complex enterprises are facing in a rapidly changing world. The participants of the working conference share a belief that dealing with these challenges requires rigorous and scientific solutions, focusing on the design and engineering of enterprises. The goal of EEWC is to stimulate interaction between the different stakeholders, scientists, as well as practitioners interested in making EE a reality.

May 2018

David Aveiro
Giancarlo Guizzardi
Sérgio Guerreiro
Wided Guédria

Organization

EEWC 2018 was the eighth Working Conference resulting from a series of successful CIAO! Workshops and EEWC Conferences over the past few years. These events were aimed at addressing the challenges that modern and complex enterprises are facing in a rapidly changing world. The participants in these events share the belief that dealing with these challenges requires rigorous and scientific solutions, focusing on the design and engineering of enterprises.

This conviction has led to the effort of annually organizing an international working conference on the topic of enterprise engineering, in order to bring together all stakeholders interested in making enterprise engineering a reality. This means that not only scientists are invited, but also practitioners. Moreover, it also means that the conference is aimed at active participation, discussion, and exchange of ideas in order to stimulate future cooperation among the participants. This makes EEWC a working conference contributing to the further development of enterprise engineering as a mature discipline.

The organization of EEWC 2018 and the peer review of the contributions to the conference were accomplished by an outstanding international team of experts in the fields of enterprise engineering. The following is the organizational structure of EEWC 2018.

Advisory Board

Antonia Albani	University of St. Gallen, Switzerland
Jan Dietz	Delft University of Technology, The Netherlands

Conference Chairs

Henderik A. Proper	Luxembourg Institute of Science and Technology, Luxembourg
Jan Verelst	University of Antwerp, Belgium

Program Chairs

David Aveiro	University of Madeira and Madeira Interactive Technologies Institute, Portugal
Giancarlo Guizzardi	Free University of Bozen-Bolzano, Italy

Organizing Chair

Wided Guédria	Luxembourg Institute of Science and Technology, Luxembourg

Program Committee

Alberto Silva	INESC and University of Lisbon, Portugal
Carlos Pascoa	University of Lisbon, Portugal
Christian Huemer	Vienna University of Technology, Austria
David Aveiro	University of Madeira, Portugal
Duarte Gouveia	University of Madeira, Portugal
Eduard Babkin	Higher School of Economics, Nizhny Novgorod, Russia
Florian Matthes	Technical University Munich, Germany
Frank Harmsen	Maastricht University and Ernst & Young Advisory, The Netherlands
Geert Poels	Ghent University, Belgium
Giancarlo Guizzardi	Free University of Bozen-Bolzano, Italy
Graham McLeod	University of Cape Town and Inspired.org, South Africa
Hans Mulder	University of Antwerp, Belgium
Jan Dietz	Delft University of Technology, The Netherlands
Jan Hoogervorst	Sogeti Netherlands, The Netherlands
Jens Gulden	University of Duisburg-Essen, Germany
Joao Paulo Almeida	Federal University of Espírito Santo, Brazil
Jose Tribolet	INESC and University of Lisbon, Portugal
Joseph Barjis	Institute of Engineering and Management, San Francisco, CA, USA
Junichi Iijima	Tokyo Institute of Technology, Japan
Marcello Bax	Federal University of Minas Gerais, Brazil
Martin Op 't Land	Capgemini, The Netherlands; University of Antwerp, Belgium
Mauricio Almeida	Federal University of Minas Gerais, Brazil
Miguel Mira Da Silva	INESC and University of Lisbon, Portugal
Monika Kaczmarek	University Duisburg Essen, Germany
Niek Pluijmert	INQA Quality Consultants, The Netherlands
Peter Loos	University of Saarland, Germany
Petr Kremen	Czech Technical University in Prague, Czech Republic
Philip Huysmans	University of Antwerp, Belgium
Rony Flatscher	Wirtschaftsuniversität Wien, Austria
Sérgio Guerreiro	INESC and University of Lisbon, Portugal
Steven van Kervel	Formetis, The Netherlands
Stijn Hoppenbrouwers	HAN University of Applied Sciences, The Netherlands
Sybren de Kinderen	University of Luxembourg, Luxembourg
Tatiana Poletaeva	Higher School of Economics, Nizhny Novgorod, Russia
Tiago Prince Sales	University of Trento, Italy
Ulrik Franke	Swedish Defense Research Agency, Sweden

Contents

On Architecture

The Institutional Logic of Harmonization: Local Versus Global Perspectives

Maximilian Brosius[(⊠)], Stephan Aier, M. Kazem Haki, and Robert Winter

Institute of Information Management, University of St. Gallen, St. Gallen, Switzerland
{maximilian.brosius,stephan.aier, kazem.haki,robert.winter}@unisg.ch

Abstract. Perspectives in organizations differ to which extent information systems (IS) should be tailored towards local (e.g., business unit) needs or toward organization-wide, global goals (e.g., synergies, integration). For contributing to overall IS performance success, the harmonization of different perspectives becomes essential. While many scholars have highlighted the role of IS management approaches, institutional studies argue that harmonization is not solely the result of managerial action, but a consequence of institutional pressures that guide organizational decision-making. In the paper at hand, we follow the call for adopting institutional theory on the intra-organizational level of analysis and study the logic of attaining harmonization along institutional pressures. By means of a revelatory case study, we find harmonization attained in a dynamic interplay between different institutional pressures. Mimetic pressures influence normative pressures, which in turn influence coercive pressures. Our findings as well as our implications for enterprise engineering guide prospective research in studying the attainment of harmonization through an institutional lens.

Keywords: Institutional theory · Institutional pressures · Harmonization

1 Introduction

In virtue of ever-growing complex organizational environments, perspectives on the development of information systems (IS) differ on whether to meet local business needs or organization-wide, global IS performance goals [1]. While tailored IS solutions may support local business unit operations [2], cost efficiencies and synergies are said to become realized through aligned and consistent IS landscapes at the global level, which requires harmonization efforts [3]. Consequently, it has become the underpinning rationale of numerous IS management approaches to harmonize local (i.e. business unit) needs with global (i.e. organization-wide) goals [4]. Yet, Mignerat and Rivard [5, p. 369] posit that researchers might not be able to explain "everything that happens in organizations by considering only rational actions of managers". For studying how global goals are achieved, the *institutional logic* that surrounds decision-makers in exercising their tasks needs to be considered, and requires a closer investigation [6].

© Springer Nature Switzerland AG 2019
D. Aveiro et al. (Eds.): EEWC 2018, LNBIP 334, pp. 3–17, 2019.
https://doi.org/10.1007/978-3-030-06097-8_1

Institutional logic is defined as the patterns of rules, values, assumptions, and beliefs by which individuals (re-)produce their material subsistence, organize time and space, and provide meaning to their social reality [7]. It intends to explain the formal and informal rationales of action and interaction for accomplishing organizational goals and tasks [8, 9]. Institutional logic is promoted by institutional theory, which is among the most vibrant theoretical lenses in IS research [5]. However, to date, institutional theory has been applied mainly at the *inter-organizational* level, i.e. explaining harmonization between organizations.

In the paper at hand, we follow several calls in the root discipline of institutional theory [10–13] as well as in IS research [5] and take an *intra-organizational* perspective through a revelatory case study of a highly decentralized organization. High decentralization is a well-suited structure for our purpose as it helps to translate the setting of pressures among different organizations into a setting of pressures among different units within an organization. We thus aim to learn how the distinctive influence of each pressure alone as well as the dynamic influence of pressures interacting (e.g., shaping, constraining, or constituting each other among different units) contribute to the attainment of harmonization. We seek to answer the following research question:

What is the institutional logic of harmonization in a decentralized organization?

The remainder of this paper is structured as follows: first, we provide the theoretical foundation, i.e. institutional theory, its state of research in IS, as well as the research gap along which we position our contribution. Next to the research method, the case analysis is presented, following the reflection of institutional pressures and their influence. We conclude by discussing implications of our insights for future research.

2 Theoretical Background

2.1 Institutional Theory

Institutional theory [14–16] understands organizations as social constructions, which seek to gain legitimacy in their environment. To gain legitimacy, organizations must adhere to assumptions, values, beliefs, and rules that are prevailing in their environment. In turn, adhering to a common set of assumptions, values, beliefs, and rules leads organizations to become homogenous over each other, i.e. a state of harmonization, which shapes and constrains organizational action and behavior [8].

Numerous theorists have contributed to explain how harmonization becomes attained. More prominently, regulative, normative, and cultural systems have been associated by theorists as "vital ingredients of institutions" [8, p. 59]. These associations are particularly reflected in the three *institutional pressures* introduced by Dimaggio and Powell [16], namely, *coercive*, *normative*, and *mimetic pressures*. Theory further argues that each pressure is catered by types of *carriers*, namely, symbolic systems (coded meaningful information), relational systems (horizontal and vertical structures fostering commitment), activities (actions, routines), and artifacts (objects, materials) [8]. Coercive pressures build on the logic of instrumentality, through which organizations constrain and regularize behavior. Rules, laws, or sanctions are prominent carriers. Normative pressures introduce an obligatory dimension into social life to which behaviors can be compared. Normative pressures are typically carried by values, norms, and standards, building on the logic of appropriateness and social obligations. Finally, mimetic pressures result from similar responses to uncertainty and refer to the imitation of one organization seen by another as more legitimate or successful, following the logic of perceived benefits. Observation, communication, and the work climate are prominent carriers of mimetic pressures.

IS research has applied institutional theory as a lens on a variety of settings, such as IS innovation, IS implementation, and IS adoption [5, 17]. A growing body of work thereby explicates the importance of institutional pressures on the inter-organizational level, leading to harmonized courses of action between organizations [5]. For instance, Teo et al. [18] found that all three pressures work in parallel and respectively have an influence on an organization's intention to adopt IS. However, they found that pressures' effects vary in strength with regards to the level of exertion (competitors, parent organization, customers, and suppliers). Pressures also vary due to different firm characteristics (i.e. dominant/less dominant market player), a perspective that has been promoted by Bala and Venkatesh [19]. While working simultaneously, pressures are also shaped by external influences: Liang et al. [20], for instance, examined mediating effects on external institutional pressures, highlighting the role of top management on information technology (IT) assimilation. Furthermore, the combination of institutional pressures may vary over time. For instance, Benders et al. [21] found varying effects and strengths of institutional pressures over several IS adoption phases. Finally, Nielsen et al. [17] demonstrated that organizations change their responses to institutional pressures over time. Their findings broadened the understanding of institutional pressures, reflecting organizational concerns of conformity and nonconformity.

2.2 Intended Contribution

To date, the existing discourses in IS research on institutional theory mainly refer to the *inter-organizational level*, studying the influence of pressures on harmonization between organizations [5]. According to Mignerat and Rivard's [5] review of 53 IS studies that adopt institutional theory, only two focused the intra-organizational level. In line with Greenwood et al.'s [13] outline in organization science, Mignerat and Rivard [5] motivate the adoption of institutional theory on the intra-organizational level —such as on/among units—for future IS research. We follow their call and study the attainment of harmonization along institutional pressures on the *intra-organizational level*.

Furthermore, the discourses in IS research illustrate pressures to work in combination [5], in different organizational contexts [e.g., 18], as well as in different temporal circumstances [21]. By shifting the focus from the organization as such to different units within an organization, we assume that harmonization may be explained by more than just the distinctive influence of each pressure separately. Particularly, we aim to account for the dynamics of institutional pressures interacting among different units, which may be shaping, constraining, or even constituting one another.

To develop a first understanding of how institutional pressures lead to harmonization in an intra-organizational setting, we study the *institutional logic*. Institutional logic intends to explain the patterns of rules, values, assumptions, and beliefs (i.e. carriers of institutional pressures) by which individuals (re-)produce their material subsistence, organize time and space, and provide meaning to their social reality [7]. It explains the formal and informal rationales of action and interaction for accomplishing organizational goals and tasks [8, 9]. For our purpose, it may help to explain how local (i.e. business and IS) needs become harmonized with global business and IT goals. As organizations are infused with various (often competing) rationales of what constitutes global goals and how to pursue these, institutional logic may be well-suited to explain the distinctive as well as the dynamic influence of institutional pressures in place [22]. In recent years, institutional logic has been pertinently used for explaining how intra-organizational processes affect organizational goals, change, and success [23–25].

3 Research Method

Case studies are a dominantly used approach for studying institutional logic [23, 26, 27]. We selected a single case along the criteria of criticalness and revelatory insights, conducting a series of twelve semi-structured interviews [28]. Following our research objective, we opted for a highly decentralized organization, operating under labor division and granted autonomy. This structure may be well-suited to explain how unbounded local units, focused on meeting specific demands of their respective customers, may become guided toward global goals. High decentralization also helped us magnifying the focus on the (dynamic) influence of institutional pressures within and between different units as well as between local and global levels.

3.1 Case Description

The case organization is one of the Europe's leading providers of public services in its respective field. With a yearly operating budget of over €200 million and more than 3,000 employees, it supplies its services to over 8,000 international customers on three continents namely, South America, Europe, and Eastern Asia. Additionally, the organization has over 50 partnership agreements with peer organizations around the world. The organization is structured highly decentralized: while adhering to shared global goals, the attainment of these goals is left autonomously in the hands of its local units. Overall, the organization offers four types of services. The first is a standardized service for a heterogeneous market of about 7,000 customers. The second is specialized and tailored to an exclusive market of around 1,000 customers. The third service type is a knowledge-centered public service, offered to a small market of international experts. The fourth service type is also knowledge-centered, however, mostly offered locally.

Global Business. The organization is operating under a global management board. Its president is temporarily elected out of the over 100 local business unit managers, being responsible for supervising the legitimacy of internal decisions. Three vice-presidents support the president in the fields of services, internal operations, and international relations. While decisions are exercised through the board of management, decision-making is commissioned by an authorized committee. This committee consolidates goals and interests of local units by the leading business unit managers, who are members of this committee.

Global IT. The global IT department employs around 50 full-time equivalents and is headed by the Chief Information Officer (CIO). The CIO manages the project portfolio and stands in close contact with the global business. In total, up to 50 projects on different levels of complexity are run simultaneously by the global IT department, ranging from large, global transformation projects to daily business incidents.

Local Business. In total, there are over 1,000 local employees and over 100 leading service managers in around 40 business units. While specialized on their respective market segment, they operate autonomously. For service types 1 and 2, business units are interdependent and have to align their activities with other local units and the global business level. Service types 3 and 4 follow individual market segments. As local units are not interdependent in service 3 and 4, no alignment is necessary there.

Local IT. The local IT are independently operating units in the organization and complement the global IT. The business support as well as their modes of operation lie autonomously in the hands of the local IT. Currently, five business units exclusively employ local IT for their operational support. The strengths of the local IT are primarily a quicker and more flexible mode of operation—as compared to the global IT—such as in technological (e.g., tool support, incidents) and business process solutions.

3.2 Data Collection

The data collection took place between November 2016 and November 2017. The collection comprised empirical data from primary and secondary sources.

Primary sources refer to the interviews conducted in the organization. In total, we conducted twelve semi-structured interviews under the thematic frame of the three institutional pressures. Each of the three interview parts started with a structured question, followed by an open discussion for collecting carriers of institutional pressures:

(1) Coercive: "What are the rules, laws, regulations, guidelines or sanctions that direct local goals to global goals?"
(2) Normative: "What are the behaviors, norms, values, ideals, or philosophies that direct local goals to global goals?"
(3) Mimetic: "What are your perceptions, thoughts, beliefs, routines or best-practices that direct local goals to global goals?

Following our research objectives of understanding the logic of harmonization from an organizational (not solely IS-specific) perspective, interviewees were chosen from four distinct areas (Table 1): business global, business local, IT global, and IT local. All interviews were recorded and transcribed. Complementing our interviews by secondary sources allowed a triangulation of the data. We used different sources to gain an in-depth understanding of the organization's structure, goals, functions, roles, and dependencies. We studied organigrams, regulations, job descriptions, annual reports, strategies, mission/vision statements, newspaper articles and the content of webpages.

Table 1. Profiles of interviewees

Role		Function (length)
Global business	Vice-president	Director of internal operations (60 min)
	Vice-president	Director of administration (60 min)
	Vice-president	Director of corporate services (60 min)
Global IT	CIO	Director of IT administration and services (90 min)
	Head of global unit	Responsible for service evolution (60 min)
Local business	Head of local unit	Mainly engaged in service 1, 2, and 3 (60 min)
	Head of local unit	Mainly engaged in service 4 (60 min)
	Head of local unit	Engaged in service 1, 2, 3, and 4 (60 min)
	Head of local unit	Engaged in service 1, 2, 3, and 4 (60 min)
	Member of local unit	Mainly engaged in service 1 and 3 (90 min)
Local IT	IT service manager	Engaged in central IT administration (60 min)
	Head of local IT	Engaged in local IT administration/services (90 min)

3.3   Scheme-Guided Analysis

Following Miles and Hubermann [29] as well as Eisenhardt [30], the data analysis was divided into two phases: *coding* and *case analysis* (next section). The coding scheme was developed based on the three institutional pressures promoted by institutional theory [8]. These were studied on both local (operational units) and global (administrative units) levels. Table 2 illustrates our analysis scheme (adapted from [8]).

Table 2. Coding scheme (adapted from [8])

Pressures	Coercive	Normative	Mimetic
Global level	Examples:	Examples:	Examples:
Local level	• Rules, regulations	• Values, norms	• Thoughts, beliefs
	• Sanctions	• Standards	• Shared understanding
	• Incentives	• Expectations	• Work culture/climate

We coded the entire case transcript using Atlas.ti software. In order to identify institutional pressures, we followed Scott's [8, p. 60] theoretical descriptions as well as illustrative examples of carriers (Table 2). Consistent with Scott [8], we considered the reflection of pressures via symbolic systems, relational systems, activities, and artifacts.

4   Case Analysis

In the following, we describe the identified carriers reflecting the pressures that contribute to the attainment of harmonization in the organization. Consistent with our focus of analysis, we study the reflection of pressures on global and local business and IT levels. We report on the both distinctive (i.e. separate) as well as dynamic (i.e. interacting) influence of pressures.

4.1   Institutional Pressures

Coercive Pressures. At the global business level, coercive pressures are carried by the overall vision and strategy. Vision and strategy reflect negotiated compromises of the organization's committee. They comprise a global business orientation, which is used to initiate and direct local change and development projects. Furthermore, the global business monitors and evaluates standards of local business service. Together with the global business, the global IT develops IT-related parts of the overall strategy. For operationalizing IT-related strategies, the global IT is in constant negotiation with the global business for the allocation of budgets. Toward the local business, the global IT is required to steer IT developments that either operationalize global goals or non-standardized business support solutions. Despite these regulations, the global IT is granted autonomy in pursuing technological support for the local business.

On the local business level, coercive pressures are reflected in the standardization of services, in strict definitions of service processes and minimum quality requirements. For developing technological solutions to which no standardized products exist, the global business requires mandatory consultancies from local business units with the IT. Despite these consultancies and the minimum quality requirements, there are no coercive pressures on the operations of local business units. Moreover, autonomy is granted by the regulation not to regulate local units' operations. By granted autonomy, local units specialize in tasks and labor to supply their services to their respective market, guided by the global frame of vision and strategies. The local IT is constrained by budgets, which are allocated by the global IT and the local business level. For services that support the global IT, the local IT takes advantage of financial subsidies from the global IT. Yet, the operationalization of local business demands lies autonomously in the hands of the local IT and is not further regulated.

Normative Pressures. At the global business level, normative pressures are carried by norms, values, and the overall identity. Norms focus the generation of quality and innovativeness in outputs and services, comprising desired performance toward the customer. Values refer to the organization's brand and reputation, creating a common desire of belonging and foster the motivation to actively engage in corporate development. Another major carrier of normative pressures is the committee, which comprises over 100 representatives from global and local levels with the goal of corporate development. While decisions are executed at the global business level, the committee collects and negotiates contesting and potentially conflicting local goals and expectations, fostering a compromise among these. Compromises then become externalized in vision and strategies. Finally, identity is among the normative pressures, carrying the meaning attached to goals that are negotiated among local and global levels. Moreover, identity encompasses shared expectations, such as toward roles and contributions. The global IT shares values and norms of the global business, understanding its role as supporting function for the global business. In order to excel support, the global IT employs high standards of technical resources deployment as well as personnel capabilities. Due to high standards, the global IT becomes involved in organizational development regarding IT-related aspects in global vision and strategies.

As local units serve different markets, they differ with regards to norms and values. Expectations to pursue these values are also specific, differing particularly within local units: while having a strong team focus, unit members value specializations in tasks as well as their different levels of knowledge and expertise. In turn, they value pro-active engagement in corporate development. As local unit representatives are members of the committee, contesting and potentially conflicting goals, norms, values, and expectations become mutually negotiated toward a global compromise. Operating autonomously, the local IT understands its role as a flexible business support provider. Local IT units operate directly with the business, independently from global supervision. Service orientation, while not directly delivering on the organization's output, drives the local IT. The mode of working within the local IT is similarly characterized by a high degree of flexibility in pursuing operations (emphasizing a service way of thinking).

Mimetic Pressures. At the global business level, mimetic pressures are triggered by transparent communication channels and an endorsed feedback culture. Transparent channels of communication foster the exchange of knowledge and experience among global and local levels. Thereby, the global business learns how overall goals are operationalized, and what best practices or performance challenges resulted. In this vein, personal contact and bilateral communication between global and local representatives is valued and encouraged for a shared understanding on corporate development. Besides, the global business learns from the observation of industry competitors. At the global IT level, mimetic pressures are also triggered by observations: on the one side, the global IT observes the global business in joint operations, learning from a centralized body operating in a comparable administration function. On the other side, global IT units observe industry competitors in regular peer meetings, where project management practices, success stories, and field reports are shared. Communication and reporting channels as well as bilateral contact among global IT representatives follow this relation. Learnings and experience are also shared with the local IT based on personal contacts as well as the bilateral exchange of knowledge and best practices.

At the local business level, mimetic pressures are reflected in mutual perception and communication, supported by the work climate. Business units closely observe their counterparts' performance. Based on communicated knowledge, success stories, and best practices, they learn and derive benchmarks for their own operations. By the same token, learning and the derivation of benchmarks occurs within local business units: unit members value different qualifications of their colleagues (e.g., education backgrounds, specialized skills), by which they individually contest toward a greater performance of the respective unit. Especially trust, reliability, curiosity as well as the willingness to learn are important factors of the work climate that support communication and observation. The comparably small size of the local IT unit permits close physical colocation for mutual observation, helping local IT units' members to gather an understanding of best practices and success stories. As a result of pro-active endorsement of the local IT's supervisors, experience, knowledge, and learnings are collectively shared. Likewise, trust and reliability support communication and interaction on the local IT level.

4.2   Institutional Logic of Harmonization

Building on our analysis, in the following, we synthesize our findings into six pressure-specific propositions on explaining the institutional logic of harmonization attained in a decentralized organization. We further report on the dynamics between institutional pressures, deriving a seventh proposition on the interplay of pressures (Table 3).

Table 3. Propositions on institutional pressures and their dynamics

P1	In decentralized organizations,…	While local units adhere to their own coercive mechanisms, globally-enforced coercive pressures reflect a set of mutually negotiated compromises among local units	Coercive pressures
P2		Global coercive pressures foster guided interaction among local units by providing a general orientation frame for decision-making	
P3		Local units retain their own distinctive norms and values, that are shared by the market segments in which they operate and compete	Normative pressures
P4		Distinctions in norms and values among local units are negotiated at the global level toward a mutually-generated identity	
P5		The appreciation of distinct qualifications and perception of best practices set the benchmarks within local units	Mimetic pressures
P6		The appreciation of distinct norms/values and perception of best practices set the benchmarks among local units	
P7		Harmonization becomes attained in a dynamic interplay between institutional pressures, i.e. between mimetic and normative as well as normative and coercive pressures	Dynamics of pressures
$P7_a$		Coercive pressures are influenced by normative pressures	
$P7_b$		Normative pressures are influenced by mimetic pressures	

In decentralized organizations, coercive pressures are not enforced from one level to another. They are a product of local and global negotiations of individual expectations to pursue valued ends. This leads to a compromise of goals and expectations, becoming reflected in a set of mutually-agreed mechanisms (e.g., vision) (P1). In effect, these mechanisms harmonize differences among local units and provide an orientation frame for decision-making toward valued ends (e.g., outputs) as well as guided interaction (e.g., transparency in communication) among local and global levels (P2).

Local levels adhere to individual norms and values. This mainly results from the specialization of local units as they operate and compete in different market segments. Therefore, each local unit shares the prevailing norms and values of their respective market segment (P3). In turn, normative pressures are also found to stimulate the adherence of local levels to global values (feeling of belonging). That is, local units engage in the negotiation of goals and expectations, which contributes not only to the finding of compromises, but also to an overall identity due to shared expectations (P4).

Communication channels allow for mimetic behavior within and among local units. Within local units, members appreciate different qualifications of their colleagues, all contesting toward greater performance of the respective unit. Simultaneously, best practices are perceived as benchmarks for members' performance in their own unit (P5). This fosters the formation of cross-market knowledge among local units, which perform to different market segments, and eventually leverages mimetic behavior based on lessons learned from other market segments. Also, local units perceive best practices as benchmarks, triggering output performance on the global level (P6).

Coercive pressures are externalized in the organization's overall vision and strategies. Coercive carriers are the result of mutual agreements among local units on how to regulate and develop the overall business at the global level. The resultant compromises comprise norms, values, and expectations among global and local levels. This brings us to a dynamic interplay between coercive and normative pressure, in which coercive pressures are impacted by normative pressures that cater negotiated norms, values, and expectations of local units (P7a). At the local level, two types of normative pressures are reflected. One type originates in the specific market segment to which the respective local unit belongs. Consequently, local units try to gain legitimacy in their respective market through compliance with the given market's norms and values. The other type of normative pressures stems from the organization itself: as such, local units gain legitimacy in the organization through respecting shared norms and values among different local units. In effect, local units appreciate their differences, while deriving benchmarks from each other based on success stories and best practices. This fosters the rise and acquisition of common norms and values as local units try to mimic the behavior of their successful counterparts (P7b).

To conclude, the institutional logic of harmonization in highly decentralized organizations can be explained through a dynamic interplay between institutional pressures (P7). As local units try to mimic behavior of their successful counterparts, shared norms and values among local units become leveraged. In turn, shared norms and values become reflected in means to communicate and regulate them in the organization.

5 Discussion and Conclusion

Our research responds to recent calls for conducting institutional research on the *intra-organizational level of analysis* [13]. We make two contributions: firstly, our results provide six pressure-specific propositions on the institutional logic of harmonization at the intra-organizational level, which are similarly supported by IS literature at the inter-organizational level [19, 21, 31–35]. Secondly, our results show the dynamics of institutional pressures, which are mutually interacting and constitutive. For prospective research, this finding provides new insights and offers a vantage point for discussion.

5.1 Contribution

For coercive pressures, we found diverging goals and expectations of local levels reflected in a set of mutually-negotiated mechanisms (*P1*). IS literature supports this finding at the inter-organizational level. For example, Bala and Venkatesh [19] found that inter-organizational business process standards are co-developed by organizations to standardize their business processes as well as to strengthen their relations to other firms. Asset connectedness, resource synergies, and collaboration are aimed for mutually-developed standards. Our proposition that coercive pressures foster guided interaction among local units by providing an orientation frame for decision-making (*P2*) is also line with the inter-organizational IS literature: mechanisms that routinize decision-making, for instance the allocation of material or authorization of human resources, are shown to provide a regulative frame for guided decision-making [31, 32].

Furthermore, we proposed normative pressures along distinctive norms, values, and beliefs of local levels (*P3*) as well as their negotiation at the global level toward a mutually-generated identity (*P4*). The distinctiveness of norms and values corresponds to the inter-organizational perspective [33]. A general assumption is that due to different spatial and hierarchical levels, norms, values, and beliefs differ in an organization [36]. Simultaneously, values, rationales, and opinions are shared within the organization and thus yield a collective, assimilated social structure [33]. Davidson and Chismar [34], among others, discuss that expectations between actors may spill over to behavioral obligations. In turn, these obligations foster an overall "structure", which shapes and provides meaning to organizational behavior [34].

Mimetic pressures were reflected in the appreciation of distinct qualifications and perception of best practices that set benchmarks among local units (*P6*) as well as their members (*P5*). This is similarly uphold in inter-organizational IS studies, such as by Bala and Venkatesh [19], who maintain that organizations have a competitive interest in expanding their relations to others to benefit from shared knowledge, IT/IS assets, and routines. According to Nicolaou [35, p. 140], communication and social relations among personnel help organizations to learn about each other's solutions and "whether they intend to or not, facilitate imitation of each others' developments and decisions." Benders et al. [21] show that IS managers are attracted by best practices, which simultaneously leads to industry-wide standardized practices as a result of competitors that perceive successful practices as an opportunity to catch up in competition.

Finally, we discovered a distinctive logic, in which harmonization becomes attained in a dynamic interplay between pressures (*P7*). We find that mimetic pressures influence normative pressures (*P7_b*), which in turn influence coercive pressures (*P7_a*). Further, coercive pressures carry normative reflections throughout the organization. In the inter-organizational IS literature, we selectively found indications that coercive pressures may derive from normative pressures [e.g., 19]. Further, we found evidence that normative pressures are influenced by mimetic pressures [e.g., 33, 34, 36]. However, our findings on the institutional logic, occurring dynamically from local to global levels in a distinctive interplay of mimetic, normative, and coercive pressures, respectively, lacks evidence in the existing IS literature. This is where our research contributes with new insights and simultaneously opens an avenue for prospective IS research.

5.2   Implications

Our findings have implications for the understanding of institutional theory on the intra-organizational level (*explanatory findings*) and the discipline of *enterprise engineering*.

Explanatory Findings. Our findings show that harmonization emerges in a dynamic interplay between institutional pressures, a finding that goes beyond existing explanations on the distinctive influence of pressures. While IS research has studied how institutional pressures work in parallel [5], in different organizational contexts [18], as well as in different temporal circumstances [21], little is known about their dynamic, i.e. their interacting influence. Hence, we motivate to consider the dynamic influence of institutional pressures for future research.

While pressures are dynamic and their influence may change over time, there are also continuities, i.e. features that are highly stable and persisting in organizations. This is what institutional theory refers to as "imprinting" [8]. Such continuities may reflect particular norms, beliefs, rules or combined configurations of them [8]. Our case shows one major continuity – the institutional logic – that was discovered as a persisting process, stable due to the constant negotiation of norms, values, and goals. Although IS scholars have started to focus more on longitudinal and historical examinations of institutional processes [e.g., 37–39], a large extent of research so far neglects explicit considerations of stable and persisting features of organizations [5]. Due to this shortcoming, we outline organizational imprinting as a topic for future research.

Enterprise Engineering. In enterprise engineering (EE), a common discourse addresses the empowerment of individuals for accomplishing organizational goals and tasks [40]. Research has propagated to mitigate the Taylorist separation of global ("thinkers") and local ("workers") actors. To this end, our finding of local actors who negotiate global goals and tasks to pursue these has major implications for any approach to engineer the organization. For example, approaches that are coercive (e.g., strict architecture rules) and not balanced against goals, values, and expectations of local actors may risk ineffectiveness or non-conformity. This brings us to the following outline.

Regarding our findings on normative and mimetic pressures, it becomes evident that harmonization is a dynamic process that occurs along constantly re-negotiated institutional demands. Consequently, we motivate a more dynamic perspective on EE. In line with Hoogervorst [40] who suggests to consider the unplanned, self-organizing, and emerging nature of organizational environments, we motivate to establish and pursue EE as a continuous process of considering and continuously negotiating goals, goals, values, beliefs, and best practices among different organizational levels [e.g., see also 41, 42]. In line with our findings and EE research [43, 44], feedback sessions, communication channels, and alignment meetings within and between organizational units may provide a pertinent avenue to dynamically establish and pursue EE over time.

5.3 Limitations

This research has limitations. In line with our research objective, we purposefully chose a highly decentralized organization. Yet, organizations differ by contextual factors and personal motives [45]. In consequence, they also respond differently to institutional pressures. In order to generalize the discovered logic independent from contextual factors and motives, we suggest extending our single case approach by multiple case studies, enriching our qualitative data and conducting cross-case analyses.

Another limitation reconciles with this study's lack of considering timeliness. While demonstrating the attainment of harmonization as a dynamic process through interplaying pressures, our study neglects further insights on their temporal evolvement. Moreover, institutionalization is a process that occurs over time and thus raises the consideration of timeliness [8]. Historic conflicts, changes, or unforeseen events could lead to a deeper understanding of why some pressures are meaningful in a given situation or environment, while others are not. A longitudinal perspective may allow for deeper insights. Hence, we outline the consideration of timeliness in studying the attainment of harmonization [10] complementarily to the future progress of this research.

Acknowledgement. This work has been supported by the Swiss National Science Foundation (SNSF).

References

1. Williams, C.K., Karahanna, E.: Causal explanation in the coordinating process: a critical realist case study of federated IT governance structures. MIS Q. **37**(3), 933–964 (2013)
2. Peterson, R.: Crafting information technology governance. Inf. Syst. Manag. **21**(4), 7–22 (2004)
3. Pawlowski, S.D., Robey, D.: Bridging user organizations: knowledge brokering and the work of information technology professionals. MIS Q. **28**(4), 645–672 (2004)
4. Sambamurthy, V., Zmud, R.W.: Research commentary: the organizing logic for an enterprise's IT activities in the digital era—a prognosis of practice and a call for research. Inf. Syst. Res. **11**(2), 105–114 (2000)
5. Mignerat, M., Rivard, S.: Positioning the institutional perspective in information systems research. J. Inf. Technol. **24**(4), 369–391 (2009)

6. Orlikowski, W.J., Barley, S.R.: Technology and Institutions: what can research on information technology and research on organizations learn from each other? MIS Q. **25**(2), 145–165 (2001)
7. Thornton, P.H., Ocasio, W.: Institutional logics and the historical contingency of power in organizations: executive succession in the higher education publishing industry, 1958–1990. Am. J. Sociol. **105**(3), 801–843 (1999)
8. Scott, W.R. (ed.): Institutions and Organizations: Ideas, Interests, and Identities, 4th edn. Sage, Thousand Oaks (2014)
9. Ocasio, W.: Towards an attention-based view of the firm. Strateg. Manag. J. **18**, 187–206 (1997)
10. Dacin, M.T., Goodstein, J., Scott, R.: Institutional theory and institutional change: introduction to the special research forum. Acad. Manag. J. **45**(1), 43–56 (2002)
11. Greenwood, R., Hinings, C.R.: Understanding radical organizational change: bringing together the old and the new institutionalism. Acad. Manag. Rev. **21**(4), 1022–1054 (1996)
12. Pache, A.-C., Santos, F.: Embedded in hybrid contexts: how individuals in organizations respond to competing institutional logics. In: Lounsbury, M., Boxenbaum, E. (eds.) Research in the Sociology of Organizations, pp. 3–35. Emerald Group Publishing Limited, Bingley (2013)
13. Greenwood, R., et al. (eds.): The SAGE Handbook of Organizational Institutionalism. Sage Publications, London (2008)
14. Meyer, J.W., Rowan, B.: Institutionalized organizations: formal structure as myth and ceremony. Am. J. Sociol. **83**(2), 340–363 (1977)
15. Zucker, L.G.: The role of institutionalization in cultural persistence. Am. Sociol. Rev. **42**(5), 726–743 (1977)
16. DiMaggio, P.J., Powell, W.W.: The iron cage revisited institutional isomorphism and collective rationality in organizational fields. In: Economics Meets Sociology in Strategic Management, pp. 143–166 (2000)
17. Nielsen, J.A., Mathiassen, L., Newell, S.: Theorization and translation in information technology institutionalization: evidence from Danish home care. MIS Q. **38**(1), 165–186 (2014)
18. Teo, H.H., Wei, K.K., Benbasat, I.: Predicting intention to adopt interorganizational linkages: an institutional perspective. MIS Q. **27**(1), 19–49 (2003)
19. Bala, H., Venkatesh, V.: Assimilation of interorganizational business process standards. Inf. Syst. Res. **18**(3), 340–362 (2007)
20. Liang, H., et al.: Assimilation of enterprise systems: the effect of institutional pressures and the mediating role of top management. MIS Q. **33**(1), 59–87 (2007)
21. Benders, J., Batenburg, R., Van der Blonk, H.: Sticking to standards; technical and other isomorphic pressures in deploying E.R.P.-systems. Inf. Manag. **43**(2), 194–203 (2006)
22. Friedland, R., Alford, R.R.: Bringing society back. In: symbols, practices, and institutional contradictions. In: Powell, W.W., DiMaggio, P.J. (eds.) The New Institutionalism in Organizational Analysis. University of Chicago Press, Chicago (1991)
23. Currie, W.L., Guah, M.W.: Conflicting institutional logics: a national programme for IT in the organisational field of healthcare. J. Inf. Technol. **22**(3), 235–247 (2007)
24. Almandoz, J.: Arriving at the starting line: the impact of community and financial logics on new banking ventures. Acad. Manag. J. **55**(6), 1381–1406 (2012)
25. Tilcsik, A.: From ritual to reality: demography, ideology, and decoupling in a post-communist government agency. Acad. Manag. J. **53**(6), 1474–1498 (2010)
26. Gosain, S.: Enterprise information systems as objects and carriers of institutional forces: the new iron cage? J. Assoc. Inf. Syst. **5**(4), 151–182 (2004)

27. Jensen, T.B., Kjaergaard, A., Svejvig, P.: Using institutional theory with sensemaking theory: a case study of information system implementation in healthcare. J. Inf. Technol. **24**(4), 343–353 (2009)
28. Yin, R.K.: Case Study Research. Design and Methods, 3rd edn. Sage Publications Inc., Thousand Oaks (2003)
29. Miles, M.B., Huberman, A.M.: Qualitative Data Analysis: An Expanded Sourcebook, 2nd edn. Sage Publications Inc., Thousand Oaks (1994)
30. Eisenhardt, K.M.: Building theories from case study research. Acad. Manag. Rev. **14**(4), 532–550 (1989)
31. Son, J.-Y., Benbasat, I.: Organizational buyers' adoption and use of B2B electronic marketplaces: efficiency- and legitimacy-oriented perspectives. J. Manag. Inf. Syst. **24**(1), 55–99 (2007)
32. Miranda, S.M., Kim, Y.M.: Professional versus political contexts: institutional mitigation and the transaction cost heuristic in information systems outsourcing. MIS Q. **30**(3), 725–753 (2006)
33. Chatterjee, D., Grewal, R., Sambamurthy, V.: Shaping up for e-Commerce: institutional enablers of the organizational assimilation of web technologies. MIS Q. **26**(2), 65–89 (2002)
34. Davidson, E.J., Chismar, W.G.: The interaction of institutionally triggered and technology-triggered social structure change: an investigation of computerized physician order entry. MIS Q. **31**(4), 739–758 (2007)
35. Nicolaou, A.I.: Social control in information systems development. Inf. Technol. People **1**(2), 130–147 (1999)
36. Lewis, W., Agarwal, R., Sambamurthy, V.: Sources of influence on beliefs about information technology use: an empirical study of knowledge workers. MIS Q. **27**(4), 657–678 (2003)
37. Cousins, K.C., Robey, D.: The social shaping of electronic metals exchanges: an institutional theory perspective. Inf. Technol. People **18**(3), 212–229 (2005)
38. Wang, P., Swanson, E.B.: Launching professional services automation: institutional entrepreneurship for information technology innovations. Inf. Organ. **17**, 59–88 (2007)
39. Nickerson, J.V., Zur Muehlen, M.: The ecology of standards processes: insights from internet standard making. MIS Q. **30**, 467–488 (2006)
40. Hoogervorst, J.A.P.: Enterprise Governance and Enterprise Engineering. Springer, Berlin (2009). https://doi.org/10.1007/978-3-540-92671-9
41. Faller, H., de Kinderen, S., Constantinidis, C.: Organizational subcultures and enterprise architecture effectiveness: findings from a case study at a European airport company. In: 49th Hawaii International Conference on System Sciences (2016)
42. Faller, H., de Kinderen, S.: The impact of cultural differences on enterprise architecture effectiveness: a case study. In: 8th Mediterranean Conference on Information Systems (2014)
43. van Steenbergen, M.: Maturity and Effectiveness of Enterprise Architecture. Utrecht University, Utrecht (2011)
44. Rouse, W.B., Baba, M.L.: Enterprise transformation. Commun. ACM **49**(7), 67–72 (2006)
45. Oliver, C.: Strategic responses to institutional processes. Acad. Manag. Rev. **16**(1), 145–179 (1991)

Systems Approaches in the Enterprise Architecture Field of Research: A Systematic Literature Review

Jarkko Nurmi, Mirja Pulkkinen[✉], Ville Seppänen,
and Katja Penttinen

Faculty of Information Technology, University of Jyvaskyla,
P.O. Box 35, 40014 Jyväskylä, Finland
{jarkko.nurmi,mirja.pulkkinen,ville.r.seppanen,
katja.penttinen}@jyu.fi

Abstract. This study explores the use of the systems approaches (systems thinking and systems theories) as the theoretical underpinnings for Enterprise Architecture (EA) research. Both the academic and the practitioner communities have maintained an interest in EA due to its potential benefits, promising for the recent technological and business advances. EA as a research area is, however, characterized by diversified views depicted in different definitions of the concept, and no acknowledged common theoretical foundation. A number of prior studies have noticed this gap in the EA field of research, and called for a strengthening of the theory of EA. Variegated systems approaches have been suggested as a theory base. The aim of this study is to examine if, and to what extent the systems approaches could provide a common theoretical foundation. We contribute with a systematic literature review on the state-of-art of systems approaches in EA research. We find that the systems approaches are, indeed, frequently referred to in the EA studies. However, as of yet, the application of these theories appears to be fragmented, and the approaches are rarely systematically used in empirical studies. We discuss the findings, reflecting to the types of theory and the use of theory in our area of research.

Keywords: Enterprise architecture · Systems thinking · Systems theory
Systems approaches · Literature review

1 Introduction

Enterprise architecture (EA) appears to maintain some interest in research. This might be due to the potential solutions it offers to some of the present problems organizations face with the current emerging technologies and growing complexity [33]. EA presents a tool for alignment between business and IT, an issue still judged as one of the top three management concerns [34]. Further, some evidence of business benefits attained with this approach have been brought up recently [49].

Definition of enterprise architecture varies by its use [6, 32, 39, 55]. However, we start out by defining EA loosely as an approach to manage, plan and develop enterprises and their IT. As a unit of analysis, enterprises or organizations, that, even if

© Springer Nature Switzerland AG 2019
D. Aveiro et al. (Eds.): EEWC 2018, LNBIP 334, pp. 18–38, 2019.
https://doi.org/10.1007/978-3-030-06097-8_2

networked or federated and thus depending on their environments, have some decision-making authority over their own resources and their goal setting (See e.g. [22]; Definition 2.7). The need for an architectural approach to the management of the business-IT alignment emerged with the diffusion of IT and the emergence of networking technologies already decades ago [6]. Technology developments today keep driving the need, giving new emphasis to the vision: "enterprise analysis tools that are growing in importance and are likely to become mandatory for any business that continues to grow and evolve" [62]. This outlines the need for an approach to apply to at least medium or large size organizations. The need appears in the context of the use of IT in organizations. The term 'enterprise architecture', was coined later, and its focus has been enlarging to cover also the strategic planning [27, 42], to support the business and IT alignment [6, 44].

Various systems approaches are applied in EA research, and the idea of viewing enterprises as systems finds support in the related research areas. In management science, the research of management and organizations, systems theory used to have a strong resonance [15], summarized in a related special issue of the Academy of Management Journal [1], however, the interest appearing to fade over time [3].

For EA, an early example of systems theory use is the Systemic EA Method (SEAM) [59]. Recently, Santana et al. [46] conducted a literature review and a description of EA network analysis that sees enterprises as complex networks. Fu et al. [16] discussed complexity cybernetics in relation to EA, and, based on an analysis of 33 papers, concluded that despite growing interest, neither EA cybernetics, nor other systems approaches have been yet established as a theoretical foundation for studies in this field. Lapalme [32] encourages taking on the systems thinking and system-in-environment paradigms for the evolving EA approach.

The need for an acknowledged theoretical foundation for EA has been noted by previous research [e.g. 7, 25, 26]. Several other studies [e.g. 19, 21] have discussed the systems nature of an enterprise, and researchers have noted a need to strengthen the theoretical roots of enterprise architecture as well as to study its relations to other fields, such as systems thinking [5, 33]. For example, Kappelman and Zachman [28] point that "[…] the EA trend of applying holistic systems thinking, shared language, and engineering concepts, albeit in the early stages of their application, is here to stay". Furthermore, [42] state the "importance of systems thinking and, especially, of adopting the open systems principle, for managing EA design and evolution".

The aim of this study is to find indications, if, and to what extent, the systems approaches could provide a common theoretical foundation for EA. We conduct a systematic literature review to answer the research questions:

- RQ1: To what extent different systems approaches are already in use in EA research?
- RQ2: What aspects of theory do the systems approaches cover in earlier studies?

The remainder of this paper is structured as follows: First, the concept of enterprise architecture is presented in Sect. 2. Next, Sect. 3 presents and briefly discusses the systems approaches, and the elements shared across the different approaches. Additionally, we take a look into the significance of theory for a research area. In Sect. 4, the research method of this study, the systematic literature review (SLR) protocol is presented. Sections 5 and 6, respectively, present the analysis and discussion of the SLR results. Finally, we conclude with some remarks on the state-of-art account of the systems approaches to the field of EA, and questions opening for future research.

2 Enterprise Architecture as an Evolving Research Area

Some work regarding the various definitions of EA already exists. For example, Schönherr [48] discusses a total of 126 references from 1987 to 2008 and concludes that majority of these do not define EA in a comprehensive way. Different language communities are discussed by Schelp and Winter [47]. Rahimi et al. [42] and Saint-Louis et al. [45] conducted comprehensive systematic literature reviews in order to find definitions of EA, and Kappelman et al. [29] discuss the development of EA definition. Also, Korhonen et al. [31] discuss the possible reconceptualization of EA. While these studies make valid contributions, the nature of the complex field of enterprise IT and systems is still not captured in a single definition for EA, even if the need is pointed to by several authors [e.g. 45].

In the field of information systems (IS) research, the area to which IT in an organizational setting is foremost related to, the basic unit of analysis is traditionally an information system. EA, however, as an approach is suggested to cope with the planning and management of a number of systems within an enterprise. The unit of analysis thus is the enterprise, or organization, with numerous systems that is naturally leading to the idea of *a system of systems*. As a baseline theory, the systems thinking, and related theories thus seem to come close.

According to Romero and Vernadat [43], EA, in the form of the EA frameworks, has historically been developed parallel in two different communities – the IS, and the industrial engineering community [6]. Bernus et al. [5] state that EA originates in the disciplines of management, IS and engineering. In IS and management science, the work of e.g. Zachman [63], and Spewak and Hill [51] have been seminal. Within the engineering community, the focus is to engineer the information and material flows of the whole enterprise – hence the term enterprise engineering (EE) [6]. Later, the scope of the engineering community extended to cover the whole enterprise and its business networks, including e.g. supply chain [43] and to further rationalize and specify the focus on essential elements of EA [41]. Ambiguity concerning the definition of EA may be partly due to its origins, and Bernus et al. [5] point, that there is a gap between originally intended scope and the present-day scope of EA. However, for the engineering communities (software, systems and enterprise engineering), the "system of systems" engineering (SoSE) the systems nature of the research area is self-evident [17]. We acknowledge this as a related area, but not included in our study.

In order to explore the literature in the EA area, an initial definition should be stated. We cite Lapalme et al. [33], who build their definition upon the ISO/IEC/IEEE 42010 standard: "EA should be understood as being constituted of the essential elements of *a socio-technical organization*, their relationships to each other and to their changing environment as well as the principles of the organization's design and evolution. Enterprise architecture management is the continuous practice of describing and updating the EA in order to understand complexity and manage change".

3   Systems Approaches – A Theory for the EA Research Area?

According to Mingers and White [37], systems approaches emerged in early to mid-1900's, and were developed, among others, by von Bertalanffy [57] in the form of Systems Theory, and further, by Wiener [61] and Beer [4], who discussed with these approaches among other things cybernetics. Arnold and Wade [2] note that systems thinking was coined by Barry Richmond in the late 1980's, and define systems thinking consisting of elements, interconnections and a purpose. Probably the most applied General Systems Theory (GST) approach in the IS field of research is the nine-fold hierarchy of Boulding [8] presented initially to the management field of science (see e.g. [1]). It has found resonance in the study of IS-related semiotics through the work of Stamper [52, 53], that continues to impact as an underlying theory in foundational research on enterprise modeling [8]. Relying on Boulding, Daft and Weick [13] lay out a theoretical baseline for organizational information and the management and processing of information in organizations, well-cited within the IS field.

As a practical application, Checkland [12] developed the Soft Systems Methodology to support the systemic organizational design and change, and in order to serve these goals, to enhance the involvement of stakeholders at the implementation of technical systems. In the same vein, Senge's [50] learning organization as a further application of systems idea to organizational development take on this approach to stress the interdependencies within the organizational subsystems, and the socio-technical system perspectives. Mingers and White [37], use the generic term *systems approaches* to cover systems related lines of research ("theory" or "thinking" [23]). They discover the following common elements, reflected here for the setting of EA.

- Systems consists of wholes comprising of parts, or sub-systems.
- Systems exist in the midst of their environment and are defined by their boundaries.
- A system can be described as a static entity (system structure), or through its dynamics, i.e. the processes, or transformations in the system.
- Systems change (evolve) over time.
- Systems (and subsystems) appear as hierarchical, and there is a hierarchy of levels of complexity.
- Within the system and at its boundaries, there are feedback loops (positive and negative) between the structural elements, potentially influencing the system dynamics.
- Systems entail information processing, regarding both the system and in exchange with its environment.
- System and subsystems are normally "open", i.e. they are taking inputs from and sending outputs to the environment, and possible adjacent (sub-)systems. (This influences the analysis of a system, its components and their evolution.)
- System thinking is a holistic approach, i.e. taking into consideration the whole also in the examination of parts of the system.
- Systems approaches afford for an observer, i.e. a point of view, or a position taking a holistic perspective to the system.

For the EA-related EE research area, we find a thorough elaboration on enterprise engineering *theories* [14]. Further, some questions on the role and the nature of theories in the field of IS have been elaborated [18]. In accordance, to find a theory or theories for a research focus area, the following points or basic questions are involved:

- *Establishing the domain.* What are the characteristics of the domain of interest? What phenomena are in the focus of the study, and what problems are to solve? [18]. The outlining of the disciplinary boundaries is done by applying a standard definition of organization for enterprise. Further delineation are the problems related to the IT in the organizations in questions going *beyond one information system.* Single information systems (with their entire life cycles) are dealt with in various research areas within the IS field of study.
- The *ontological* theories [14], or the structural or *ontological* questions [18]. Although theory for EA is claimed missing, it appears that the research has indeed brought forth several suggested ontologies, the Zachman [64] Framework as the most prominent one. Suggested structures ("contributions to knowledge", or expressions of theory [18]) for the area are abundant, but none commonly accepted. Neither are patterns for research questions or the resulting claims [18].
- The *epistemological* questions relate to the nature of knowledge in the research area [18]. This raises questions of how to capture, and by which methods to validate and verify knowledge. Dietz et al. [14] thus join with epistemology also logics, mathematics and phenomenology. With the complexity of the research target, this apparently presents challenges to both the research, and to the question of the theoretical base. With different viewpoints to EA, different epistemological foundations and research methods not only apply but are fundamental.
- Gregor [18] points also to the broader environment, where the research is undertaken: The influential socio-political questions, seen by Dietz et al. [14] as a category of *ideological theories.* The related questions remind of the role of diverse stakeholders within and outside of the research area, and further, the complexity of social behaviors, and the challenges of objectivity in research.
- Further, Dietz et al. [14] see the *technological theories* as a distinct category in their theory framework. This seems to map to the theory for "design and action" [18]: to know how to accomplish something in reality.

For EE, Dietz et al. [14] propose eight specific kinds of theory for the different aspects of enterprise and the diverse systems belonging to enterprises. Systems approaches, or their applications [e.g. 10, 12, 57] are pointed at as the basis of several of these theory classes, emphasizing the relevance to the enterprise systems area. In our exploration on theories in the area of study, it is of interest what the theory offers for the research, and to what extent it is indeed applied. The five functions of theory listed in [18] give a starting point:

1. *Analysis:* 'what is', i.e. the ontology and structure of the focus area. At this level, the theory remains descriptive, showing elements and relationships, but not making inferences to causality, or making predictions.

2. *Explanation* – extends analysis with explanations, also attempting to answer the questions how, why, when, and where. However, this does not imply prediction or hypotheses.
3. *Prediction* – the theory allows for developing predictions and hypothetical propositions but does not explain causalities.
4. *Explanation and prediction* – the theory answers the questions what is, how, why, when, where, what will be. It allows for developing testable hypotheses, predicts the future states, and provides causal explanations.
5. *Design and Action* – an applicable theory, that *prescribes* how to do or achieve something, meaning the development of articulate instructions (as e.g., methods, techniques, principles of form and function) for constructing an artifact.

We seek to find out, how the systems approaches are reflected in the EA research and in the use of theories in it presently, and discuss if a potential could be detected for a common theoretical foundation.

4   Method of Study: Literature Review Protocol

According to Templier and Paré [56], leading researchers, e.g. Webster and Watson [58], have noted the relevance of publishing quality standalone literature reviews. In an attempt to strengthen the theoretical foundations of EA, we conducted a comprehensive systematic literature review. We followed the guidelines proposed by [56], hence our work included the following phases: (1) formulating the problem, (2) searching the literature, (3) screening for inclusion, (4) assessing quality, (5) extracting data, and (6) analyzing and synthesizing data.

To ensure a comprehensive look into the contributions of systems paradigms on EA we chose to look for relevant literature from three databases: Google Scholar, Scopus and IEEE Xplore Digital Library. We used the following search phrases appearing anywhere in either the title of the article, in abstracts or in keywords: "enterprise architecture" AND ("system thinking" OR "systems thinking" OR "system theory" OR "systems theory"). The search was conducted in February 2018.

Initially, a total of 3457 results was found, 3380 of these from Google Scholar, 71 from Scopus and 6 from IEEE Xplore Digital Library. The amount of initial results was extensive, mainly due to Google Scholar's search algorithms and limited options in filtering the search results. Google Scholar's "Advanced search" allows search terms to appear either in the title of the article, or anywhere in the article. To find all the relevant articles, the search terms were allowed to appear anywhere in the article. In terms of literature coverage, we aimed to conclude the search and selection process when the research material was saturated [56, 58]. In order to gather all relevant literature, the first 960 papers from Google Scholar and all papers from Scopus and IEEE were screened. At this stage, we read the titles, abstracts and keywords of the articles, and included those that mentioned EA and referenced "systems thinking" or some systems theory. We included journal and conference articles as well as books. We excluded articles that were not written in English as well obviously those that were inaccessible. 156 articles and books were chosen for a more thorough inspection. Also, 18 articles found with forward search were included. After crossing out the doubles and excluding articles that did not contribute to the research question, we ended up with a total of 47 publications (see Appendix A).

5   Results and Analysis

The included studies were published in various journals and conferences, although the systems nature of enterprises has been mostly discussed at the Hawaii International Conference on System Science (7 items), IEEE International Conference on Systems, Man and Cybernetics, International IEEE EDOC Conference, and the Journal of Enterprise Architecture (5 each). In retrospective, a broad search covering also less well-known journals and conference proceedings was needed. Our sample shows varying quantity per annum. Eight articles were published 2012 (most publications), while only one article was published in 2008 and 2015, none in 2004. Although we did not have preconceived inclusion or exclusion criteria concerning the year of publication, all the included articles were published 2000 onwards.

Several systems theories, e.g. General Systems Theory [e.g. 21], Living Systems Theory [e.g. 60] and Complex Adaptive Systems [e.g. 24] are taken as underlying theory. Further, Viable System Model [e.g. 64], simply System of Systems [e.g. 54], and own coinages such as "complex adaptive living system" [#27], appear in EA studies. Most studies did not name a particular theory, but refer to Systems Thinking [e.g. 40], (which however has been theorized as well [11]), or merely to "systems theory" [e.g. 36], without specifying which approach the study relies on. Notably, not only several different approaches came up, but multiple studies mention more than one systems approach.

According to the analysis of the articles included, *enterprises* are perceived as a type of *system*. There are mentions of *a system of systems,* some kind of a *complex system*, such as a *[complex] socio-technical system,* or *complex network,* if not a *Complex Adaptive System.* GST, Systems Thinking and an unspecified "systems theory" are the most frequent theoretical starting points. Enterprise architecture is defined in a number of ways, most often as a comprehensive view of an interconnected and networked whole of an organization with multiple information systems, possibly in two different states: as-is and to-be.

- This reflects to the first fundamental question to develop theory: Establishing the research domain, in this case EA. We can conclude that the systems nature of the target domain is widely recognized.

For the question on ontology, systems elements have been suggested. E.g. Wegmann [#1] notes that "an enterprise is a system in which the components are the enterprise's resources". Schuetz et al. [#32] see that "Following a system theoretical perspective we consider EA as a system, consisting of components (or 'things') and relations", also making a very clear relation between the two and reflecting the basic concepts of systems approaches. Santana et al. [#44], reflecting the ideas of the theory of Complex Adaptive Systems, define EA as a "complex network" and elaborate it as an "interwoven system of strategic goals, business processes, applications and infrastructure components", which "is subject to a variety of relationships and dependencies among its several components".

Table 1 classifies the 47 articles based on the dominant systems approach referenced in each study. We classify the studies according to the purpose of the theory (first column) following roughly the aristotelian classification [18], see above. We also distinguish, whether the article presents only conceptual or theoretical ideas, or if the study is based on, or supported by, evidence from empirical work (second column).

Table 1. Classification based on systems approach and type of article

For the advancement of	Argumentation	Systems approach (n): Paper ID #	Total	
1. Theory or discipline	Conceptual or theoretical	STH (9): #14; #20; #23; #24; #31; #37; #41; #42; #43 CYB (3): #11; #29; #36 GST (2): #39; #47 VSM (1): #21 CAS (1): #44 ORT (1): #38	17	19
	Based on or supported by empirical evidence	STH (1): #34 MHS (1): #28	2	
2. Ontologies and frameworks	Conceptual or theoretical	STH (3): #3; #15; #16	3	6
	Based on or supported by empirical evidence	GST (1): #10 SM (1): #13 MHS (1): #8	3	
3. Methods and modelling	Conceptual or theoretical	STH (8): #1; #17; #25; #30; #33; #35; #45; #46 VSM (2): #26; #27 GST (1): #19 CYB (1): #22 LST (1): #2	13	20
	Based on or supported by empirical evidence	STH (2): #9; #32 GST (2): #12; #18 VSM (1): #40 CAS (1): #5 LST (1): #7	7	
4. Software tools	Conceptual or theoretical	LST (2): #4; #6	2	2
	Based on or supported by empirical evidence		0	

Legend: CAS = Complex Adaptive Systems (2), CYB = Cybernetics (4), GST = General Systems Theory (6), LST = Living Systems Theory (4), MHS = Theory of Multilevel Hierarchical Systems (2), ORT = Orientor Theory (1), STH = 'Systems Theory', 'Systems Thinking' etc. (23), VSM = Viable Systems Model (5)

Comparing to the theory functions (p. 6), the results show that to a good portion, 'systems' idea is seen as an analytical expedient of the research domain, i.e. analytical tool for managing enterprises and their IT. Missing the theories for explanation and prediction is likely due to the research methodologies used, and further, the complicated nature of the research target. To pinpoint causalities and develop predictions would require simplified views, loosing from sight the holistic systemic nature of the research target. However, with a more established theoretical outline, the reduction needed to study causal relationships could become possible.

Most often, systems approaches appear in the studies of methods and modeling, i.e. the practicable knowledge "for design and action", for which, empirically founded studies are more frequent. Even if frameworks used to be often on the fore in discussions on EA, the systems approaches appear less often as a basis for explicit ontological structuring for EA study, and only half of the studies for this purpose rely on empirics.

- A commonly acknowledged, consistent systems theoretical ontology for EA remains to be established.

To summarize, despite of keen interest on the systems approaches, they seem still more rarely contribute to empirical efforts. Different systems approaches, and some specific models are used in the studies. In the following, we present and discuss the individual systems approaches found in this study.

6 Discussion

It appears plausible to anchor EA in the field of system sciences, a discipline providing the necessary theoretical foundations to design, model and manage socio-technical systems. The literature review results show maybe a more fragmented theory base than could be expected. The specified systems approaches that appear in the included papers have, however, each contributed to an understanding of the problem field of EA. We attempt to summarize with a brief characterization of each theory or model in the following paragraphs.

GST – As an early systems approach, especially in the studies of organization and management, the General Systems Theory suggests hierarchically layered systems at nine distinct levels, with growing autonomy and increasing complexity towards the top levels [9]. Human deliberation enters at level 7, leading to less predictable actions and introducing complexity. Enterprises as such at level 8 of the GST hierarchy, as social (or rather socio-technical) systems, consist of several, both more and less complicated and complex (sub)systems. EA elements, such as the technical systems on one, and the human activity systems on the other hand, can be described, and their behaviors to an extent also explained through GST. Openness (cf. Open Systems, [57]) is assumed, meaning interactions with the environment and across system boundaries, as no enterprise exists in isolation, but within an environment with which it is in multiple relationships. The purpose of GST is to be "a body of systematic theoretical constructs which will discuss the general relationships of the empirical world" [9], and it has found application in empirical EA work both on ontologies or frameworks [#10], and methods or modelling [#12] [#18].

LST – In addition to an eight-level hierarchy, building on the GST, the Living Systems Theory [38] purports a division of labor between the system components. In LST, processing and transmission of information is in focus, making it apt to the study of IS and IT in organizations. The parts of a living system are classified to those processing either matter and energy, or information, or both [30]. In addition to this division, more refined roles are specified, e.g. for enabling managed interactions with the system environment at its boundaries. Openness is naturally also an attribute of an LST. System states and event cycles, as well as the 'in-, out- and throughput' concepts are a root for the current understanding of enterprises as a set of (business) processes, transforming inputs to outputs. The LST has been seminal in early EA research, especially in the extensive, well known work on the SEAM methodology [#1], [#2], [#4], [#6], [#10], leaning on the LST, but also supported by GST. Following SEAM, with LST as a theoretical base, a process meta-model for EA management has been presented in an empirical study investigating the partitioning of the complex whole to manageable parts in EA ("EA domains") [#7]. In alignment with the systems approach, feedback loops in this model ensure informed decisions by the upper levels in the systems hierarchy. The LST is conceptually rich, and has found application both in organization and management, and e.g. in industry automation, where it is the basis for Multilevel Hierarchical Systems **MHS**, [35]. MHS has been tapped on also directly in an EA study [#28] included in our SLR.

VSM – The Viable Systems Model proposes a simplified view for formal modelling to a system "capable of independent existence". A viable system, however, in also exchange with its environment (which may be another viable system, as implied by the recursion principle). The challenge of a VS is to cope with 'variety', and it is deploying 'intrinsic control' as means to sustain its viability. Cybernetics (CYB) as such complements the theory, rather than being an independent systems theoretical approach. Cybernetics is presented as an aspect of information processing and diffusion within the VSM.

From a Viable System Model perspective, [#13] analyzes EA management functions, proposes a method framework for EAM, and describes the results from a case study. Here, VSM provides a framework through which complex management systems can be described from a systemic perspective, and with five subsystems – operation, coordination, control, planning and identity. In the context of EA, operation is formed via EA projects, by the enterprise-level management functions, whereas the communication function of EAM forms systems two – coordination [#13]. Control systems forms the reactive function of EAM, establishing higher level control over the coordination system function, i.e. ensuring stability in the enterprise-level management process interaction. Furthermore, the authors argue that EAM encompasses a proactive function (planning), which anticipates and addresses environmental changes. Lastly, identity system concerns EAM governance – the scope and reach of EAM. [#11] is another paper deploying the VSM. Similarities between EA and the Viable System Model, as well as with Cybernetics have been found in other studies as well [#26, #27].

An adaptation of **Cybernetics** is applied in [#21] that the authors call Enterprise Architecture Cybernetics as the research framework for their study, to formulate methods to calculate and reduce the structural complexity of collaborative networks. Furthermore, they use the extension of Axiomatic Design Theory as an approach to treat complex systems whose operation cannot be fully predicted. The decisions regarding such systems are based on incomplete information, and therefore the ability to estimate and control their complexity can yield better guided decisions. The paper provides an interesting example of the use of systems approaches to propose an applicable method as a solution to a problem that stems from a high structural complexity of the domain.

CAS – Complex Adaptive Systems has raised interest more recently, likely following the technological developments with non-human agents interacting alongside of humans within networks [20]. The main emphasis is in the system adaptive behavior conditional to the signals received from the environment and explained through the common characteristics of evolution, aggregate behavior (parts or subsystems contributing to the overall system behavior), and anticipation, where the system aims at adapting in anticipation to the changes of the environment [#5].

The Orientor Theory (**ORT**) complements the views to system with the orientors defining the overall desired system outcomes (or system states). As pointed out by [#38], in the case of EA, the orientors can be seen the desired EA principles to follow in design and development activities.

The highest number of studies fall into the category Systems Thinking that may, or may not be explained in the individual studies in more detail. The high occurrence of the Systems Thinking or unspecified systems theory may indicate that the field of research does rely on some generic system related truths, as maybe a common 'mental model' [50] that potentially supports the research community in learning on the subject. As pointed out for organization and management [3], maybe in the EA field of research there are also "missed opportunities", for not more consistently relying on the systems approach. Rather than mere metaphorical use, a systems paradigm tuned for EA could support the description, explanation and even prediction of the enterprise and its information systems phenomena. We assume that this is a call for unifying the view of this paradigm in the EA field of research. The common features presented in this paper (based on [37], cf. Sect. 3) is an attempt in this vein. As a summary (Table 2), where the EA research stands, with examples we suggest how the common systems features reflect to well-known EA concepts in use in the EA studies. Further, we consider with these concepts, what challenges could be ahead for the systems related EA research.

Table 2. Common systems features vs. EA concepts, and EA research challenges

Common features of systems approaches	EA concepts and challenges
Systems consists of wholes comprising of parts, or sub-systems	View of 'organizations' or 'enterprises', the unit of analysis in EA studies, as systems/systems of systems (with different characterizations)
Systems exist in the midst of their environment and are defined by their boundaries	EA as a tool for managing enterprise IT and information resources, a tool corporate and business strategy within these limits *Challenge:* EAM for the extended, federated enterprises, networks and ecosystems
A system can be described as a static entity (system structure), or through its dynamics, i.e. the processes, or transformations in the system	EA modelling, EA descriptions; Business architecture descriptions; E.g. business processes as an element ("layer") *Challenge:* Modelling of the evolving/constantly changing enterprise
Systems change (evolve) over time	EA current and future stage ("as-is", "to-be") *Challenge:* The synchronized evolution of related enterprise subsystems and sub-subsystems
Systems (and subsystems) appear as hierarchical, and there is a hierarchy of levels of complexity	Enterprise and enterprise segments ("domains"), EA describing systems-of-systems *Challenge:* EA Management for systems consisting of complex systems, where also the sub-systems change independently
Within the system and at its boundaries, there are feedback loops (positive and negative) between the structural elements, potentially influencing the system dynamics	The EA Process/The EAM Process *Challenge:* Understanding and supporting the nature of feedback as signals from (sub) system to system within the enterprise
Systems entail information processing, regarding both the system and in exchange with its environment	Information Architecture Dimension of EA *Challenge:* Inclusion of Information and Data Architectures and their management as an integral part of EA and EAM
System and subsystems are normally "open", i.e. they are taking inputs from and sending outputs to the environment, and possible adjacent (sub-)systems	EA acknowledges the enterprise environment as source of diverse influences for enterprise behavior *Challenge:* EAM for the open systems-of-systems emerging with the evolution of technologies (e.g. Industrial Internet of Things) and digitalization; with federated, loosely-coupled and independently managed systems collaboration

(continued)

Table 2. (*continued*)

Common features of systems approaches	EA concepts and challenges
System thinking is a holistic approach, i.e. taking into consideration the whole also in the examination of parts of the system	The essence of EA, the strength of EA methodology *Challenge:* With the above mentioned challenges, how well are the current EA methods equipped for this, especially with the new technology developments?
Systems approaches afford for an observer, i.e. a point of view, or a position taking a holistic perspective to the system	The 'Enterprise Architect' *Challenge:* In large enterprise and networked settings, the task is too broad for any one role; but requires coordinated, collaborative activity, presenting a challenge to methodology

7 Conclusions

The purpose of this study was to discuss firstly, to what extent the systems approaches are already in use in EA research (RQ1). Secondly, we wanted to examine the specific aspects of theory in this regard. This means, we look into the basic theory types or basic questions on theory, and further, the functions of theory (analytical, predictive, causal or "technological", i.e. for design and action), and aimed to find out if the EA research already deploys the systems approaches for these purposes (RQ2). In order to account for the contribution of the systems approaches in the field of EA, we look into the use of the theories in the studies we examine, and take account where empirical work supports the theory development in these studies. Further, we count the occurrence of the different systems theories and models, and discuss their contribution to this field of inquiry.

The common elements of systems theories that are discussed with reflections to existing concepts in the EA studies could be seen as signifying a systems theoretical starting point for EA, with the various theories and models providing further support for specific cases of inquiry. With this summarizing view also some further challenges are presented, that in our view are emerging for EA with the evolving technology landscapes.

More consistent use of the systems paradigm could move the research closer to being on the same page. To an extent, testing and validation of the theories in empirical efforts is taking place, but a common account of general systems ontology as the EA core is yet to develop. Beyond analysis and explanation, the use of systems paradigm for design and action seems to be taking place: There are already numerous empirical examples for methodologies and modelling, where also the strengths of EA as an approach lie for the enterprise information and systems management and development.

Systems paradigm is promising also from the point of view of the combination of formal, semi-formal and non-formal approaches. As noted in prior research [5]: "EA must encompass both soft and hard systems problems, model complex systems behavior through self-design, and add the human interpretive behavior and cognition to organizations as living systems". Systems theories are feasible candidates for extending and enriching EA research in order to achieve exactly that effect. Systems models are used for formal modelling, and this aspect indeed is successfully made use of. However, the paradigm can also be a starting point for exploratory approaches. A comprehensive paradigm depicted already in the GST, from mechanistic, simple systems to highly complex social systems, further explicated with the diverse constant roles and sub-system relationships as the strength of the LST approach, seems to be fitting for EA.

The question is, however, not which systems approach to take, but how the specific approaches complement the overall systems approach for EA. The more recently introduced CAS paradigm that emphasizes the independent decision making within systems – and their subsystems, a facet not so much emphasized! – as well as the autonomous (re-)orientation of systems, illustrates in our view very well the challenges of EA management. In engineering, the mindset can be to manage systems, or even systems of systems, where the decision making can remain with the systems engineer, or manager. In EA, or especially EAM, relating to management and organization, the task is to manage the complexity of influences within the enterprise(s) and their segments (subsystems and sub-subsystems), that have decision making power over their own resources and strategy setting.

According to the soft systems methodology, there is a distinction between problems faced by soft systems and hard systems. While hard systems discuss types of problems that can be seen as engineering problems, soft systems deal with problems related to e.g. organizational or social problems [5] - both of which can thus be seen as dealing with problems also considered in EA. Furthermore, Bernus et al. [5] note that Cybernetics can provide a theoretical backbone for analysis of relationships between social and psychological systems – for example organizations and individuals. From the early, basic systems theories (GST and LST) emphasizing the composition of the systems and hierarchical levels of complexity, indeed the shift of focus seems to be towards the dynamic features of the systems in models like VSM and Cybernetics, as well as CAS. For EA, and its management, both the structural and the dynamical views will be needed. The diverse theories and models can be seen as complementary – for the management, also the analytical views to the structures and dynamics in EA are, however, still needed.

There is an extensive volume of prior work discussing the systems nature of enterprises, as well as the systems approaches, as a means of solving various problems also considered in the field of EA. A limitation of our study is that prior work spread out to various fields, such as cybernetics [16] and EA network analysis [46], and not covered in detail here. Further, comparisons with the work in SoSE [17] as another promising line of research, is out of the scope of this study. In terms of literature coverage, we could have used additional search phrases, concerning for example enterprise architecture and various specified systems theories, enterprise engineering, and system-of-systems related keywords. Still, as stated by [56], a developmental literature review strives to include a sample of articles covering important aspects of concerned topic. We believe that this sample enables us to answer the research questions at an adequate level. Beyond the list of all included ones (Appendix A), the authors retain the list of papers excluded (see Sect. 4 for the exclusion criteria) at different phases of the search process for future referral.

We strive to contribute to the discussion on EA to solidify the theoretical foundations. We hope that this study elucidates the current knowledge and academic endeavors concerning Systems Thinking, Systems Theories and Enterprise Architecture. Further research is obviously necessary, as well as probing by practitioners, in order to establish EA as a field of study within the broader systems research area. It could learn from insights in related fields, e.g. Systems of Systems Engineering, Enterprise Engineering and Organization Design.

A Appendix

Included articles	ID
Wegmann, A. (2002). The systemic enterprise architecture methodology (SEAM). Business and IT alignment for competitiveness (No. LAMS-REPORT-2002-009)	#1
Wegmann, A., & Preiss, O. (2003, September). MDA in enterprise architecture? The living system theory to the rescue. In Enterprise Distributed Object Computing Conference, 2003. Proceedings. Seventh IEEE International (pp. 2–13). IEEE	#2
Harmon, K. (2005, October). The "systems" nature of enterprise architecture. In Systems, Man and Cybernetics, 2005 IEEE International Conference on (Vol. 1, pp. 78–85). IEEE	#3
Le, L. S., & Wegmann, A. (2005, January). Definition of an object-oriented modeling language for enterprise architecture. In System Sciences, 2005. HICSS'05. Proceedings of the 38th Annual Hawaii International Conference on (pp. 222a–222a). IEEE	#4
Janssen, M., & Kuk, G. (2006, January). A complex adaptive system perspective of enterprise architecture in electronic government. In System Sciences, 2006. HICSS'06. Proceedings of the 39th Annual Hawaii International Conference on(Vol. 4, pp. 71b–71b). IEEE	#5
Lê, L. S., & Wegmann, A. (2006, January). SeamCAD: object-oriented modeling tool for hierarchical systems in enterprise architecture. In System Sciences, 2006. HICSS'06. Proceedings of the 39th Annual Hawaii International Conference on (Vol. 8, pp. 179c–179c). IEEE	#6
Pulkkinen, M. (2006, January). Systemic management of architectural decisions in enterprise architecture planning. four dimensions and three abstraction levels. In System Sciences, 2006. HICSS'06. Proceedings of the 39th Annual Hawaii International Conference on (Vol. 8, pp. 179a–179a). IEEE	#7
Winter, R., & Fischer, R. (2006, October). Essential layers, artifacts, and dependencies of enterprise architecture. In Enterprise Distributed Object Computing Conference Workshops, 2006. EDOCW'06. 10th IEEE International (pp. 30–30). IEEE	#8
Wegmann, A., Regev, G., Rychkova, I., Lê, L. S., & Julia, P. (2007, October). Business and IT alignment with SEAM for enterprise architecture. In Enterprise Distributed Object Computing Conference, 2007. EDOC 2007. 11th IEEE International (pp. 111–111). IEEE	#9

(*continued*)

(*continued*)

Included articles	ID
Wegmann, A., Kotsalainen, A., Matthey, L., Regev, G., & Giannattasio, A. (2008, September). Augmenting the Zachman enterprise architecture framework with a systemic conceptualization. In Enterprise Distributed Object Computing Conference, 2008. EDOC'08. 12th International IEEE (pp. 3–13). IEEE	#10
Buckl, S., Matthes, F., & Schweda, C. M. (2009, October). A viable system perspective on enterprise architecture management. In Systems, Man and Cybernetics, 2009. SMC 2009. IEEE International Conference on (pp. 1483–1488). IEEE	#11
Sousa, P., Lima, J., Sampaio, A., & Pereira, C. (2009). An approach for creating and managing enterprise blueprints: A case for IT blueprints. In Advances in enterprise engineering III (pp. 70–84). Springer, Berlin, Heidelberg	#12
Buckl, S., Matthes, F., & Schweda, C. M. (2010). Towards a method framework for enterprise architecture management–a literature analysis from a viable system perspective. In 5th International Workshop on Business/IT Alignment and Interoperability (BUSITAL 2010) (pp. 46–60)	#13
Kloeckner, S., & Birkmeier, D. (2010). Something is missing: Enterprise architecture from a systems theory perspective. In Service-Oriented Computing. ICSOC/ServiceWave 2009 Workshops (pp. 22–34). Springer, Berlin, Heidelberg	#14
Kotzé, P., & Neaga, I. (2010). Towards an enterprise interoperability framework	#15
Meschke, M., & Baumoel, U. (2010). Architecture Concepts for Value Networks in the Service Industry. In ICIS (p. 266)	#16
Bider, I., Bellinger, G., & Perjons, E. (2011, November). Modeling an agile enterprise: reconciling systems and process thinking. In IFIP Working Conference on The Practice of Enterprise Modeling (pp. 238–252). Springer, Berlin, Heidelberg	#17
Dietz, J. L., & Hoogervorst, J. A. (2011, May). A critical investigation of TOGAF-based on the enterprise engineering theory and practice. In Enterprise Engineering Working Conference (pp. 76–90). Springer, Berlin, Heidelberg	#18
Hoyland, C. A. (2011, October). An analysis of enterprise architectures using general systems theory. In Systems, Man, and Cybernetics (SMC), 2011 IEEE International Conference on (pp. 340–344). IEEE	#19
Wang, S., Xu, L., Li, L., Wang, K., & Choi, J. (2011, October). Features of enterprise information systems integration: A systemic analysis. In Systems, Man, and Cybernetics (SMC), 2011 IEEE International Conference on (pp. 333–339). IEEE	#20
Kandjani, H., & Bernus, P. (2012, June). The enterprise architecture body of knowledge as an evolving discipline. In International Conference on Enterprise Information Systems (pp. 452–470) Springer, Berlin, Heidelberg	#21
Kandjani, H., Wen, L., & Bernus, P. (2012). Enterprise Architecture Cybernetics for Collaborative Networks: Reducing the Structural Complexity and Transaction Cost via Virtual Brokerage. IFAC Proceedings Volumes, 45(6), 1233-1239	#22
Lapalme, J. (2012). Three schools of thought on enterprise architecture. IT professional, 14(6), 37–43	#23
Wan, H., & Carlsson, S. (2012, September). Towards an understanding of enterprise architecture analysis activities. In European Conference on Information Management and Evaluation (p. 334). Academic Conferences International Limited	#24

(*continued*)

(*continued*)

Included articles	ID
Wang, S., Li, L., Wang, K., & Jones, J. D. (2012). e-Business systems integration: a systems perspective. Information Technology and Management, 13(4), 233–249	#25
Zadeh, M. E., Millar, G., & Lewis, E. (2012a). Reinterpreting the TOGAF® enterprise architecture principles using a cybernetic lens. Journal of Enterprise Architecture, 8(2), 9–17	#26
Zadeh, M. E., Millar, G., & Lewis, E. (2012b, January). Mapping the enterprise architecture principles in TOGAF to the cybernetic concepts–An exploratory study. In System Science (HICSS), 2012 45th Hawaii International Conference on (pp. 4270–4276). IEEE	#27
Abraham, R., Tribolet, J., & Winter, R. (2013, May). Transformation of multi-level systems–theoretical grounding and consequences for enterprise architecture management. In Enterprise Engineering Working Conference (pp. 73–87). Springer, Berlin, Heidelberg	#28
Kandjani, H., Bernus, P., & Nielsen, S. (2013, January). Enterprise architecture cybernetics and the edge of chaos: Sustaining enterprises as complex systems in complex business environments. In System Sciences (HICSS), 2013 46th Hawaii International Conference on (pp. 3858–3867). IEEE	#29
Kappelman, L. A., & Zachman, J. A. (2013). The enterprise and its architecture: ontology & challenges. Journal of Computer Information Systems, 53(4), 87–95	#30
Korhonen, J. J., & Poutanen, J. (2013). Tripartite approach to enterprise architecture. Journal of Enterprise Architecture, 9(1), 28–38	#31
Schuetz, A., Widjaja, T., & Kaiser, J. (2013). Complexity in enterprise architectures-conceptualization and introduction of a measure from a system theoretic perspective. In 21st European Conference on Information Systems, Utrecht (pp. 1–12)	#32
Bernus, P., Noran, O., & Molina, A. (2014). Enterprise architecture: twenty years of the GERAM framework. IFAC Proceedings Volumes, 47(3), 3300–3308	#33
du Preez, J., van der Merwe, A., & Matthee, M. (2014, September). Enterprise architecture schools of thought: An exploratory study. In Enterprise Distributed Object Computing Conference Workshops and Demonstrations (EDOCW), 2014 IEEE 18th International (pp. 3–12). IEEE	#34
Hoyland, C. A., M. Adams, K., Tolk, A., & D. Xu, L. (2014). The RQ-Tech methodology: a new paradigm for conceptualizing strategic enterprise architectures. Journal of Management Analytics, 1(1), 55–77	#35
Kandjani, H., Tavana, M., Bernus, P., & Nielsen, S. (2014). Co-Evolution Path Model (CePM): Sustaining Enterprises as Complex Systems on the Edge of Chaos. Cybernetics and Systems, 45(7), 547–567	#36
Noran, O., & Romero, D. (2014). A Pluralistic Approach towards Sustainable Eco-Industrial Networking. IFAC Proceedings Volumes, 47(3), 4292–4297	#37
Schneider, A. W., & Matthes, F. (2014). Using Orientor Theory for Coherent Decision Making for Application Landscape Design. In CSDM (Posters) (pp. 161–172)	#38
Syynimaa, N. (2013). Theoretical perspectives of enterprise architecture	#39

(*continued*)

(continued)

Included articles	ID
Zadeh, M. E., Lewis, E., Millar, G., Yang, Y., & Thorne, C. (2014, October). The use of Viable System Model to develop guidelines for generating Enterprise Architecture Principles. In Systems, Man and Cybernetics (SMC), 2014 IEEE International Conference on (pp. 1020–1026). IEEE	#40
Bernus, P., Goranson, T., Gøtze, J., Jensen-Waud, A., Kandjani, H., Molina, A., ... & Turner, P. (2016). Enterprise engineering and management at the crossroads. Computers in Industry, 79, 87–102	#41
Korhonen, J. J., Lapalme, J., McDavid, D., & Gill, A. Q. (2016, August). Adaptive enterprise architecture for the future: Towards a reconceptualization of EA. In Business Informatics (CBI), 2016 IEEE 18th Conference on (Vol. 1, pp. 272–281). IEEE	#42
Lapalme, J., Gerber, A., Van der Merwe, A., Zachman, J., De Vries, M., & Hinkelmann, K. (2016). Exploring the future of enterprise architecture: A Zachman perspective. Computers in Industry, 79, 103–113	#43
Santana, A., Fischbach, K., & Moura, H. (2016, January). Enterprise architecture analysis and network thinking: A literature review. In System Sciences (HICSS), 2016 49th Hawaii International Conference on (pp. 4566–4575). IEEE	#44
da Silva, N. M. C., & da Silva, M. L. B. M. (2017a, July). Modelling the evolution of enterprise architectures using ontologies. In Business Informatics (CBI), 2017 IEEE 19th Conference on (Vol. 1, pp. 79–88). IEEE	#45
da Silva, N. M. C., Da Silva, M. L. B. M., & De Sousa, P. M. V. A. (2017b, October). A Viewpoint for Analyzing Enterprise Architecture Evolution. In Enterprise Distributed Object Computing Conference (EDOC), 2017 IEEE 21st International (pp. 20–29). IEEE	#46
Syynimaa, N. (2017). The Quest for Underpinning Theory of Enterprise Architecture: General Systems Theory. In ICEIS 2017: Proceedings of the 19th International Conference on Enterprise Information Systems. Volume 3, ISBN 978-989-758-249-3. SCITEPRESS	#47

References

1. Academy of Management Review: Theme issue: general systems theory. Acad. Manag. Rev. **15**(4), (1972)
2. Arnold, R.D., Wade, J.P.: A definition of systems thinking: a systems approach. Procedia Comput. Sci. **44**, 669–678 (2015)
3. Ashmos, D.P., Huber, G.P.: The systems paradigm in organization theory: correcting the record and suggesting the future. Acad. Manag. Rev. **12**(4), 607–621 (1987)
4. Beer, S.: What has cybernetics to do with operational research? J. Oper. Res. Soc. **10**(1), 1–21 (1959)
5. Bernus, P., et al.: Enterprise engineering and management at the crossroads. Comput. Ind. **79**, 87–102 (2016)
6. Bernus, P., Nemes, L., Schmidt, G. (eds.): Handbook on Enterprise Architecture. Springer, Heidelberg (2012). https://doi.org/10.1007/978-3-540-24744-9
7. Bernus, P., Noran, O., Molina, A.: Enterprise architecture: twenty years of the GERAM framework. Annu. Rev. Control **39**, 83–93 (2015)

8. Bjeković, M., Proper, H.A., Sottet, J.S.: Embracing pragmatics. In: Yu, E., Dobbie, G., Jarke, M., Purao, S. (eds.) ER 2014. LNCS, vol. 8824, pp. 431–444. Springer, Cham (2014). https://doi.org/10.1007/978-3-319-12206-9_37

9. Boulding, K.E.: General systems theory—the skeleton of science. Manag. Sci. **2**(3), 197–208 (1956)

10. Bunge, M.: Mechanism and explanation. Philos. Soc. Sci. **27**(4), 410–465 (1997)

11. Cabrera, D., Colosi, L., Lobdell, C.: Systems thinking. Eval. Program Plan. **31**(3), 299–310 (2008)

12. Checkland, P.B.: Soft systems methodology. Hum. Syst. Manag. **8**(4), 273–289 (1989)

13. Daft, R.L., Weick, K.E.: Toward a model of organizations as interpretation systems. Acad. Manag. Rev. **9**(2), 284–295 (1984)

14. Dietz, J.L., et al.: The discipline of enterprise engineering. Int. J. Organ. Des. Eng. **3**(1), 86–114 (2013)

15. Forrester, J.W.: System dynamics, systems thinking, and soft OR. Syst. Dyn. Rev. **10**(2–3), 245–256 (1994)

16. Fu, J., Luo, A., Luo, X., Liu, J.: Charting the landscape of enterprise architecture complexity cybernetics: a systematic literature analysis. In: 2016 12th World Congress on Intelligent Control and Automation (WCICA), pp. 1393–1397. IEEE, June 2016

17. Gorod, A., Sauser, B., Boardman, J.: System-of-systems (2008)

18. Gregor, S.: The nature of theory in information systems. MIS Q. **30**(3), 611–642 (2006). University of Minnesota. http://www.jstor.org/stable/25148742

19. Harmon, K.: The "systems" nature of enterprise architecture. In: 2005 IEEE International Conference on Systems, Man and Cybernetics, vol. 1, pp. 78–85. IEEE, October 2005

20. Holland, J.H.: Complex adaptive systems, pp. 17–30. Daedalus, Sawtry (1992)

21. Hoyland, C.A.: An analysis of enterprise architectures using general systems theory. In: 2011 IEEE International Conference on Systems, Man, and Cybernetics (SMC), pp. 340–344. IEEE, October 2011

22. ISO/IEC 38500:2015(en) Information technology—Governance of IT for the organization (2015)

23. Jackson, M.C.: Fifty years of systems thinking for management. J. Oper. Res. Soc. **60**(1), S24–S32 (2009)

24. Janssen, M., Kuk, G.: A complex adaptive system perspective of enterprise architecture in electronic government. In: Proceedings of the 39th Annual Hawaii International Conference on System Sciences, HICSS 2006, vol. 4, pp. 71b-71b. IEEE, January 2006

25. Kandjani, H., Bernus, P.: The enterprise architecture body of knowledge as an evolving discipline. In: Cordeiro, J., Maciaszek, L.A., Filipe, J. (eds.) ICEIS 2012. LNBIP, vol. 141, pp. 452–470. Springer, Heidelberg (2013). https://doi.org/10.1007/978-3-642-40654-6_27

26. Kandjani, H., Bernus, P., Nielsen, S.: Enterprise architecture cybernetics and the edge of chaos: sustaining enterprises as complex systems in complex business environments. In: 2013 46th Hawaii International Conference on System Sciences (HICSS), pp. 3858–3867. IEEE, January 2013

27. Kalpic, B., Pandza, K., Bernus, P.: Strategy as a creation of corporate future. In: Bernus, P., Nemes, L., Schmidt, G. (eds.) Handbook on Enterprise Architecture, pp. 213–253. Springer, Heidelberg (2003). https://doi.org/10.1007/978-3-540-24744-9_4

28. Kappelman, L.A., Zachman, J.A.: The enterprise and its architecture: ontology & challenges. J. Comput. Inf. Syst. **53**(4), 87–95 (2013)

29. Kappelman, L., McGinnis, T., Pettite, A., Sidorova, A.: Enterprise architecture: charting the territory for academic research. In: AMCIS 2008 Proceedings, p. 162 (2008)

30. Katz, D., Kahn, R.L.: The Social Psychology of Organizations, vol. 2, p. 528. Wiley, New York (1978)

31. Korhonen, J.J., Lapalme, J., McDavid, D., Gill, A.Q.: Adaptive enterprise architecture for the future: Towards a reconceptualization of EA. In: 2016 IEEE 18th Conference on Business Informatics (CBI), vol. 1, pp. 272–281. IEEE, August 2016

32. Lapalme, J.: Three schools of thought on enterprise architecture. IT Prof. **14**(6), 37–43 (2012)

33. Lapalme, J., Gerber, A., Van der Merwe, A., Zachman, J., De Vries, M., Hinkelmann, K.: Exploring the future of enterprise architecture: a Zachman perspective. Comput. Ind. **79**, 103–113 (2016)

34. Luftman, J., Ben-Zvi, T.: Key issues for IT executives 2010: judicious IT investments continue post-recession. MIS Q. Exec. **9**(4), 263–273 (2010)

35. Mesarovic, M.D., Macko, D., Takahara, Y.: Theory of Hierarchical, Multilevel, Systems, vol. 68. Elsevier, Amsterdam (2000)

36. Meschke, M., Baumoel, U.: Architecture concepts for value networks in the service industry. In: ICIS, p. 266 (2010)

37. Mingers, J., White, L.: A review of the recent contribution of systems thinking to operational research and management science. Eur. J. Oper. Res. **207**(3), 1147–1161 (2010)

38. Miller, J.G.: Living Systems. McGraw-Hill, New York (1978)

39. Niemi, E., Pekkola, S.: Using enterprise architecture artefacts in an organisation. Enterp. Inf. Syst. **11**(3), 313–338 (2017)

40. Noran, O., Romero, D.: A pluralistic approach towards sustainable eco-industrial networking. IFAC Proc. Vol. **47**(3), 4292–4297 (2014)

41. Proper, H., Lankhorst, M.M.: Enterprise architecture – towards essential sensemaking. Enterp. Model. Inf. Syst. Arch. – Int. J. Concept. Model. **9**(1), 5–21 (2014)

42. Rahimi, F., Gøtze, J., Møller, C.: Enterprise architecture management: toward a taxonomy of applications. Commun. Assoc. Inf. Syst. **40**(1), 7 (2017)

43. Romero, D., Vernadat, F.: Enterprise information systems state of the art: past, present and future trends. Comput. Ind. **79**, 3–13 (2016)

44. Ross, J.W., Weill, P., Robertson, D.: Enterprise Architecture as Strategy: Creating a Foundation for Business Execution. Harvard Business Press, Brighton (2006)

45. Saint-Louis, P., Morency, M.C., Lapalme, J.: Defining enterprise architecture: a systematic literature review. In: 2017 IEEE 21st International Enterprise Distributed Object Computing Workshop (EDOCW), pp. 41–49. IEEE October 2017

46. Santana, A., Fischbach, K., Moura, H.: Enterprise architecture analysis and network thinking: a literature review. In: 2016 49th Hawaii International Conference on System Sciences (HICSS), pp. 4566–4575. IEEE, January 2016

47. Schelp, J., Winter, R.: Language communities in enterprise architecture research. In: Proceedings of the 4th International Conference on Design Science Research in Information Systems and Technology, p. 23. ACM, May 2009

48. Schöenherr, M.: Towards a common terminology in the discipline of enterprise architecture. In: Feuerlicht, G., Lamersdorf, W. (eds.) ICSOC 2008. LNCS, vol. 5472, pp. 400–413. Springer, Heidelberg (2009). https://doi.org/10.1007/978-3-642-01247-1_40

49. Shanks, G., Gloet, M., Someh, I.A., Frampton, K., Tamm, T.: Achieving benefits with enterprise architecture. J. Strat. Inf. Syst. **27**, 139–156 (2018)

50. Senge, P.M.: The fifth discipline, the art and practice of the learning organization. Perform. Improv. **30**(5), 37 (1991)

51. Spewak, S.H., Hill, S.C.: Enterprise Architecture Planning: Developing a Blueprint for Data, Applications and Technology. QED Information Sciences, Inc., Wellesley (1993)

52. Stamper, R.K.: Informatics without the computer. In: Proceedings of the CAFRAD Conference, Algiers (1976)

53. Stamper, R.K.: Organizational semiotics: Informatics without the computer? In: Liu, K., Clarke, R.J., Andersen, P.B., Stamper, R.K. (eds.) Information, Organisation and Technology, pp. 115–171. Springer, Boston (2001). https://doi.org/10.1007/978-1-4615-1655-2_5

54. Syynimaa, N.: The quest for underpinning theory of enterprise architecture: general systems theory. In: Proceedings of the 19th International Conference on Enterprise Information Systems, ICEIS 2017, vol. 3. SCITEPRESS (2017). ISBN 978-989-758-249-3

55. Tamm, T., Seddon, P.B., Shanks, G.G., Reynolds, P.: How does enterprise architecture add value to organisations? CAIS **28**, 10 (2011)

56. Templier, M., Paré, G.: A framework for guiding and evaluating literature reviews. Commun. Assoc. Inf. Syst. **37** (2015)

57. Von Bertalanffy, L.: The History and Status of General Systems Theory (1950)

58. Webster, J., Watson, R.T.: Analyzing the past to prepare for the future: writing a literature review. MIS Q. **26**, xiii–xxiii (2002)

59. Wegmann, A.: The systemic enterprise architecture methodology (SEAM). Business and IT alignment for competitiveness (No. LAMS-REPORT-2002-009) (2002)

60. Wegmann, A., Preiss, O.: MDA in enterprise architecture? The living system theory to the rescue. In: 2003 Proceedings of the Seventh IEEE International Enterprise Distributed Object Computing Conference, pp. 2–13. IEEE, September 2003

61. Wiener, N.: Cybernetics. Sci. Am. **179**(5), 14–19 (1948)

62. Zachman, J.A.: Business systems planning and business information control study: a comparison. IBM Syst. J. **21**(1), 31–53 (1982)

63. Zachman, J.A.: A framework for information systems architecture. IBM Syst. J. **26**(3), 276–292 (1987)

64. Zadeh, M.E., Lewis, E., Millar, G., Yang, Y., Thorne, C.: The use of Viable System Model to develop guidelines for generating Enterprise Architecture Principles. In: 2014 IEEE International Conference on Systems, Man and Cybernetics (SMC), pp. 1020–1026. IEEE October 2014

Affordance-Driven Software Assembling

Ondřej Dvořák[✉], Robert Pergl[✉], and Petr Kroha[✉]

Czech Technical University in Prague, Faculty of Information Technology,
Prague, Czech Republic
{ondrej.dvorak,robert.pergl,petr.kroha}@fit.cvut.cz
http://ccmi.fit.cvut.cz

Abstract. Nowadays, the pace of technology innovation and disruption accelerates. This poses a challenge of transforming complex functionalities of enterprise systems to a new technological environment. In this paper, we explain how enterprise engineering τ-theory and β-theory may help to manage the relationship between system function and its construction (F/C), thus facilitating changing technology challenges more rigorously and efficiently. We introduce the notion of Affordance-Driven Assembling (ADA) and its simplified version Objectified Affordance-Driven Assembling (O-ADA), which together with the so-called Semantic Descriptions represent a software-engineering approach enabling reasoning about users and their purposes versus components and their properties. Our experiments show that engineering methods based on these theories may increase reusability of code and improve important metrics such as costs, time reduction and error rate decrease, especially when switching to a new technology. We also discuss existing approaches related to ADA and O-ADA.

Keywords: Component-based systems · Semantic descriptions
Software architecture · EE theories · ADA · O-ADA

1 Introduction

1.1 Motivation

Most of current industries rely on services provided by software solutions. These solutions age over time and become legacy information systems. Assuming that these software services are crucial for the overall business activity, companies must either invest to keeping these systems operational and up to date, replace them at some point with functionally equivalent systems, or (sadly) adjust their business to the limits of the systems.

Evidence shows that companies spend currently most of their available budgets on maintenance [2]. "By some estimates, seventy-five percent of the IT budgets of banks and insurance companies are consumed maintaining existing systems" [10]. Anxiously, these maintenance budgets rise in time as confirmed by research of Mannaert et al. [21]: "continuing IT builds as before yield more and

© Springer Nature Switzerland AG 2019
D. Aveiro et al. (Eds.): EEWC 2018, LNBIP 334, pp. 39–54, 2019.
https://doi.org/10.1007/978-3-030-06097-8_3

more complexity and thus increase build and maintenance costs". Yet, usually costs and risks of switching to a new technology are still higher than its maintenance and there is a high psychological barrier of investing in an expensive project where the technology is switched, but the functionality does not change considerably.

To encourage companies to innovate more frequently to new technology, thus to prefer switching over maintenance, we would need to considerably reduce costs on the system switch. Such a cost is influenced by multiple factors, e.g., an effort on re-engineering the legacy system, integrating it into the current infrastructure, retraining employees to use it and taking an operational risk associated with the use of the new system.

We argue that systems composed of components (component-based systems, CBS), where function and construction (F/C) are explicitly expressed and distinguished, can be replaced in a controlled way with considerably lower costs and risks.

We approach this goal by exploring the relationship between F/C. In particular, we apply a software design approach to build component-based systems by clearly defining the function, construction, and F/C relationship of components.

1.2   Structure of the Paper

First, we briefly introduce formal foundations of our research in Sect. 2 – we explain the key terms affordance, function, construction and their relationship. In Sect. 3, we refine the terms in the context of component-based software systems. In Sect. 4, we bring the term "affordance-driven assembling" (ADA) and we objectify it in Sect. 5. We present first part of our case study in Sect. 6 and demonstrate the introduced terms on it. Then, in Sect. 7, we explain the construct called "semantic description", a formal description of ADA. Further in this section we continue with our case study and we exemplify the use of "semantic descriptions" on that. In Sect. 8, we evaluate how applying the formulated method helped in an existing financial system separating its F/C in two conceptually different technologies – desktop and web. We discuss related work in Sect. 9, and we conclude in Sect. 10 by outlining further research in this field.

2   Formal Foundations

Enterprise engineering (EE) τ-theory and β-theory discuss the concepts of function, construction and their relation thoroughly. At the same time, EE theories primarily address broad understanding of core notions of organizations [15].

The question is whether these theories can be directly applied to the area of software engineering. The next question is whether these theories can be in particular applied to the area of component-based systems (CBS) built from components. Such components are defined by Szyperski [9]: "A software component is a unit of composition with contractually specified interfaces and explicit context dependencies only. A software component can be deployed independently and is subject to composition by third-parties."

We argue that the theories mentioned above can be applied. Rooted in general Bunge's system ontology [7,8], EE theories are based on the notion of *system* [12]. According to them, each subsystem of a system is an ontological system by itself. Thus, the theories are recursively applicable to ontological subsystems, as well. Now, an enterprise being a system, ICT infrastructure is clearly one of its subsystems, so we can conclude that general theories of enterprise systems can be applied to ICT infrastructures, as well (CBS being a specific class of such systems).

2.1 Affordances

To explain the F/C, it is important to introduce the notion of *affordances*. Merriam-Webstern defines them as "the qualities or properties of an object that define its possible uses or make clear how it can or should be used". However, a more formal definition is provided by the τ-theory. Among others, the theory studies the relation between subjects with purposes, and objects with properties. It defines the affordance as follows:

Definition 1. *Affordance is a subject-object relationship, which can be represented by the formula below. The symbol $*$ denotes "is in relation"*

$$affordance : (subject * purpose) * (object * properties)$$

Thus, the affordance is a term bridging teleological and ontological points of view [13]. From the Theory of Affordances [17] comes that subjects observe and manipulate objects to satisfy their needs and desires. However, by themselves, the objects with properties are not what satisfies their needs and desires. Rather, it is the affordance of objects doing so.

2.2 Functions

As τ-theory [13] reminds, subjects also create objects, these newly created objects are called *artefacts*. They are usually designed and created with some affordance in mind to provide a corresponding function. Dietz and Hoogervorst [13] explain: "A chair may offer an affordance sit-on-able while providing a function sit-on to a subject." Following this reasoning, a hammer is hit-able (function hit), knife is cut-able (function cut), thermometer is measure-temperature-able (function measure-temperature), etc.

Obviously, a number of affordances (and functions) can be assigned to a single artefact. It depends on the purpose to which the subjects want to use them. Formally, all the functions of a given artefact can be decomposed into a hierarchically organized structure called a functional decomposition – a Blackbox model that captures how the system can be used.

In software engineering, there are several established methods for functional analysis to capture the Black-box model, e.g., UML Use-Case model [16], Extreme Programming User Stories [4], or COCOMO II Object Points [5].

Summarized, [13]: "artefacts are created with an affordance in mind, which is commonly called a function of the artefact". The functions can be organized into a structure called a functional decomposition. Dietz and Hoogervorst [13] remark that "because of the unlimited imagination of the human mind, the number of affordances of an object is basically unlimited".

2.3 Constructions

There is a notion of construction discussed by the τ-theory. Dietz and Hoogervorst [13] clarify: "the function of an artefact is made possible by its construction". They describe the construction as "the parts it is composed of, their interconnections, and the substances the parts are made of". Next, the notion of a system is defined by [13]:

Definition 2. *Something is a system if and only if it has the following properties:*

- Composition: *a set of elements that are atomic in some category (physical, social, etc.).*
- Environment: *a set of elements of the same category; the composition and the environment are disjoint.*
- Structure: *a set of interaction bonds among the elements in the composition, and between them and the elements in the environment.*

The construction of an artefact can be decomposed into a hierarchically organized structure called a constructional-decomposition – a white-box model. As Dietz [12] clarifies in terms of Definition 2: "It is, in fact, a technique to compose a system as a construction of parts (elements or subsystems).". Typically, a white-box view of a system is captured in software engineering by the UML Component diagram [1].

2.4 F/C Relationship

To conceive the relationship between a function and its construction, we follow the τ-theory and the β-theory.

The τ-theory perceives a relationship between subjects with purposes and objects with properties, which we described earlier.

Next, the β-theory concerns the design of systems, as defined by the τ-theory. The theory grounds the notion of an architecture and it elaborates on the so-called *Generic System Development Process (GSDP)* illustrated in Fig. 1. According to that, "an architecture is a collective name for functional and constructional principles" [14]. The β-theory covers important notions of distinguishing F/C design. A given set of functional requirements typically has more

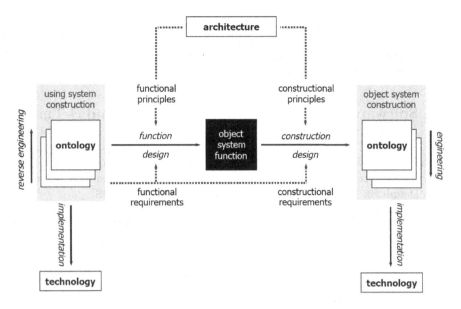

Fig. 1. Generic system development process [14]

constructions satisfying them. For example, there can be several differently looking houses, yet based on the same set of functional requirement. This difference
is explained by a substantial amount of a design freedom that architects may
exercise. When building a house, an architect can choose from various technologies and materials. The same is valid for software engineering. Today, a software
architect can choose from a substantial amount of technologies and components
to build a software from (as outlined on Fig. 1).

However, because of the subjectivity of functional decomposition and because
of the possibly multiple different constructions of each function, Dietz warns [12]:
"It is a misunderstanding that one could choose the components in a functional
decomposition such that they coincide with constructional components, but that
is just impossible. Black-box models and White-box models are fundamentally
different types of models. There is no way of simply mapping one to the other."
He concludes [12]: "The constructional designers have to bridge the mental gap
between function and construction".

Having said that, we argue that the ad-hoc mental bridge between a function and construction is one of key reasons of complicated switching from old
to new technologies, as introduced in Sect. 1. While fully agreeing with Dietz on
the general level, we suggest that if we are able to limit conditions to a certain
degree, the gap can be bridged more systematically within the software design
approach where subjective aspects are minimized and where the set of construction elements is limited and clearly defined. This suggestion is based on a simple
mental experiment: Let us assume that the naturally infinite set of functions is
(arbitrarily) limited. Then making a cartesian product with a (naturally) limited set of possible constructions and a limited design freedom (given by software

best practices), we come to a bounded relation between functions and constructions. Thus, our stance is that for software engineering, it is possible to devise at least a semi-rigorous engineering way of designing software systems. In the next section, we introduce such an approach.

3   A Software System Founded on τ-Theory and β-Theory

A system founded in τ-theory and β-theory must be composed of components that suit the needs of a given user with a specific purpose. As we know from Sect. 2.1, such a relationship is captured by the term affordance. Now, we reformulate Definition 1 in terms of a component-based system (CBS):

Definition 3. *Affordance is a user-component relationship, which can be represented by the following formula:*

$$affordance : (user * purpose) * (component * properties).$$

Definition 3 is a key to building systems considering F/C division. We may now reformulate this relation into a function, which takes users, their purposes, and components with their properties, and it outputs the final construction. Figure 2 visually depicts this function in CBS. We can see that components and properties are inherently bound together. This function actually expresses a software design process that results in a construction of the resulting CBS from the appropriate components.

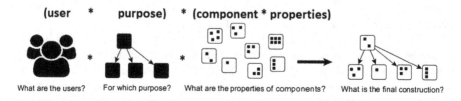

Fig. 2. Affordances in component-based systems

A mapping algorithm that selects proper components for user-purpose relationship is the key means of software design process here. The algorithm may be manual (assisted), semi-automated, or even automated (as is the case of NSX mentioned in Sect. 9). Figure 3 visualises the essence of such an algorithm in a 3-dimensional space. It shows that each component can satisfy specific purpose of a given user to some extent (affordance). The degree of satisfaction is fuzzy. It means that it may range between completely true (best fit) and completely false (worst fit), which is here represented by shades of gray.

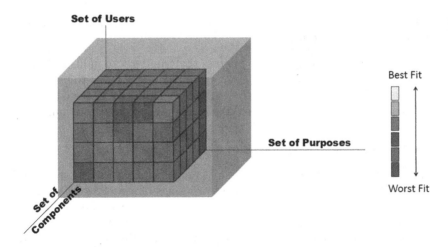

Set of Users

Best Fit

Worst Fit

Set of Purposes

Set of Components

Fig. 3. CBS affordances in a 3-dimensional space

Finally, when designing systems founded on the τ-theory and the β-theory, we need to define a semantic meaning of objects on the axes of Fig. 3, which means a description of specific users and their purposes on one side, and components and their properties on the other side. We call software design approach based on these descriptions *affordance-driven*, and we investigate it deeper in the next section.

4   Affordance-Driven Assembling

In Sect. 2.1, we explained that Dietz reminds that an individual can identify an unlimited number of purposes for which the system can be used. To make the F/C relation manageable, we deliberately limit the number of imaginable users, purposes, and components. Let us now formulate a definition based on the previous thoughts:

Definition 4. *Affordance-Driven Assembling (ADA) is a software design approach for development of component-based systems following Definition 2, where all the following points hold:*

1. *There is a bounded set of **ADA-users** AU, which we are able to formally describe.*
2. *There is a bounded set of **ADA-purposes** AP, which we are able to formally describe.*
3. *There is a bounded set of **ADA-components** AC. Each component has its construction and properties, and it manifests its possible ADA-purposes for all possible ADA-users.*
4. *ADA-components are either atomic, or they consist of other ADA-components being their constructional decomposition according to the τ-theory.*
5. *There exists a relation **ADA-relation:** $(AU * AP) * AC$.*

Definition 5. *The union of ADA-users, ADA-purposes and ADA-components forms the set of* **ADA-elements**.

We use the term "Assembling" to express that similarly to industrial assembly lines, the resulting product is merely assembled from ready-to-use components instead of involving human-centred design principles, as expressed in Fig. 1.

Let us now elaborate more on the ADA-elements and ADA-relation.

4.1   ADA-Purposes Decomposition

Principles, according to which a "process of organising a knowledge of an application domain into hierarchical rankings or orderings of abstractions", are commonly referred to as *abstraction principles* [23]. As purposes (and thus ADA-purposes) can be seen as a type of knowledge, the same principles may be applied to them. Thus, the purposes can be logically grouped into higher level of abstraction organised hierarchically [23] "in order to obtain a better understanding of the phenomena in concern". The set of ADA-purposes then becomes a tree structure. In the end, we can observe that the decomposition is actually the functional decomposition from the τ-theory. For the case of ADA, it describes all the possible ADA-purposes related to all the possible users for which a system within a specific domain can be used.

4.2   Realising ADA-Relation

The realisation of ADA-relation can have two forms:

1. A function $(AU * AP) \rightarrow AC$, which assigns a set of ADA-components to ADA-users and ADA-purposes. This situation corresponds to Fig. 2 and can be seen as generating of software from specifications.
2. A function $AC \rightarrow (AU * AP)$, which gives possible ADA-users and ADA-purposes of a given ADA-component. This is a means of reusability, i.e. discovery of existing components suitable for a certain combination of ADA-user and ADA-purpose, thus facilitating software design process.

5   Objectified Affordance-Driven Assembling

In UFO-C[1], the purpose may be mapped to a *desire*, which is existentially dependent on its bearer. This means that in ADA, we need to classify independently various types of users, various purposes, and to relate them.

However, we may make a simplification by assuming "standard" users and their typical purposes. This means, the kind of a shared desire become "extracted" from its bearer to form an existentially independent object – an objectified desire. According to τ-theory, this is an intended affordance disconnected from the purpose someone can have. The theory refers to that by the term "function". Then we may formulate a simplified notion of ADA:

---

[1] Unified Foundational Ontology of Social Entities [18].

Definition 6. *Objectified Affordance-Driven Assembling (O-ADA) is a special type of ADA, where*

1. *Instead of ADA-Users and ADA-Purposes, there is a bounded set of* **O-ADA-Functions** *OAF, which we are able to formally describe.*
2. *We replace ADA-relation by* **O-ADA-relation:** $OAF * AC$.

Again, we need to deal with an unlimited number of purposes, as remarked by Dietz and Hoogervorst [13]. However, we can assume that we can objectify the decomposition into a form on which "everybody can agree". Additionally, we can limit the decomposition to a domain of a specific system. In the next section, we bring a case study of a system in a domain of viewing tabular data. We further demonstrate one possible O-ADA-Function decomposition in Fig. 6.

6   Mapping User Requirements to O-ADA-Functions

Let us now relate the traditional requirements analysis performed in software engineering to the concepts formulated above. We present this mapping on a case study of the tabular data viewer. For simplicity, let us work with O-ADA[2]. First, we describe the case study more precisely, analyse it using the traditional UML Use-Case Diagram, and demonstrate a sample wireframe of the demanded system.

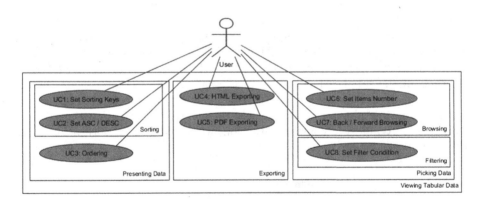

Fig. 4. Use-case diagram of a tabular data viewer

Case Study (Part 1): *Tabular data viewer is a component for viewing, filtering, and exporting tabular data, e.g., relational data from a database. It operates in a scope given by tabular data O-ADA-Functions. The system must implement*

---

[2] This will be probably the most common situation in practice, as we need to work with ADA just in case we need to distinguish special types of users, such as users with various inabilities.

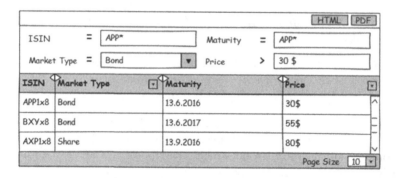

Fig. 5. Wireframe of a tabular data viewer

use-cases depicted in Fig. 4. The wireframe of its possible construction can look like in Fig. 5. We can see that UC_1 and UC_2 can be performed by using the header of each column, one can sort data ascending or descending using a little black arrow. UC_3 is covered by using the left/right arrows directly in the header – they switch the order of columns. The exporting functionality demanded by UC_3 and UC_4 is triggered by HTML/PDF buttons. The number of displayed items demanded by UC_6 can be set in the footer using a page size selector. The back and forward browsing in UC_7 can be performed using a scroll bar, and the filter condition in UC_8 can be set in a filter.

Now, we need to map the use-cases onto O-ADA-Functions. In a general situation, this would result in a mapping onto several O-ADA-Function decomposition trees (called a *forest* in computer science). However, in our simple case, all the use cases map onto a single O-ADA-Function decomposition of the tabular data viewer. The result is depicted in Fig. 6. The black nodes mark O-ADA-Functions of the tabular data viewer in the case study. The grey nodes mark O-ADA-Functions that are not needed, yet generally, they belong to the same domain of viewing tabular data. Obviously, the involved O-ADA-Functions result in a subtree. Again, in a common situation, we would end up with a forest of O-ADA-Function trees.

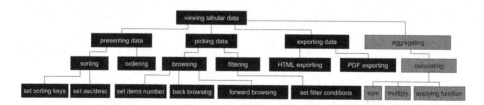

Fig. 6. O-ADA-Functions decomposition of the tabular data viewer

In Fig. 7, the constructional decomposition is displayed using a traditional UML Component Diagram. Generally, the relation between a node from the

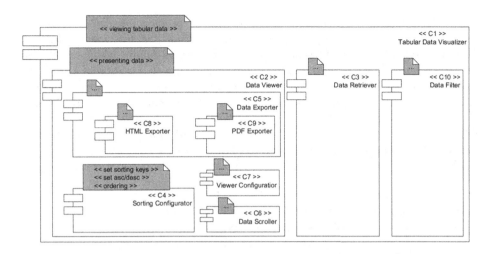

Fig. 7. UML Component diagram representing a constructional decomposition

functional decomposition and the nodes in the constructional decomposition is M:N, as one function may be (and it typically is) realised by several constructional nodes and vice versa, one constructional node may realise several functions (reusability). In this particular case, the constructional decomposition is very similar to the functional one, however in principle the nodes represent constructional elements, and as such they may be reused in different systems.

7 Semantic Descriptions

Now, having an ADA system defined, the next question is how to describe the ADA-elements (ADA-users, ADA-purposes, and ADA-components). We propose to call these descriptions *semantic descriptions* (SD):

Definition 7. *A **Semantic Description in ADA** is a formal description of an ADA-element that specifies its essence in such a way that the ADA-relation can be realised.*

Then, similarly:

Definition 8. *A **Semantic Description in O-ADA** is a formal description of an O-ADA-element that specifies its essence in such a way that the O-ADA-relation can be realised.*

The realisation of the relations refers here to Sect. 4.2. Below, we continue with our case study, and we detail it to a simplistic financial system. We show an example of an implementation of basic SD of a component for viewing bonds in a tabular data viewer.

Case Study (Part 2): *The tabular data viewer is a component of a simple financial system. This component is used for sorting and filtering bonds. We declare that an O-ADA component for filtering should ignore its international security identification number ISIN – an attribute uniquely identifying a tradable financial assest, i.e. the component must handle the notion of ignoring things. Additionally, when having an O-ADA-Function to present bonds, we want them to be sorted ascendantly by name. We further require that the string attribute CFICode follows ISO 10962, being a classification of financial instruments and that the component can filter and sort bonds according to this code.*

This is how we may describe these O-ADA-Functions in a natural language:

1. Set FilteringFunction to ignore the ISIN field.
2. Set SortingFunction to sort by Name field ascending.
3. Set the type[3] of the CFI field to CFICodeType.

For machine processing, we need to encode the semantic description into a formal language: a general-purpose programming language (GPL), a descriptive language (like XML) or a domain-specific language (DSL)[4]. In Listing 1.1, we show the example of semantic descriptions expressed in the C# language.

```
class BondDescriptor : IClassDescriptor<Bond> {
  void Descriptor(IClassDescription<Bond> bondDescr) {
    bondDescr.Function<IFiltering>()
       .Field(x => x.ISIN).Ignore();
    bondDescr.Function<ISorting>()
       .Field(x => x.Name).SortAsc();
    bondDescr.Field(x => x.CFI)
       .Type(new CFICodeType());
    }
}
```

Listing 1.1. Semantic description of O-ADA-Functions to filter and sort bonds

Expressing SD in DSL (or in a descriptive language) instead of a GPL[5], brings additional effort of implementing a parser/processor. However, for a certain number of SD, this pays off, because once a switch to a new programming language occurs, the SD do not have to be recoded, just the parser/processor is reimplemented. For typical large enterprise systems like the one described below, the savings of costs and decrease of risks of bugs are considerable.

---

[3] We may use the standard *type* concept from computer science, as it is defined a set of admissible values and operations upon them.

[4] "A domain-specific language (DSL) is a programming language or executable specification language that offers, through appropriate notations and abstractions, expressive power focused on, and usually restricted to, a particular problem domain" [11].

[5] General-purpose programming language (GPL).

8   Evaluating the Approach in Practice

We contribute to an implementation of a system `corima`. It is an application framework developed by company COPS. It can host applications in various business domains[6]. The portfolio of `corima` financial applications mostly covers the needs of the whole treasury department of banking/corporate customers. Most of the applications are data-centric, focused on displaying data in standardized components, e.g., pivot tables, grids, charts, edit forms, etc. The system `corima` traditionally offered WPF[7] desktop components. We started implementing sample O-ADA components in the system across about 40 applications and we now make the use of semantically-described components as follows: Data Editor (630 usages), Data Filter (513 usages), Data Viewer (564 usages). For each new usage, a new component is installed based on its semantic description – in a declarative way, which saves a lot of code and errors compared to standard customisation of components.

Lately, we started porting `corima` to web technologies (JavaScript). This is where we realised that expressing SD in a descriptive language (or a DSL) is a great help, as future technological switches will not require rewriting the SD (possibly just syntactically rewritten), just the code of high-cohesion, low-coupling O-ADA-components must be recoded.

9   Related Work

In software engineering, the efforts to improve reusability and code quality are traditional. However, we are not aware of any approach that builds on the enterprise engineering theories. Here, following representative examples of classes of approaches, we find the most relevant to our effort.

Today's programming languages package repositories like NuGet (C#), NPM (NodeJS), RubyGems (Ruby), Hackage (Haskell), Clojars (Clojure), and many others store libraries and components annotated by tags and sorted in categories, enabling searching and discovery by various queries. Moreover, dependencies are managed, so we may say that they store trees of components. This is a clear demonstration of approach 2 in Sect. 4.2. However, F/C is currently not explicitly separated and semantically described, so there is no automation possible of finding suitable constructions for given functions.

ASP.NET MVC[8] offers a feature called *data annotations*. The annotations are similar to our proposal of SD. They declaratively state the semantic meaning of a given data. A suitable UI component for manipulating them is selected automatically. For instance, we can annotate a data property with [Email].

---

[6] The business domain is meant to be the area of a business, e.g., finance, medicine, etc.

[7] Windows Presentation Foundation (WPF) is a graphical subsystem created by Microsoft to support a development of Windows-based applications.

[8] Microsoft's edge technology intended to develop web pages following a general Model-View-Controller (MVC) pattern.

This means that its value must be a valid email address. ASP.NET MVC technology will automatically create a text field validating the user's input against the known email pattern, which is a demonstration of approach 1 in Sect. 4.2. However, the expressiveness of annotations for describing a more complex functionality is limited, and they are tightly coupled with .NET. Nevertheless, it is a good inspiration of how a basic annotation system may look like.

A holistic example of approach 1 in Sect. 4.2 is offered by Normalized Systems theory (NS) [21], namely the NS Expanders technology based on it. It is focused on building evolvable software architectures. These systems "can be long-lived and correspond to changes in a cost-effective way" [6]. Therefore, such an approach is fully aligned with our motivation. NS comes up with a systematic methodology for a modular design with the objective of creating these evolvable systems [21]. The creators of NS propose that "in order to spare developers from all the complexity of NS theory, and to eliminate human errors" [20], the systems should be generated based on formally proven NS theorems. The NSX company has built so-called "NS Expanders" to generate Java Enterprise client-server applications based on NS descriptions. From the theoretical point, this approach is based on specifying functions and automatically generating construction for it. The concrete construction may be customized (e.g. selecting a specific JavaScript framework or a database backend), however, it does employ annotated components reusable out of scope of NS. Also, the functional description expresses structure and behaviour, but not declarative-style affordances. Moreover, the generated structures mostly aim at providing "basic out-of-the-box functionalities such as CRUD[9] screens, waterfall screens, data import, document upload/download, basic user management, basic reporting, etc." [24].

Last but not least, our research of capabilities relates to ADA approaches described in this paper. Azvedo et al. [3] discuss this notion in context of ArchiMate. They investigate how the capability and resource contribute to the field of enterprise architecture, and how ArchiMate framework can be extended in order to include these notions appropriately. Further, Miranda et al. [22] present an analysis of capability-related concepts in the domain of defense. The first article refers to the definition of capability as [19] "the ability (of a static structure element, e.g., actor, application component, etc.) to employ resources to achieve some goal". Our research is purpose-oriented and thus shares some similarity with the goal-oriented capabilities. Our future work is to investigate these similarities and reflect them in current ADA research.

10   Summary and Conclusions

We tried to tackle the traditional challenge of software code expressiveness and reusability, yet in a different way – by applying enterprise-engineering τ-theory and β-theory to software engineering, specifically to component-based

---

[9] In computer programming, CRUD is an acronym to Create, Read, Update, Delete.

systems development. We defined principles of so-called affordance-driven assembly (ADA) and its simplified version O-ADA. Together with that, we brought semantic descriptors (SD) to distinguish and capture function and construction in a managed way. We demonstrated the concepts on the case study of a tabular data component and we evaluated a real application in a large enterprise software system.

We conclude that the presented approach has a potential of becoming a basis for (semi-)automated software systems composition from ADA-components based on functional specification, as well as increasing components reusability through improved discoverability (Sect. 4.2). These become crucial especially for switching technologies of existing systems.

This paper opens several research topics. We have not discussed ADA in more detail, especially with the respect to categorising and describing users, which may become interesting if dealing with users with special needs (disabilities) or cultural specifics. Also, we did not discuss in detail challenges of analysis and design of complex ADAs, i.e., encompassing many different ADA-components and complex architectures. One broad research topic are semantic descriptors, both with the respect to theory and implementation, and of course continuing with ways of leveraging them for (semi-)automated components discovery and software design process.

Acknowledgement. This research has been supported by SGS17/211/OHK3/3T/18.

References

1. OMG Unified Modeling Language (OMG UML). Superstructure, V2.1.2 (2007)
2. Alija, N.: Justification of software maintenance costs. Int. J. Adv. Res. Comput. Sci. Softw. Eng. **7**, 15–23 (2017)
3. Azevedo, C., Iacob, M.E., Almeida, J., van Sinderen, M., Ferreira Pires, L., Guizzardi, G.: Modeling resources and capabilities in enterprise architecture: a well-founded ontology-based proposal for archimate. Inf. Syst. **54**, 235–262 (2015)
4. Beck, K., Andres, C.: Extreme Programming Explained: Embrace Change, 2nd edn. Addison-Wesley, Boston (2004)
5. Boehm, B.W., Madachy, R., Steece, B., et al.: Software Cost Estimation with COCOMO II with CDROM. Prentice Hall PTR (2000)
6. Breivold, H.P., Crnkovic, I., Eriksson, P.: Evaluating software evolvability. In: Software Engineering Research and Practice in Sweden, p. 96 (2007)
7. Bunge, M.: Treatise on Basic Philosophy: The Furniture of The World, vol. 3. World D. Reidel Publishing Company, Dordrecht (1977)
8. Bunge, M.: Treatise on Basic Philosophy: A World of Systems, vol. 4. World D. Reidel Publishing Company, Dordrecht (1979)
9. Szyperski, C.: Component Software: Beyond Object-Oriented Programming, 2nd edn. Addison-Wesley, Boston (2002)
10. Crotty, J., Horrocks, I.: Managing legacy system costs: a case study of a meta-assessment model to identify solutions in a large financial services company. Appl. Comput. Inf. **13**(2), 175–183 (2017)
11. van Deursen, A., Klint, P., Visser, J.: Domain-specific languages: an annotated bibliography. SIGPLAN Not. **35**, 26–36 (2000)

12. Dietz, J.: Enterprise Ontology: Theory and Methodology. Springer, Heidelberg (2006). https://doi.org/10.1007/3-540-33149-2
13. Dietz, J., Hoogervorst, J.: Theories in Enterprise Engineering Memorandum - TAO
14. Dietz, J., Hoogervorst, J.: Theories in Enterprise Engineering Memorandum - BETA (2014)
15. Dietz, J., Hoogervorst, J.: Technical Report TR-FIT-15-01 (2015)
16. Gemino, A., Parker, D.: Use case diagrams in support of use case modeling: deriving understanding from the picture. J. Database Manag. **20**(1), 1–24 (2009)
17. Gibson, J.J.: The theory of affordances. In: Perceiving, Acting and Knowing. Towards an Ecological Psychology. Wiley, Hoboken (1977)
18. Guizzardi, G., de Almeida Falbo, R., Guizzardi, R.S.: Grounding software domain ontologies in the unified foundational ontology (UFO): the case of the ode software process ontology. In: CIbSE, pp. 127–140 (2008)
19. Iacob, M.E., Quartel, D., Jonkers, H.: Capturing business strategy and value in enterprise architecture to support portfolio valuation. In: 2012 IEEE 16th International Enterprise Distributed Object Computing Conference (EDOC), pp. 11–20. IEEE (2012)
20. van der Linden, D., Neugschwandtner, G., Mannaert, H.: Towards evolvable state machines for automation systems. In: Proceedings of the 8th International Conference on Systems (ICONS), pp. 148–153 (2013)
21. Mannaert, H., Verelst, J., De Bruyn, P.: Normalized Systems Theory, From Foundations for Evolvable Software Towards a General Theory for Evolvable Design. Normalized Systems Institute (2016)
22. Miranda, G., Azevedo, C., Guizzardi, G., Almeida, J.: An ontological analysis of capability modeling in defense enterprise architecture frameworks (2017)
23. Taivalsaari, A.: On the notion of inheritance. ACM Comput. Surv. (CSUR) **28**(3), 438–479 (1996)
24. Vanhoof, E., De Bruyn, P., Aerts, W., Verelst, J.: Building an evolvable prototype for a multiple GAAP accounting information system. In: Aveiro, D., Pergl, R., Gouveia, D. (eds.) EEWC 2016. LNBIP, vol. 252, pp. 71–85. Springer, Cham (2016). https://doi.org/10.1007/978-3-319-39567-8_5

Understanding Architecture Principles as Working Mechanisms

Mark Paauwe(✉)

Wageningen, The Netherlands
mark.paauwe@dragon1.com

Abstract. This paper is the introduction of a new way of formulating architecture principles as working mechanisms by enterprise architects. This alternative way of formulating is aimed at producing more effective architecture principles than enterprise architects are currently producing. This new way of formulating architecture principles aligns with practices in physics and building architecture. Architecture principles need to be made much more effective because in them lies the added value of working with enterprise architecture: using principles to guide the design and realization of enterprise-wide solutions compliant to strategy and stakeholders requirements. In this paper, principles are proposed to be formulated as working mechanisms rather than general rules (guidelines). This will make them communicate contextual truths and will have them cause more effect in guiding the design and engineering of systems. This paper presents intermediate results of an ongoing research on architecture principles.

Keywords: Architecture principles · Concepts · Concepts principles
Working mechanisms · Formulating principles · Definitions

1 Introduction

Architecture principles are largely produced, accepted and valued, but not largely approved and effectively used by enterprise architects, designers, developers, CIOs and managers.

One can imagine that the lack of high quality approved and used architecture principles lead to slower innovation and to a lower quality of enterprises than the strategy of the enterprises requires the quality to be.

Because of this problem of not approving and using (proposed) architecture principles, we want to answer the question if architecture principles are approved more and used more effectively when they are formulated in a different way, as working mechanisms, becoming contextual truths.

In this paper, we are going to introduce a new (working mechanism based) definition for architecture principle [12] for the field of enterprise architecture and introduce a suggested practice with rules for formulating architecture principles, aligned with building architecture.

© Springer Nature Switzerland AG 2019
D. Aveiro et al. (Eds.): EEWC 2018, LNBIP 334, pp. 55–65, 2019.
https://doi.org/10.1007/978-3-030-06097-8_4

2   Constructing a Research Question and Approach

The origin of architecture principles lies in fields of science such as physics, biology, building architecture, landscape architecture and engineering which are thousands of years ahead of enterprise architecture. Scientists and architects in these fields formulate principles as working mechanisms of concepts [17] and visualize researched design principles and architecture principles as patterns [12] (recurring, repeatable and scalable generic solutions). So why not only copy terms, like principles, from these fields of architecture into enterprise architecture but also copy the best practices, definitions and purposes of these terms? This is one of the reasons why we research the effectiveness of architecture principles and look at working mechanisms.

If we want to understand the relationship between formulating architecture principles and their impact and effectiveness in the design and engineering of the enterprise, we need to have a research question that is measurable. But the term architecture is very vague to many people and not that measurable. If we see architecture as a total concept, then architecture principles are principles of concepts that are made part of the architecture. Concepts are much better measurable than architecture because there is less discussion on what a concept is and there is a lot of literature available on concepts.

A focused question for our research, therefore, would be *"If we formulate the concept principles in the form of working mechanisms, how much more effective will they be approved and used in designs and engineering and have an impact on the enterprise?"*

In this ongoing research on architecture principles, we make use of the scientific method and the Design Science research methodology of Hevner [2] to guarantee the quality of our findings. In this research, we do not only introduce a new definition for principles and do experiments and predictions, but we also look at claims made in the past on architecture, principles and architecture principles [3, 7, 11]. Later on in this paper, as it will become apparent, various principle formulations and claims done by scientists, for example, the ISO definition for architecture and principle, do not withstand a critical inspection.

3   Architecture Principles Usage Analysis

It is our observation that architecture principles in enterprise architecture (EA) are produced, but not largely used. Our surveys, collecting data from 105 architects in 11 countries, show this problem is manifest [16].

The lack of consensus and availability of a successful approach, for working with architecture principles has resulted in the situation that many architects in the field of EA has their own truth and approach for working with architecture principles.

Based on the interviews held with architects and other roles, several problems with architecture principles are felt and recognized [16].

The architects were asked questions like: (1) are architecture principles formulated compliant to a standard, (2) do they have a status, owner, version, (3) are they visualized, (4) are they documented, (5) are they used and (6) are they communicated?

Most often the architecture principles were formulated by the architects in the form of optional normative statements, much compliant to theories of methods and standards.

What they really did was labeling rules and requirements as principles. Many architects just do not track and trace their principles in decision documents, design documents and the realized solutions. With that they don't get the insight quick enough their principles are not used (well enough). Long afterward they notice that this is the case.

When discussed all architects agreed that any architecture principle can be seen as the way a concept works and they agreed that principles always can be rewritten as working mechanisms and visualized as patterns.

Also, they agreed that you can first have concept principles (from theory), and once they are approved (and or used) they become architecture principles.

The direction we thus are now looking in is to understand architecture principles and concept principles as working mechanisms, as the way things work, and formulate them as mechanisms and visualize them as patterns (i.e. an arrangement of entities).

4   Exploring and Redefining Architecture and Principles

Now we need to establish a context for what we regard to be architecture and what we regard to be principles.

In the field of EA, we have an ISO standard for Enterprise Architecture: IEEE 1471/ISO 42010 [4]. This ISO standard defines the word **architecture** as follows:

> Architecture: (system) fundamental concepts or properties of a system in its environment embodied in its elements, relationships, and in the principles of its design and evolution.

Four criteria for correctly formulated definitions are [12]:

(1) All used words in the definition must be (pre)defined.
(2) There may be no counterexamples for the definition.
(3) The definition must qualify and quantify.
(4) The definition may not be subject to circular reasoning in itself or together with adjacent definitions.

The ISO definition of architecture conflicts with three of the four criteria for good definitions. For instance, not all used terms in the definition have been (pre)defined, such as the terms fundamental concepts, properties, elements, evolution or principles. Therefore we cannot measure and not know exactly when something is or is not architecture and we cannot do predictions using this definition. There is no reason or argument provided why principles are split up or disconnected from concepts in this ISO definition.

As we read the ISO documentation, we suspect that the ISO definition was not created based on the outcomes of experiments, but by desk research. In order to get a clear relationship between architecture, concept and principle we will dismiss the ISO definition of architecture and construct a new one reusing the architecture theory from building architecture.

The added value of designing and building structures with architecture is that the structure will be more durable (via a construction), utilizable (via operations) and beautiful (via decoration), answering thousands of (conflicting) requirements than it would without designing and building it with architecture. This is accomplished by designing and building a structure using a set of coherent and proven concepts that works in a specific way (their principles) and provides construction, operation and decoration.

With these insights, we can construct a definition of architecture. A definition for the architecture may be: **the architecture of a structure is the total concept or set of coherent concepts (to be) applied onto that structure, that provides for the construction, operations and decoration**.

Enterprises, organizations, companies, processes, information systems and IT Infrastructures all can be regarded as structures. So the enterprise structure can have an enterprise architecture, and designing and building enterprises with architecture will lead to more sustainable enterprises.

The definition of the architecture of an enterprise may be: **the architecture of an enterprise structure is the total enterprise concept or a set of coherent concepts applied to an enterprise structure, that provides for the construction, operations and decoration.**

The term concept we define as an idea, approach or abstraction of an implementation [12]. Preferably only concepts backed by enough sound and solid literature and best practices are used in architecture to build churches, houses and bridges or megastructures. This is also preferred for enterprises.

4.1   An Overview of Definitions for Architecture Principles

The next step is that we take a look at how authors in dictionaries and methods defined the word principle and architecture principle. Below we present definitions that are commonly referred to in scientific papers [3, 7, 11] in the field of EA:

Source	Definition
Oxford Dictionary, 2018	(1) A fundamental truth or proposition that serves as the foundation for a system of belief or behavior or for a chain of reasoning (2) A general scientific theorem or law that has numerous special applications across a wide field
Taylor, 1912	A principle is a truth or a philosophy, differing from and replacing an ordinary rule-of-thumb
Hammer and Mangurian [10]	Hammer believes that a physical information architecture is a manifestation of beliefs or principles of the organization's leadership
Richardson [6]	Principles are an organization's basic philosophies that guide the development of the architecture. [re-using Hammer]
Chen and Lillehagen [1]	Architecting principles are rules to use when elaborating enterprise architectures
Lindström [5]	Architectural principles define the underlying general rules and guidelines for the use and deployment of all IT resources and assets across the enterprise
TOGAF 9.1, 2017 [8]	Principles are general rules and guidelines, intended to be enduring and seldom amended, that inform and support the way in which an organization sets about fulfilling its mission. [Author unknown] Architecture principles define the underlying general rules and guidelines for the use and deployment of all IT resources and assets across the enterprise. [5]
ArchiMate 3.1, 2017 [14]	A principle represents a qualitative statement of intent that should be met by the architecture
BIZBOK 4.1, 2017 [13]	A principle is an agreed upon truth that can guide one's reasoning
* Dragon1 v5, 2003 [12]	A principle is the enforced way a system (f.i. a concept or entity) works, producing results. A principle is a working mechanism. An architecture principle is the principle of a concept that is made part of an architecture (i.e. a total concept)

*) This is the definition being introduced in this paper.

Definitions are scientific claims, they claim something to be true. The problems with these definitions for principles, especially the ones by Richardson and TOGAF, are that they are only assertions without evidence and that they do not have predefined all words they use in the definitions. There are counterexamples presentable that conflict with the definitions and there were no experiments undertaken to falsify these definitions before they were put up as truth or theory. A counterexample, for instance, is "We do not want to have viruses on our computers." This example fits the definitions of TOGAF and Richardson, it is a general rule, but can't be guaranteed, is not always true and will not guide design and engineering directly. Therefore it is not a principle, concept principle or architecture principle.

Without any reason or argument Richardson splits up principles into guidelines and rationales (to explain why the guideline is a smart thing to do). The rationale that Richardson proposes is more likely to be the principle itself as it describes a mechanism and his principle statement is actually the guideline to implement the principle.

4.2   Discovering Principles as the Way Concepts Work as Part of an Architecture

Every architecture of a structure, like a pyramid, church, library, museum or bridge can be broken down into the concepts that were used to build the structure. The Colosseum of Rome had applied the concepts of Arena, Portal, Tribune, Stadium, etc....

The same we can do with enterprises, organizations, companies, etc.... Sony, Toyota and Walt Disney all have applied the concepts of modularity, cloud computing, business process automation, single source of truth, mass production and online strategy. Together these concepts form (a part) of their enterprise architecture.

For all these concepts working mechanisms (i.e. concept principles) can be recognized, formulated and measured. Then we do not believe how it works, but we **know** how it works, by means of experiments, testing and observation.

This overwhelming evidence of the presence of concepts and working mechanisms makes a case for principles being working mechanisms and not being general rules (or guidelines). **We now claim and define that the principle of a concept (a concept principle) is the enforced way a concept works, producing results.**

Take, for instance, the principle of the concept of Single Source of Truth (SSOT). "By storing and retrieving a data element only (once) to and from its official source, it is prevented that inconsistent and outdated versions of that data element exist and can be (retrieved from other sources and) used."

This statement clearly describes a way of working with a context and produced results. With this, we can predict behavior and measure outcomes. Just like we want to do.

Does a concept have only one principle? No, a concept principle describes one of the unlimited numbers of working mechanisms inside a concept. The principle that describes the whole of the concept in general, we call the first principle of the concept. One principle can contain many direct and indirect benefits.

If literature mentions the key elements (logical parts) of a concept, the concept principle will tell us how these key elements need to collaborate in order for the concept to produce results and realize benefits. By measuring the availability of key elements, one can determine how mature the concept is implemented in the organization and how well the concept works.

We predict that if all key elements of a concept, as stated in the literature, are implemented, the produced results of the concept will benefit the enterprise.

5   Introducing a Practice for Formulating Architecture Principles

We have done an experiment with a few building architects and provided them with the following three sentences and we asked what they thought was the most correct formulation of an architecture principle for durability:

(1) We always and only use wind energy and solar energy.
(2) Use as much wind energy and solar energy solutions as possible when building a house.

(3) By using only wind energy and solar energy as sources of energy for appliances in a house, it is ensured that dependency on traditional fossil fuel is reduced or removed by using these environmental friendly solutions and thus making the house more durable.

All building architects chose the third sentence as most correct formulation of a principle, in fact, a concept principle, the principle of the concept Green Energy or Sustainable Energy. The third sentence describes a working mechanism with a clear produced beneficiary result. Even if you do not use solar energy when building a house, this statement is true.

This notion of a principle as a working mechanism, we are testing and applying more and more in practice in the field of enterprise architecture and we see many positive results with it.

Writing down the principles as working mechanisms, the statements are no longer optional statements, but they are explanations of how things work and you have to take it into account. They are always contextual true, as this concept principle:

The Principle of Modularity - By building a system only consisting out of loosely coupled components, the cost of maintenance is significantly lower than otherwise, [9].

This example concept principle describe the way the concept work. Concept principles written down in working mechanism style are much more clear for everyone to understand. Based on these kinds of short statements it is easy to visualize the principles (with a concept diagram and principle diagram) and understand what it takes to realize the benefits of the way of working (f.i. the rules, standards and technologies). This in contrast to normative statements labeled as a principle.

5.1 Basic Parts of the Formulation of a Concept Principle

Architects should not have the intention to constantly invent new concept principles. The literature on a concept is likely to reveal the key elements (logical parts) of a concept that need to collaborate in order to produce a beneficiary result. It is a good practice to mention all of these key elements in the short statement of a concept principle.

Looking at many principles and concept principles written down as working mechanisms and analyzing them, we have discovered five main parts in the short statement [12]:

- Action part: **By...**
- Reaction part: **It is ensured...**
- Enforcement part: **Always, through/as is stated in..**
- Result part: **Resulting...**
- Context part: **When...**

The parts assembled together to give this template for the short statement of a principle or concept principle: [**By** [**always**] building a system out of components with minimal dependence or loosely coupled [as is stated in the policy XYZ]], [**it is ensured** that it is much easier to replace components in an active and running system than without minimal dependence or loosely coupling], [**resulting** in a significant decrease of the overall maintenance cost of the system].

If every concept principle would be formulated in this way, the statement itself will describe a situation that is always contextually true, assuming that the theory of the principle is researched and proven to be correct. Therefore it is very necessary to refer to solid and sound literature describing the theory.

5.2   Ten Concept Principles to Work with

When we want to study concept principles in enterprises and want to improve their effect and usage, thus becoming a real architecture principle, we should have a sample set of concepts we can test.

Ten random, but basic concepts, that many enterprises (want to) make use of because of their strategy are: Modularity & Complexity, Adaptivity, Service Orientation, Mass Production, Zero Waste & Green Energy, Artificial Intelligence, Cloud Computing, Digitization, Single Source of Truth and Data Privacy.

Together these concepts could form a subset of the architecture of the enterprise, the enterprise architecture.

6   Working Toward a Meta Model

Part of the ongoing research is building a database with principles for study, reference, review and benchmarking. As we want to store and measure the quality and quantity of principles, we need to have a formal meta model.

From the definitions of architecture and principle follow certain relationships between entities. In the text below we outline the entities and relationships we think should be part of the meta model for architecture principles:

- **Architecture** is a total concept or set of concepts for a structure providing construction, operations and decoration
- An architecture always consists of layers and domains per layer
- **Enterprise Architecture** is the total concept or set of concepts for an enterprise structure
- A **structure** is a system with a constructive, operative and decorative dimension
- A structure can have many topical architectures (total concepts) for many different periods (states)
- A structure always consists of **layers** and domains per layer
- A **domain** is an area of responsibility and accountability
- A **concept** is an idea or approach, abstracted from its implementation
- A concept can have many principles
- A **principle** is the enforced way a system works, producing results
- A **concept principle** is the enforced way a concept works, producing results
- An **architecture principle** is a concept principle where the concept is part of an architecture
- A principle must be formulated as a **working mechanism** and visualized as a **pattern**

- A system is a coherent set of interacting elements realizing common goals
- A principle must have one or more references to **literature**
- A concept or principle always refers to **rules, standards** and **technologies**
- **Domains** contain concepts, principles, rules, standards and technologies
- A principle has a **workflow status**, has an **owner** and has a **context** within it is always true
- At a logical level of abstraction, a concept consists of **elements**, at the physical level of abstraction, a concept consists of **components** and at the implementational level of abstraction a concept consists of **technical products**.

Together these rules, roles and constraints form the core of a meta model for enterprise architecture and architecture principles.

In a next paper, this meta model will be researched further.

7 Provided Arguments Against Principles as Working Mechanisms

Are architecture principles only correct and effective when they are formulated as working mechanisms and are the statements always true and can they be always true?

What architects argue is that it is hard to formulate a statement that is always true. And especially in IT many people agree that there are no absolute truths. Also, there is the social and cultural notion that what is true for one is not true for the other. So not all architects are immediately convinced that architecture principles always can be seen and should always be formulated as working mechanisms and that the statements always can be contextual truths.

Most architecture principles that were documented the past 30 years, like for instance at government agencies worldwide, have been making use of the TOGAF approach for architecture principles. These architecture principles are often produced compliant to this approach. An example architecture principle statement from the State of Ohio in the United States is: "Applications are easy to use." In other architecture principle statements the word "should" is often used and reveals the normative character. For example: "Customers should be able to serve themselves and the State should encourage the use of the self-service applications."

When defining that architecture principles are only correct when they are always true, as we do in this paper, it conflicts immediately with the approach referred to above.

This statement "Applications are easy to use" does work as a general rule or a guideline, so for some architects this is seen as a correct architecture principle.

The problem is that they leave out the enforcement in their principle statement that ensures that what is said here, is really always true.

In science, we do not seek the truth but reliable and accurate knowledge and explanations. Reliable and accurate knowledge and explanations contain observations, evidence, facts and experiments that form truths. We need science in order to produce or build great and better things, like phones, medicines, bridges and space stations. In science we cannot prove that something is true. We can only make something highly likely to be true in all circumstances, within a context.

So when in science we look for principles we look for the way things work, the behavioral knowledge. When we define architecture principles in enterprise architecture, in order to build better organizations, there is no reason to look for principles that are not about the way things work.

A primary biology principle is [15]: "All living cells arise from pre-existing cells by division". This statement is always true in the context of life on earth. It is observed and experimented thoroughly, it is enforced by nature. The statement "Applications are easy to use" is not always true or better said, hardly ever true. So this is NOT a principle. It is more of a requirement, rule or goal. It is not observed, it has not experimented thoroughly and it is not enforced by nature or anything other. There is no literature reference. It misses the enforcement. To support our hypothesis and get architecture principles approved and used more, these elements always need to be addressed in the principle statement.

Literally, every architecture principle can be formulated as a working mechanism. It can be formulated in such a way that the statement is always contextual true. But before that can be done, it needs to be researched, observed, tested and experimented thoroughly. So, therefore, every architecture principle needs to have a reference to sound and solid literature.

8   Summary and Further Study

We have successfully followed an approach of doing a literature review, interviewing architects and formulating principles in practice. This provided data and proof we used to suggest definitions for the terms architecture and principle and to come up with an approach to identify concepts to create an architecture with.

We introduced a new theory: an alternative way of formulating the architecture principles as a working mechanism, including definitions for architecture, concept, principle, short statement and rules for formulating principles.

We have provided a tool to measure and improve the definitions of terms. We have used that tool to highlight a few problems we observed in the ISO definition for architecture.

In the next papers, we are going to introduce a template for a concept diagram, a principle details diagram and, a set of icons for visualizing architecture principles as patterns. We are going to do experiments and tests for falsification in formulating, visualizing and applying a list of ten concept principles. And we are going to create a database with architecture principles for study and reference purposes.

Acknowledgments. This ongoing research is done under the supervision of prof. H.A. Proper, Radboud University Nijmegen, The Netherlands. We thank Bas van Gils, Strategy Alliance for providing insight and expertise that greatly assisted in the research for this paper.

References

1. Chen, D., Lillehagen, F.: Enterprise architectures – review on concepts, principles and approaches. In: Proceedings of the 10th International Conference on Concurrent Engineering (ISPE CE 2004) (2004)
2. Hevner, A.R., Chatterjee, S.: Design Research in Information Systems: Theory and Practice. Springer, Dordrecht (2010). https://doi.org/10.1007/978-1-4419-5653-8
3. Fischer, C., Winter, R., Aier, S.: What is an enterprise architecture design principle? Towards a consolidated definition. In: Lee, R. (ed.) Computer and Information Science 2010, vol. 317, pp. 193–205. Springer, Heidelberg (2010). https://doi.org/10.1007/978-3-642-15405-8_16
4. ISO: ISO/IEC/IEEE 42010, formerly IEEE Recommended Practice for Architectural Description of Software Intensive Systems (IEEE Std 1471-2000) (2000)
5. Lindström, Å.: On the syntax and semantics of architectural principles. In: Proceedings of the 39th Annual Hawaii International Conference on Systems Sciences, 04 January 2006, Los Alamitos, CA, USA. IEEE Computer Society (2006)
6. Richardson, G.L., Jackson, B.M., Dickson, G.W.: A principle based enterprise architecture: lessons from texaco and star enterprise. MIS Q.: Manag. Inf. Syst. **14**(4), 285–403 (1990)
7. Stelzer, D.: Enterprise architecture principles: literature review and research directions. In: Proceedings of the 4th Workshop on Trends in Enterprise Architecture Research (Pre-Proceedings), 23 November 2009, Stockholm, pp. 21–35 (2009)
8. The Open Group: The Open Group TOGAF Version 9 – The Open Group Architecture Framework (TOGAF) (2009)
9. Baldwin, C.Y., Clark, K.B.: Modularity-in-design: an analysis based on the theory of real options. Harvard Business School (1994)
10. Hammer, M., Mangurian, G.E.: The changing value of communications technology. Sloan Manag. Rev. **28**(4) (1987)
11. Greefhorst, D., Proper, H.A.: Architecture Principles: The Cornerstones of Enterprise Architecture. Springer, Heidelberg (2011). https://doi.org/10.1007/978-3-642-20279-7
12. Paauwe, M.A.: Text Book Dragon1 Visual Enterprise Architecture (2011)
13. Business Architecture Guild: A guide to the business architecture body of knowledge, v 4.1 (BIZBOK Guide) (2014)
14. ArchiMate 3.0 Specification: Open Group standard (2016)
15. https://www.thoughtco.com/cell-theory-373300
16. https://www.dragon1.com/blogs/markpaauwe/views-on-architecture-principles
17. http://engineering.myindialist.com/2009/lab-manual-working-principle-of-reciprocating-pump

On Security and Blockchain

Decentralized Enforcement of Business Process Control Using Blockchain

Diogo Silva[1]([✉]) [iD], Sérgio Guerreiro[1,2]([✉]) [iD], and Pedro Sousa[1,2,3]([✉]) [iD]

[1] Instituto Superior Técnico, University of Lisbon,
Av. Rovisco Pais 1, 1049-001 Lisbon, Portugal
{diogo.c.da.silva,sergio.guerreiro,pedro.manuel.sousa}@tecnico.ulisboa.pt
[2] INESC-ID, Rua Alves Redol 9, 1000-029 Lisbon, Portugal
[3] Link Consulting SA, Av. Duque de Ávila 23, 1000 Lisbon, Portugal

Abstract. Lack of traceability and control is a problem nowadays identified by industries. There are many situations that prove the existence of this problem: lack of trust between actors, lack of information about defected products within business transactions, exception handling, actors performing workarounds and not conforming prescriptions, *etc*. To tackle this problem, we consider knowledge from (i) DEMO, an Enterprise Ontology that models business transactions and human interactions on organizations, and (ii) Blockchain, a technology that eliminates the need of intermediaries, provides trust among the actors and traceability over business transactions. Hyperledger Composer (HC) is a toolset example to develop Blockchain applications. This paper relates and integrates concepts between DEMO business transactions and HC, then applies the conceptualization to a context of business transactions supporting food supply and distribution. Moreover, an initial prototype implementation, supported on HC with two-clients using a user interface, shows traceability and control capabilities.

Keywords: Blockchain · Business process · Control · DEMO Traceability

1 Introduction

Organizations intend to increase their business by providing value to one or more customers. In order to do that, it is necessary to execute certain tasks. These tasks are understood as business processes and can be defined as a collection of orchestrated activities that organizations execute in order to create value, i.e., deliver services and products to their clients [25].

In order to increase organizational functioning and efficiency within the scope of enterprise governance, it is necessary to exert control on organization's business processes [19]. Control can prevent some problems that organizations face, as the difficulty to decide on the procedure of a business process when an exception occurs, or the lack of knowledge about the exact state of a business process [17]. Since workarounds can occur, actors sometimes don't act according

© Springer Nature Switzerland AG 2019
D. Aveiro et al. (Eds.): EEWC 2018, LNBIP 334, pp. 69–87, 2019.
https://doi.org/10.1007/978-3-030-06097-8_5

to business transaction models that were previously designed, which define the design restrictions of the organization [19]. However, sometimes the problem isn't caused by actors not following what has been defined, but by the occurrence of an unexpected situation not previously defined [11].

In food retail industry, the above issues are common to occur due to the high number of business collaborations between the stakeholders in the processes of manufacturing, treating, transporting that comprise a food supply chain. Exerting control on activities, for example tracking a considerable number of transactions, may help organizations in a supply chain to take informed decisions [10] or identify some possible problems as the occurrence of a defect in a product (for example infection in a food product [23]). Furthermore, in these scenarios there are multiple actors that work together on delivering a product that must possess very specific qualities to be fulfilled, therefore traceability is required [12]. The distributed knowledge, i.e., all actors viewing the same events that occurred in the supply chain, is fundamental to handle new or unexpected situations.

The lack of trust can be another problem in a supply chain due to the high number of collaborations. It may contribute to increase the probability of occurrence of the bullwhip effect [26], information distortion in the chain which is propagated from downstream to upstream members. To prevent this, actors need to communicate and establish relationships based on trust [20,22].

To solve the above issues, namely the lack of control and traceability in collaborative business processes, a Blockchain approach, *"shared distributed ledger that records transactions and tracks assets that can be tangible, e.g. car, or intangible, e.g. patent, in a business network"* [21], appears as a possible solution. This approach eliminates the need for intermediaries, provides trust among the actors and traceability over business processes. To develop the Blockchain solution, the tool Hyperledger Composer (HC) [1] was selected. However, before proceeding to the implementation, we need to understand the existent interactions and responsibilities between organizations. DEMO [15] was selected to model and study the business, in order to model transaction kinds, actor roles and their interactions.

This work aims to provide, a meta-model of integration conceptualization that relates DEMO business transactions concepts with HC concepts. Then, to validate the meta-model, we consider and model in DEMO a real food supply chain case study. Furthermore, to complement the validation, we implement in HC the same case study in an initial prototype of the Blockchain network with two clients using a browser user interface.

This paper is structured as follows. Section 2 explains the research setting containing the definition of the problem, the methodology selected and the overview of our solution. Next, in Sect. 3, the related work and background is presented describing the current state of art of the problem. In Sect. 4, we proceed to the design of an artifact, a meta-model represented as an UML class diagram that exposes and explains how HC concepts and DEMO business transactions concepts can be mapped. In Sect. 5, the validation of the artifact takes place containing the modeling of the case study in DEMO and the presentation of an initial Blockchain prototype in HC. Finally, the authors present their conclusions and the necessary future work.

2   Research Setting

2.1   Problem Definition

Nowadays, organizations face problems regarding lack of control in business processes. Sometimes, they don't know how to proceed when a workaround occurs and with combination of occasionally not knowing the exact state of a business process, can lead to wrong decision making [17]. These issues may be materialized into lack of quality in organization's products. One real situation where these issues can occur is in a food products supply chain. In order to transform raw materials and to deliver final products to the consumer, it is necessary to execute a significant number of complex processes that involve a significant number of actors, which are linked in the chain [30]. To verify the origin and processing of products in order to prevent problems, such as creation of an infection in a food product [8,23,30], it is necessary to exist traceability in business processes. According to ISO 9001:2000 standard, traceability in a chain is the *"the ability to trace the history, application or location of an entity by means of recorded identifications throughout the entire supply chain"* [8], therefore if actors don't have traceability over the processes, they can't detect the cause of the food infection.

Lack of trust among actors in collaborative processes [32] is a very frequent problem in this kind of scenarios. Without trust, the probability of occurrence of bullwhip effect [26], information distortion in the chain propagated from downstream to upstream members is higher and the cycle times between the entities involved increase [22].

Organizations face other kind of problems regarding this matter. The environments where business processes are executed, are complex systems as the ERPs [17]. Moreover, the business process models defined by organizations, establish their design restrictions but do not ensure that actors perform according to them, because unexpected events may occur and organizations are in constant change. Therefore, actors execute sometimes only some parts of what was defined [19].

In this line of reason, we have defined our problem into **lack of control and traceability in collaborative business processes** for example in food supply chains. Poor traceability of food products, lack of trust between stakeholders, need of intermediaries and information distortion on a supply chain are some examples of this problem.

2.2   Solution Methodology

We adapted Design Science Research Methodology (DSRM) [31] for the development of our solution. Through this paper, we have established a 1:1 mapping between business processes and business transactions.

Having already defined our problem, we need to establish the solution's objectives. Thus we have defined as objective:

- Build a meta-model of integration conceptualization that maps the ontological, social and communicative concepts provided by DEMO business transactions with Hyperledger Composer concepts to conceive a blockchain network that provides traceability and control over business transactions.

On the next phase, we design and develop an artifact. This artifact, present in Sect. 4 in Fig. 2, consists in an UML domain diagram that represents the meta-model indicated in the objective. Then, we validate the artifact in Sect. 5. To validate the artifact, a case study is considered and modeled in DEMO as two representations: an Actor Transaction Diagram (ATD) and a Transaction Result Table (TRT). Furthermore, it is explained and presented an initial Blockchain network prototype implementation of the case study.

2.3   Solution Overview

We present on Fig. 1, an overview of our work. First to understand and model human interactions in organizations we have selected DEMO [15], an Enterprise Ontology that models an organization as a network of responsibilities and interactions. We have selected this methodology, because we intend to provide an ontological solution for business transactions. Furthermore, it is based in ψ theory [13], enables us to design the existent transactions types and the social and communicative aspects that actors establish in those transactions. Finally, DEMO is C4E. It is **Coherent** - it constitutes a whole; is **Consistent** - it contains no logical contradictions; is **Concise** - is as minimal as possible and is **Essential** - is independent of realization and implementation.

To implement the modeled business transactions and provide traceability over them, we have selected Hyperledger Composer (HC), a toolset to develop Blockchain applications. We choose this tool since it reduces the effort in the development of Blockchain business networks. Moreover, it is supported by Linux Foundation, IBM and other companies, is open-source and is well documented. This tool allows also to define private and permissioned networks that are appropriate for the case study considered, since it supports the Hyperledger Fabric [5] blockchain infrastructure.

Having selecting our modeling methodology and our Blockchain tool, we proceed to the construction of an artifact, a meta-model of integration conceptualization between them as indicated in Fig. 1. The meta-model explains how DEMO and HC concepts can be integrated and the kind of integrations that can be established.

To validate the meta-model, we consider a real food supply-chain case study [33] as Fig. 1 exhibits. Then we proceed to its modeling in DEMO. To complement the validation, we implement the food supply chain case study as HC blockchain business network. The implemented blockchain business network, provides traceability over business processes and validates the designed meta-model of integration conceptualization.

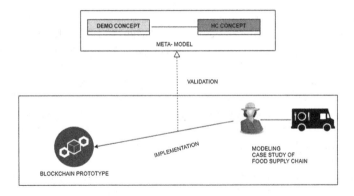

Fig. 1. The overview of our solution

3 Related Work and Background

DEMO [15] is an enterprise ontology introduced by Dietz based in the ψ theory [13] that enables the implementation of the structure and essence of organizations and the existent human interventions. According to ψ theory, in the standard pattern of a business transaction exists two actor roles: the initiator and the executor. The obtained fact when performing a business transaction, is originated by the collaboration of production and coordination acts. These acts contains three phases each one with specific steps: (1) order phase that contains the steps: request (rq), promise (pr), decline (dc) and quit (qt); (2) execution phase which contain the execution step (ex); result phase that contains: declare (da), reject (rj), stop (sp) and accept (ac). Aveiro et al. [7] proposed an ontology model based on DEMO to represent the generic control that these authors believed to exist on organizations, to increase management of organizational change.

Blockchain consists in an immutable distributed ledger that records transactions and assets [21] in a business network, where actors don't need to trust each other to interact. Its structure can be understood as a log, whose records are grouped as timestamped blocks. Each block contains a list of transactions, and it is identified by a cryptographically hash that references the hash of the block that came before it [9]. This technology has appeared with Bitcoin, a digital currency founded by Satoshi Nakamoto, not ruled by any central entity or government that resides on a peer-to-peer network to perform electronic payments between two actors [29]. On Bitcoin, payments are performed without the intervention of a third party and to validate the transactions, a consensus algorithm named proof-of-work is used. In Blockchain, smart contracts, *"agreement or set of business rules that govern a business transaction"* [21] are defined in order to participants interact with assets and other participants.

To solve the problem of lack of trust in collaborative business processes execution, Weber et al. [32] developed a technique to integrate Blockchain into the choreography of processes in order to maintain trust without the need of trust in a third party. They started to translate collaborative business processes from a supply chain scenario modeled in BPMN, into smart contracts executable in a Blockchain. After that, they have used an Ethereum Blokchain infrastructure to execute those business processes. The Blockchain enable to store the status of process execution across all involved participants, as well as to coordinate the collaborative business process execution. In order to connect the execution of processes in Blockchain to external agents, the authors implemented a Blockchain interface, responsible to convert API calls to Blockchain transactions in a smart contract, and to receive status updates from the contract converting it to API calls. To validate their work, they have used use case processes from the literature and industry prototype to evaluate the ability to record the history of the choreography processes. More specifically, the researchers evaluated if their Blockchain system could distinguish conforming traces, the set of permissible execution traces for each process model from not conforming traces. The results have shown that the system could classified the traces correctly. They have also compared public with private Blockchain and concluded that latency is higher in public. Garcia-Banuelos et al. [16] proposed an optimization of the work available at [32]. In this work, to compile a BPMN model into a smart contract in Solidity Language, the BPMN process model needs first to be translated into a reduced Petri net. After that, the reduced Petri is compiled into a Solidity smart contract. The proposed method, is compared with [32] in terms of scalability and the authors evaluation shown that their method decreases the amount paid of resources and achieves higher throughput. López-Pintado et al. [27] present a demonstration of Caterpillar, the prototype from [16] which is an open source BPMS that supports Ethereum Blockchain.

Di Ciccio et al. [12] intend, as we aim in our work, to provide traceability in inter-organizational business processes execution by using a blockchain solution. To make this, the authors considered a supply chain case study from the pharmaceutical domain and relied on the platform that runs business processes in an Ethereum blockchain from the work available at [16]. They then conceived a framework to trace the execution information about transactions recorded on-chain and demonstrated it using a prototype considering an exemplifying process. Mendling et al. [28] have discussed challenges and opportunities when applying Blockchain to Business Process Management (BPM) regarding the traditional BPM lifecycle and five BPM core capabilities. One asset that authors argue is that blockchain can improve inter-organizational processes, despite not agreeing on a trusted third party because it can help on the management of supply chains and share personal health records with service medical providers. A drawback is for example, in the implementation stage of the BPM lifecycle, the difficult to identify and define abstractions for the design of the blockchain-based business process execution.

Some researches related DEMO business transactions with Blockchain as our work relates. Guerreiro et al. [20] presented a meta-model for interoperability secure business transactions using Blockchain and DEMO. They intended to solve the security risks involved on business transactions executions increasing trust, authenticity, robustness and traceability against fraud. These authors believe that Blockchain solutions are concerned with technological aspects and not with social ones, like the existence of human interaction when performing business transactions in electronic networks. Therefore, they integrated Enterprise Operating System (EOS) [18], a model driven software system that supports the business process operation founded in the ψ theory based on DEMO methodology, with Blockchain to increase trust between stakeholders and cyber security in order to enable the operation of multiple business transactions. In their meta-model, actors of each company are responsible to initiate and execute the business transactions, where the runtime control of business transactions execution is performed by the EOS, able to execute DEMO models, at the application level. At technological level, the authors propose a private Blockchain to provide trust and security between the companies and to allow actors to consult the performed business transactions.

de Kruijff et al. [24] explained Blockchain technology using Enterprise Ontology. To turn this technology more recognize in the industry and to turn easier its understanding, these authors have described Blockchain with conceptual models in three levels of Blockchain transactions and smart contracts: datalogical, infological and essential. To make this, they used the distinction axiom from ψ theory [13,15]. Datalogical layer describes the transactions at a lower level residing on technical aspects like blocks and code. Infological level describes the transactions as a ledger system that executes them. Finally, the essential level, describes transactions in terms of business and is concerned with what is created directly or indirectly by communication.

4   Artifact Design

In the present section, we present a meta-model of integration conceptualization between DEMO business transactions and HC, exhibited in Fig. 2 and the semantics descriptions of those integrations in Table 3. In Fig. 2, exists two boundaries that corresponds to two distinct worlds: (i) DEMO business transactions and (ii) Hyperledger Composer. The identification text (Represents, Performs, *etc.*) of the relationships in Fig. 2 reads from right to left. Table 1 contains the definition for each used DEMO domain class and Table 2 contains the definition for each used HC domain class.

Starting in integration 1 from Table 3, HC **Participants** represent DEMO **Actors**. HC **Participants** are the members of the blockchain network and interact with it. DEMO **Actors** are subjects in its fulfillment of an **Actor Role**. In DEMO, an **Actor Role** is an atomic amount of authority and responsibility and is an abstraction of an **Actor**. In Hyperledger Composer, this kind of distinction between Actor and Actor role does not exists. Participant is the only concept to reference the members of the network independently of the roles that those participants play. Therefore, an HC **Participant** corresponds to a DEMO **Actor** and not to an **Actor Role**. We mapped these two concepts as a dependency where HC Participant depends from DEMO Actor because is not possible to exist an HC **Participant** without existing the corresponding DEMO **Actor**

Table 1. DEMO domain considered concepts. Adapted from [15]

HC concept	Definition
Actor	A subject fulfilling an actor role
Actor role	Atomic amount of authority and responsibility
Initiator	A role of an actor in a transaction. Responsible for performing the corresponding coordination acts, according to the transaction pattern
Executor	A role of an actor in a transaction. Responsible for performing the production act and the corresponding coordination acts, according to the transaction pattern
Business Transaction Kind	A model of a transaction whose type corresponds to the type of the production fact that is the target or result of the transaction
Business Transaction Step	An act necessary to execute a transaction kind according to the transaction pattern
Act	An atomic unit of activity, of which the effect is the creation of a fact
Coordination act	An act by which a coordination fact is created
Production act	The act in a transaction by which the executor establishes the production fact
Fact	The result or the effect of an act
Business Transaction Instance	Execution of a given business transaction kind in a certain instance in time

and an HC **Participant** corresponds to one and only DEMO **Actor**. Regarding the multiplicity, one HC **Participant** corresponds to zero or one DEMO **Actor** since a DEMO Actor can exist without existing a HC Participant, for example if a part of the business process is not persisted in Blockchain such as phone call.

As we can see in integration 2 of Table 3, we mapped a **Business Transaction Step** (BTS) with an HC **Transaction**. To justify this, we need to consider various concepts. A **Business Transaction Kind** (BTK) is a model of a business transaction of a certain type. A **Business Transaction Instance** (BTI), corresponds to the execution of a given **BTK** in a certain instance in time [20]. **BTK** type is in fact, the type of the production fact that is the result of **BTI** [15]. Since is possible to execute multiple instances of a **BTK**, for each **BTK**, there is one or more **BTI**. Both in DEMO and HC, an **Actor** may act in various business transactions. However in DEMO, a **BTK** is associated with one or two **Actor Roles** while in HC, in a **Transaction**, it can be involved one or more **Participants**. A DEMO **BTK**, is composed by one or more **BTS** (Request, Promise, Execute Declare, etc.), which are **Acts** that participants perform. These **Acts** can be **Coordination** or **Production Acts**, and their execution produce **Facts** (coordination facts and production facts). In HC, each defined **Transaction** is modeled in HC model file and is implemented by a transaction processor function [4], which is invoked by the runtime when the **Transaction** is submitted producing a change of state in the network. Therefore, it can be concluded that an HC

Table 2. The key concepts of Hyperledger Composer. Taken from [1]

HC concept	Definition
Participant	The members of the business network that may own assets and submit transactions
Identity	Digital certificate and private key that are mapped to a participant and are used to transact on a business network
Blockchain State Storage	Combination of distributed ledger that stores the submitted transactions and the blockchain state database that stores the current state of assets
Query	Return data about the blockchain world state
Transaction	Mechanism by which participants interact with assets. E.g: placing a bid on a asset in an auction
Event	Emitted by transaction processor functions to indicate to external systems that something of importance has happened to the ledger
Historian Record	Asset that contains information about a specific transaction such as its type, the participant that invoked it, date of submission, etc.
Historian Registry	Registry which records successful transactions, including the participants and identities that submitted them as Historian Records
Asset	Tangible or intangible goods, services, or property stored in registries of the business network such as cars, houses, etc.

Transaction performs the behavior of a DEMO **Business Transaction Step**. The reason of the dependency relationship is because is not possible to exist an HC **Transaction** without existing the corresponding **BTS**. Furthermore, only and only one HC **Transaction** performs the behavior of a unique **BTS**, therefore, we represented the relationship as a dependency with multiplicity 1:1 where HC Transaction depends from DEMO BTS.

In DEMO, for each **BTI** there is one or more **Facts** resulting from the steps necessary to execute it. HC **Asset** is a tangible or intangible a good that exists in the network and modified by **Transactions**. There isn't a clear HC concept that maps with **BTI**. A **BTI** may changes his status over the time and since in this work we intend to provide a solution to the problem of lack of traceability in collaborative business processes, is essential to maintain the current status of the instance and track the previous status that the instance have been through. An HC **Asset** can be understood as a resource. This means that any resource, object, good that DEMO actors use or produce are assets in the blockchain. Thus a **BTI** is represented by an **Asset**, however not all Assets correspond to BTI. Contrary to other mappings, an HC **Asset** does not depend from DEMO Business Transaction Instance since there are other Assets that do not correspond to Business Transaction Instances (a car for example). For this reason it was established a normal association between these concepts where one **Asset** corresponds to zero or one BTI, as we can view in integration 3 of Table 3 and Fig. 2.

In HC, there is an **Historian Registry** that records **Historian Records** [2], which is composed by logs of **Transactions** and **Events**, that have been submitted to the network, in order to **Participants** track what happened. **Events** may be emitted by transactions and inform external systems that relevant occurrences happened to the ledger. This provides traceability and control that we are pursuing. An **Historian Record** records information about a specific **Transaction** such as its type, who have submitted it, the time of submission and the **Events** emitted for that **Transaction**. Therefore, a **Historian Record** records a DEMO **Fact** as the integration 4 of Fig. 2 and Table 3 state. The reason of the dependency relationship is the same as the previous mappings. A **Historian Record** corresponds to only and only one **Fact** and there is not possible to exist an **Historian Record** without existing the corresponding **Fact**. Therefore we have established a multiplicity 1:1 between these two concepts.

In HC, **Blockchain State Storage** has a database that stores, the current state of **Assets**, **Participants** and **Identities**. It has also a ledger that stores all **Transactions** submitted as **Historian Records** in the **Historian Registry**. **Identities** are credentials encapsulated in business network cards, that **Participants** use to register on the network and to submit **Transactions**. When an **Identity** is issued to a participant, it allows an user to utilize the business network card that contains the **Identity** to transact on a business network as that **Participant**. An **Identity** is issued to only one **Participant**, however a **Participant** may use other if he revokes the current **Identity** and activates the new one. **Queries** in HC consist in returning and consulting data from the **Blockchain State Storage**, for example an **Historian Record** is a **Query** over the **Historian Registry**.

The attributes of HC concepts are the attributes present in the class definitions in HC documentation available at [1]. As we can see in Fig. 2, **BTI** has 3 attributes. We will explain why we defined those attributes in the next section with more detail.

5   Validation of the Artifact

In this section, to validate the meta-model of the previous section, a case study is considered. Then we proceed to its modeling on DEMO developing two diagrams: (i) ATD - Actor Transaction Diagram and (ii) TRT - Transaction Result Table. In Sect. 5.2, we present an initial Blockchain network prototype implementation in HC of the same case study.

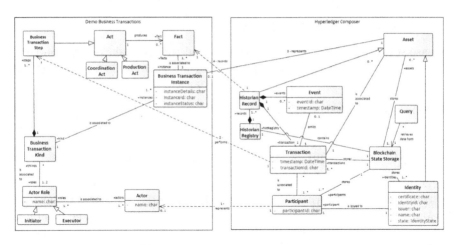

Fig. 2. Domain of the solution: Conceptualization between DEMO business transactions and Hyperledger Composer. Notation used available at [6]

Table 3. Integrations between DEMO and Hyperledger Composer

Identification of the relationship	Type of UML relationship	Semantic description of the relationship
Integration 1 represents	Dependency	This integration maps each Actor contained in DEMO in an HC Participant in order to state that a Participant represents an Actor and it cannot exists a Participant without existing the corresponding Actor
Integration 2 performs	Dependency	This integration maps each BTS in DEMO in an HC Transaction in order to state that a Transaction performs the behavior of a BTS and it cannot exists a Transaction without existing the corresponding BTS
Integration 3 represents	Association	This integration maps each BTI contained in DEMO in an HC Asset in order to state that an Asset represents a BTI
Integration 4 records	Dependency	This integration maps each Fact contained in DEMO in an HC Historian Record in order to state that an Historian Record records a Fact and it cannot exists an Historian Record without existing the corresponding Fact

5.1   Modeling of Case Study in DEMO

The case study considered [33], conceives a food supply chain in retail industry in UK. It is explained how the supply chain for bananas in the UK grocery market is designed. There are 3 major companies on the case:

– J Sainsbury - a retailer in UK
– Mack Multiples - an operation division of M & W Mack that is a distributor of J Sainsbury
– Noboa - A major family-owned plantation business in Ecuador.

The work describe in detail the processes involved in the production, testing, transporting, delivering and payment between the participants involved. The journey from Ecuador to J Sainsbury on UK takes 13 days. The plantation of bananas starts at Ecuador, in Noboa, taking account the J Sainsbury customers preferences. When the plantation is over in order to enable the growth of bananas, they are enclosed in plastic wraps. Their stem is harvest, they are cut and are transported to the packhouse. Then they are inspected by quality managers, floated through a fungicide bath to prevent infections and packaged to be transported on a ship to Zeebrugge, Belgium. At Zeebrugge the bananas are bought and inspected by Mack personnel. The merchandise are then delivered to Mack at Kent, where they are stored on ripening rooms for five to six days in order to achieve the stage of ripeness that J Sainsbury have specified. After that, the fruits are transported to Sainsbury depots in a Mack temperature controlled truck, where its staff test and pay for the bananas if they follow the specifications that have been defined. The fruits are finally delivered to J Sainsbury's stores where the customers can purchase them.

Having considering this, we have built an ATD to model the transaction kinds and the actor roles that participate on those transaction kinds. In this diagram, not only is represented intra-organization processes, but also inter-organization processes. This diagram is illustrated on Fig. 3. As we can see, four boundaries are represented that correspond to the 3 major companies above mentioned, plus the local of intermediation where bananas are inspected and bought by Mack personnel. We can observe in Fig. 3, that are some transaction kinds that appear more than one time. For example, T07 appears 5 times, since the order (the bananas) has to be transported through several locations.

To understand the results of each modeled transaction kind, we proceeded to the construction of a TRT in Table 4. Here, for each transaction kind represented in the previous ATD, is presented the resultant product kind after performing it. In Table 4, transaction kinds from T04 to T14 refer to the different phases of the orders of bananas made by diverse actors from the 3 organizations. The others refer to the creation of other artifacts, for example the execution of T01 produces a best producers report as outcome. Since we are dealing with ontological transactions, we represented all the orders of bananas (order done by Sainsbury, order done by Mack, etc.) as the same order in the ATD and TRT. In spite of being orders started by different actors, in the product kind all orders contain a phase change. For example, when A01 orders bananas to A02 and A02

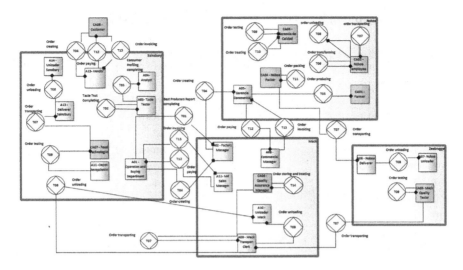

Fig. 3. Actor Transaction Diagram of the case study. The figure use DEMO notation [15]

orders bananas to A05, the product kind resultant of these transaction kinds are exactly the same (an order was created). In the same way, when bananas are transported (T07), the product kind resultant is always the same (order transported), independently from its source or destination. There are other phases of the order. For example, it is produced in Noboa, transformed, tested, transported and unloaded to packhouse, treated and packaged. Posteriorly the order is transported to Zeebrugge, unloaded, tested and payed to Noboa personnel and finally invoiced. The remaining phases of the order as well as the remaining transaction kinds are illustrated in Fig. 3 and Table 4.

5.2 Initial Prototype Implementation of the Blockchain Network

In this subsection, we present an initial blockchain prototype to validate the meta-model present in Fig. 2 of Sect. 4. First, we have started to define some concepts on HC Modeling Language [3]. An abstract class Person has been defined with the following fields: *String* email, *String* firstname and *String* lastname where the email is the parameter that identifies that class. Furthermore, two participants have been defined that extend the abstract class Person: Initiator and Executor. These participants, correspond to the actor roles of the standard transaction pattern of DEMO [15].

An asset Order has been defined, which will be represented in a future work by a Transaction Instance of Fig. 2, initiated by an Initiator and executed by an Executor. This asset can be seen as the same way as the order that is stated on the production kinds of Table 4. It establishes a relationship [3] with an Initiator and an Executor. Besides, it possess the fields: *String* orderId, *OrderStatus* orderStatus and *OrderDetails* orderDetails. As we can see, these fields are very

Table 4. Transaction Result Table of the case study

Transaction kind	Product kind
T01 - Best producers report completing	P01 - Best producers report BPR is completed
T02 - Taste test completing	P02 - Taste test TB is completed
T03 - Consumer profiling completing	P03 - Consumer profile CP is completed
T04 - Order creating	P04 - Order O is created
T05 - Order producing	P05 - O is produced
T06 - Order transforming	P06 - O is transformed
T07 - Order transporting	P07 - O is transported
T08 - Order unloading	P08 - O is unloaded
T09 - Order testing	P09 - O is tested
T10 - Order treating	P10 - O is treated
T11 - Order packing	P11 - O is packaged
T12 - Order paying	P12 - O is payed
T13 - Order invoicing	P13 - O is invoiced
T14 - Order storing and treating	P14 - O is stored and treated

similar to the Transaction Instance concept from Fig. 2. *OrderStatus* concept, is an enumeration containing all the states of the complete transaction pattern in DEMO (request (rq), promise (pm), etc.) [14] represented in Fig. 4. *OrderDetails* concept, represents the contents of the order and contains as subfields: *String* typeOfProduct, *Integer* quantity.

Some HC transactions have been developed. It has been implemented transactions, that enable to proceed on the possible paths of Fig. 4. The transaction **RequestOrder**, receives an executor and order's details as arguments and returns an asset Order identified by an id given by the system. That asset Order fills its attributes according to the values passed in the **RequestOrder** transaction. Furthermore, the status of the Order becomes "REQUESTED" and the field initiator is filled with the id of the participant that submits the **RequestOrder** transaction. The others transactions also change the status of the order, until the business transaction kind is finished. For example, the transaction **PromiseOrder**, receives an order id and changes its state from "REQUESTED" to "PROMISED". The **DeclareOrder** transaction, besides changing the state of the asset Order, it may create or change other assets. For example, for transaction kind T05, when submitting the **DeclareOrder** HC transaction, besides change the order status to "DECLARED", it is created a Banana Asset with certain properties such as source, ripening Stage, temperature, pesticides used, *etc.*

This is only a simple version of the prototype. In the future, we will have an asset **Transaction Instance** as Fig. 2 shows. This asset is an instance of a **Business Transaction Kind** and will replace the asset Order that we explained in the paragraphs above since it contains the same attributes. Furthermore we will contain in Transaction Instance asset the kind of the transaction for that instance and the number of that instance for its transaction kind. The reason of this is was already explained in Subsect. 5.1. For example, T07 in Fig. 3 appears 5 times, so in our implementation we will have 5 instances for transaction kind T07. HC participants will then submit the steps Request, Promise, Execute, Declare etc. implemented as HC transactions over a specific transaction instance.

Some conditions and permissions have been implemented in the prototype. An initiator doesn't have permission to submit acts of an executor: promise (pm), decline (dc), execute (ex), declare (da), revoke promise (rv pm), revoke declare (rv da) and stop (sp). On the same way, an executor doesn't have permission to submit acts of an initiator: request (rq), accept (ac), reject (rj), revoke request (rv rq), revoke accept (rv ac), quit (qt). To submit the transactions, some conditions are needed. For instance, in the network for an order to be promised it is mandatory that its current status is "REQUESTED". On the same way, an initiator can only accept the order if its current status is "DECLARED".

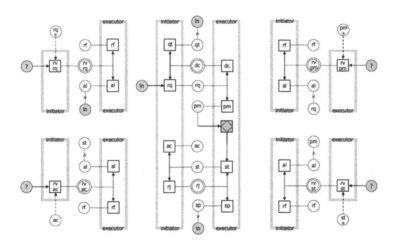

Fig. 4. DEMO complete transaction pattern [13]

The administrator of the network, the participant responsible by its deployment and which possess all the permissions, may issue identities to the participants created and then they can register on the network with those identities. We have created a transaction Setup, to be submitted by the administrator of the network that creates two participants: an initiator and an executor. After that, the identities to those participants need to be issued, in order to participants register on the network. It is possible in HC to consult the transactions that have been submitted. Each transaction may emit an event that is associated to that transaction. Figure 5 presents the Historian registry (taken from the HC Playground a browser user interface of HC) of the network after an initiator "diogosilva" submit a request at 22:54 on 9th March and an executor "sergioguerreiro" submit a promise over that request at 22:55 on the same day.

The code in JSON after the figure, shows an historian record of the transaction **RequestOrder** if the user click on "viewrecord".

Date, Time	Entry Type	Participant	
2018-03-09, 22:55:06	PromiseOrder	sergio.guerreiro@gmail.com (...	view record
2018-03-09, 22:54:40	RequestOrder	diogo.silva@gmail.com (Initiat...	view record
2018-03-09, 22:53:34	ActivateCurrentIdentity	none	view record
2018-03-09, 22:53:24	ActivateCurrentIdentity	none	view record

Fig. 5. Historian Registry after submitting the transactions RequestOrder and PromiseOrder

```
{"$class": "org.acme.supplychain.RequestOrder",
 "orderDetails": {
   "$class": "org.acme.supplychain.OrderDetails",
   "typeOfProduct": "banana",
   "quantity": 5
 },
 "initiator": "resource:org.acme.supplychain.Initiator
#diogo.silva@gmail.com",
 "executor": "resource:org.acme.supplychain.Executor
#sergio.guerreiro@gmail.com",
 "transactionId": "62e5039f-b9ee-4a41-9e90-fd035a2e4ac0",
 "timestamp": "2018-03-09T22:54:40.751Z"}
```

6   Conclusions and Future Work

We have defined the existence of the problem **lack of control and traceability in collaborative business processes** for example in food supply chains. In order to solve the problem identified, we have proposed the development of a Blockchain solution in Hyperledger Composer (HC). This solution will conceive a business network, in which various actors participate and interact with each other with trust and without intermediaries having the ability to consult all the transactions that have occurred. However, before implementing this network, we need to understand how the business operates in food supply chains. For that, we have used the knowledge of DEMO business transactions to understand the existent business processes and human intervention in organizations that participate in a food supply chain. In this line of reason, we have built an artifact, which consists in an meta-model of integration conceptualization designed in an UML domain model, that maps the key concepts existent in DEMO business transactions with the key concepts existent in HC. In this meta-model, we have found four possible integrations between DEMO and HC. To validate the artifact, we considered a case study that describes a supply chain of bananas from J Sainsbury, a big retailer in UK. We have proceeded to the modeling of that case study, where we have designed an ATD and a TRT.

An initial prototype on HC has been presented to validate the artifact too. An asset order have been defined with a field named orderStatus, which informs the current state of the order. Furthermore, two participants, an initiator and an executor, have been defined. Both can submit operations that are able to on the complete transaction pattern, changing the status of the order. It has been demonstrated the history of submitting a request by an initiator and a promise by an executor.

For future work, we establish the full implementation of the case study in HC. The asset Transaction Instance needs to be created to include the processes regarding the order of the bananas but the others as well, such as the creation of consumer profiles. The system needs to be prepared in the future to answer to some issues like: infection on the bananas, failure on its delivery and rejection of bananas for not being in accordance with the specifications defined. To conclude, a submission of other paper that integrates other modeling language with HC and compares with the integration made in this paper needs to be done.

Acknowledgments. This work was supported by national funds through Fundação para a Ciência e a Tecnologia (FCT) with reference UID/CEC/50021/2013.

References

1. Hyperledger composer. https://hyperledger.github.io/composer. Accessed 5 Feb 2018
2. Hyperledger composer historian. https://hyperledger.github.io/composer/reference/historian.html. Accessed 14 Mar 2018
3. Hyperledger composer modeling language. https://hyperledger.github.io/composer/latest/reference/cto_language.html. Accessed 28 Feb 2018
4. Hyperledger composer transaction processor function. https://hyperledger.github.io/composer/reference/js_scripts.html. Accessed 14 Mar 2018
5. Hyperledger fabric. https://www.hyperledger.org/projects/fabric. Accessed 23 Feb 2018
6. UML specification. https://www.omg.org/spec/UML. Accessed 28 Feb 2018
7. Aveiro, D., Silva, A.R., Tribolet, J.: Control organization: a DEMO based specification and extension. In: Albani, A., Dietz, J.L.G., Verelst, J. (eds.) EEWC 2011. LNBIP, vol. 79, pp. 16–30. Springer, Heidelberg (2011). https://doi.org/10.1007/978-3-642-21058-7_2
8. Bechini, A., Cimino, M.G., Marcelloni, F., Tomasi, A.: Patterns and technologies for enabling supply chain traceability through collaborative e-business. Inf. Softw. Technol. **50**(4), 342–359 (2008)

9. Christidis, K., Devetsikiotis, M.: Blockchains and smart contracts for the Internet of Things. IEEE Access **4**, 2292–2303 (2016)
10. Davenport, T.H., Prusak, L.: Working Knowledge: How Organizations Manage What They Know. Harvard Business Press, Brighton (1998)
11. Dellarocas, C., Klein, M.: A knowledge-based approach for handling exceptions in business processes. Inf. Technol. Manag. **1**(3), 155–169 (2000)
12. Di Ciccio, C., et al.: Blockchain-based traceability of inter-organisational business processes. In: Shishkov, B. (ed.) BMSD 2018. LNBIP, vol. 319, pp. 56–68. Springer, Cham (2018). https://doi.org/10.1007/978-3-319-94214-8_4
13. Dietz, J.L.: The PSI theory - understanding human collaboration, October 2017
14. Dietz, J.L., Hoogervorst, J.A.: Foundations of enterprise engineering, October 2017
15. Dietz, J.L.: Enterprise Ontology: Theory and Methodology. Springer, Heidelberg (2006). https://doi.org/10.1007/3-540-33149-2
16. García-Bañuelos, L., Ponomarev, A., Dumas, M., Weber, I.: Optimized execution of business processes on blockchain. In: Carmona, J., Engels, G., Kumar, A. (eds.) BPM 2017. LNCS, vol. 10445, pp. 130–146. Springer, Cham (2017). https://doi.org/10.1007/978-3-319-65000-5_8
17. Guerreiro, S.: Designing a decision-making process for partially observable environments using Markov theory. In: Reinhartz-Berger, I., Gulden, J., Nurcan, S., Guédria, W., Bera, P. (eds.) BPMDS/EMMSAD-2017. LNBIP, vol. 287, pp. 257–271. Springer, Cham (2017). https://doi.org/10.1007/978-3-319-59466-8_16
18. Guerreiro, S., van Kervel, S.J., Babkin, E.: Towards devising an architectural framework for enterprise operating systems. In: ICSOFT, pp. 578–585 (2013)
19. Guerreiro, S., Vasconcelos, A., Tribolet, J.: Enforcing control in the run-time business transactions. In: Advances in Enterprise Information Systems II, p. 69 (2012)
20. Guerreiro, S., Guédria, W., Lagerström, R., Kervel, S.: A meta model for interoperability of secure business transactions - using blockchain and demo, pp. 253–260, January 2017
21. Gupta, M.: Blockchain for Dummies® IBM, Limited edn. Wiley, Hoboken (2017)
22. Handfield, R.B., Bechtel, C.: The role of trust and relationship structure in improving supply chain responsiveness. Ind. Mark. Manag. **31**(4), 367–382 (2002)
23. Jacxsens, L., Luning, P., Van der Vorst, J., Devlieghere, F., Leemans, R., Uyttendaele, M.: Simulation modelling and risk assessment as tools to identify the impact of climate change on microbiological food safety-the case study of fresh produce supply chain. Food Res. Int. **43**(7), 1925–1935 (2010)
24. de Kruijff, J., Weigand, H.: Understanding the blockchain using enterprise ontology. In: Dubois, E., Pohl, K. (eds.) CAiSE 2017. LNCS, vol. 10253, pp. 29–43. Springer, Cham (2017). https://doi.org/10.1007/978-3-319-59536-8_3
25. Laudon, K.C., Laudon, J.P.: Management Information Systems-Managing the Digital Firm. Information Systems, 13 edn., vol. 25 (2014)
26. Lee, H.L., Padmanabhan, V., Whang, S.: Information distortion in a supply chain: the bullwhip effect. Manag. Sci. **43**(4), 546–558 (1997)
27. López-Pintado, O., García-Bañuelos, L., Dumas, M., Weber, I.: Caterpillar: a blockchain-based business process management system. In: Proceedings of the BPM Demo Track and BPM Dissertation Award Co-located with 15th International Conference on Business Process Modeling (BPM 2017), Barcelona, Spain (2017)
28. Mendling, J., et al.: Blockchains for business process management-challenges and opportunities. ACM Trans. Manag. Inf. Syst. (TMIS) **9**(1), 4 (2018)
29. Nakamoto, S.: Bitcoin: a peer-to-peer electronic cash system (2008)

30. Opara, L.U.: Traceability in agriculture and food supply chain: a review of basic concepts, technological implications, and future prospects. J. Food Agric. Environ. **1**, 101–106 (2003)

31. Peffers, K., Tuunanen, T., Rothenberger, M.A., Chatterjee, S.: A design science research methodology for information systems research. J. Manag. Inf. Syst. **24**(3), 45–77 (2007)

32. Weber, I., Xu, X., Riveret, R., Governatori, G., Ponomarev, A., Mendling, J.: Untrusted business process monitoring and execution using blockchain. In: La Rosa, M., Loos, P., Pastor, O. (eds.) BPM 2016. LNCS, vol. 9850, pp. 329–347. Springer, Cham (2016). https://doi.org/10.1007/978-3-319-45348-4_19

33. Wilson, N.: Supply chain management: a case study of a dedicated supply chain for bananas in the UK grocery market. Supply Chain. Manag.: Int. J. **1**(2), 28–35 (1996)

Enterprise Engineering in Business Information Security

Yuri Bobbert[1,2,3] and Hans Mulder[2,3(✉)]

[1] Radboud University, Nijmegen, Netherlands
[2] University of Antwerp, Antwerp, Belgium
[3] Antwerp Management School, Antwerp, Belgium
{yuri.bobbert,hans.mulder}@ams.ac.be

Abstract. Implementing and maintaining Business Information Security (BIS) is cumbersome. Frameworks and models are used to implement BIS, but these are perceived as complex and hard to maintain. Most companies still use spreadsheets to design, direct and monitor their information security improvement plans. Regulators too use spreadsheets for supervision. This paper reflects on ten years of Design Science Research (DSR) on BIS and describes the design and engineering of an artefact which can emancipate boards from silo-based spreadsheet management and improve their visibility, control and assurance via an integrated dash-boarding and reporting tool. Three cases are presented to illustrate the way the artefact, of which the realisation is called the Securimeter, works. The paper concludes with an in-depth comparison study acknowledging 91% of the core BIS requirements being present in the artefact.

1 Introduction

When starting this research in 2008, security was mainly IT-oriented and the main focus was on using IT controls to mitigate or detect security threats. Research has shown that the number of IT security incidents has increased over the years, as has the financial impact per data breach [1]. In 2009, an average of 25% of EU organisations experienced a data breach [2]. Mastering emerging technologies such as big data, Internet of Things, social media and combating cybercrime [3], while protecting critical business data, requires a team instead of a single IT person. To protect this data, security professionals need to know about the value of information and the impact if it is threatened [4]. Several Risk & Security methods have been developed over the last years such as CRAMM (CCTA Risk Analysis and Management Method), OCTAVE, [5], NIST, [6] and ISFs' IRAM [7], particularly into risk analysis and risk assessments in order to analyse threats, vulnerabilities and the impact on information systems as part of the risk management process. The relationship of Risk Management (RM) to Risk Assessment (RA) and information security control setting is visualized in Fig. 1 and is adopted from OCTAVE. To determine these information security controls in the form

---

A case study & expert validation in Security, Risk and Compliance artefact engineering.

© Springer Nature Switzerland AG 2019
D. Aveiro et al. (Eds.): EEWC 2018, LNBIP 334, pp. 88–112, 2019.
https://doi.org/10.1007/978-3-030-06097-8_6

of process controls, technical controls or people controls is based on the risk and impact estimation on the critical *business* assets. Therefore IT risk management requires different capabilities, knowledge and expertise from the skills of IT security professionals [8]. Hubbard [8] refers to the failure of 'expert knowledge' in impact estimations and to the importance of experience beyond risk and IT security, such as asset valuation, collaboration and reflection.

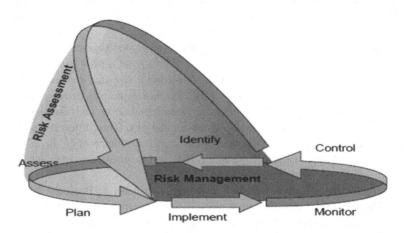

Fig. 1. The relationship between Risk Management and Risk Assessment taken from OCTAVE [9]

2 Practical Contribution

In the past [10] IT security controls were implemented based on best practices prescribed by vendors, without a direct link to risks or business objectives [10]. These controls depended on technology and the audits and assessments (in spreadsheets) were used to prove their effectiveness [11]. The problem with this approach lay in the limitations of mainly IT-focused security and security experts working in silos with limited, subjective views of the world [12]. This is important, as information security is subject to many different interpretations, meanings and viewpoints of several stakeholders [13]. Objectivism is a position that claims that social entities (e.g. 'actors' such as organisations) share exact the same observations and concepts of reality. This is often associated with the term social constructionism. Interpretivism involves the epistemology of a 'social subject'. Actors subjectively observe, analyse and interpret phenomena which they are part of. 'Intersubjective', according to Seale, relates to *"common-sense, shared meanings constructed by people in their interactions with each other and used as an everyday resource to interpret the meaning of elements of social and cultural life. If people share common sense, then they share a definition of the situation."* [14] In the case of BIS, this refers to interactions and reflection between actors e.g. the business, data owners and industry peers on the appropriate level of risk appetite and security maturity [12]. Thus objectivity relates to reality, 'truth reliability', testability and reproducibility, while subjectivity refers to the quality of personal opinions. Intersubjectivity involves the agreements between social entities and the sharing of subjective states by two or more individuals [14].

In order to design a secure enterprise which uses theories and concepts of subjectivity, intersubjectivity and objectivity, the discipline of Enterprise Engineering (EE), which focuses on collaboration in and between organisations, was expected to deliver a contribution to the field of BIS, in 2008. The EE methodology Design and Engineering Method for Organisations (DEMO) therefor was applied in this research in 2009 [15]. DEMO is used to develop an ontological model and to develop a theoretical pattern that can be validated using the artefact (tool).

The field of security in 2010 shifted towards 'information security'. ISO specifies information security as *"protecting information assets from a wide range of threats in order to ensure business continuity, minimise business risk and maximise return on investment and business opportunities"* [16]. Its core principles are Confidentiality, Integrity and Availability (CIA) [16]. Later non-repudiation and auditability were added to comply with audit and compliance regulations. Thus Information Security should ensure a certain level of system quality and assurance [17]. In 2010 many organisations used spreadsheets to practice risk and security management and also proof their assurance via spreadsheets [18, 19].

The scope of Information Security was then expanded to Business Information Security (BIS). In their book 'Information Security Governance', Von Solms and Von Solms describe the growing number of disciplines involved in *BIS* [20]. By 2011 IT managers and IT security managers were increasingly urged to engage with business to determine risk appetite and the desired state of security. Up to 2016, the subjective silo approach to BIS was designed, maintained and reported via spreadsheets [11]. Experts mapped multiple control frameworks [21] from ISO, ISF, COBIT5 in spreadsheets and these are still used by regulators such as the Dutch Central Bank [22]. Volchkov stated that collecting evidence of effectiveness of the controls via spreadsheets has limitations [23]. So Governance Risk and Compliance (GRC) tools moved towards information risk, due to the Sarbanes-Oxley Act, and were designed for large enterprises. GRC implementations are complex and their maintenance requires dedicated staff [24]. Integration of GRC tools with operational data via Security Information and Event Management (SIEM) functionality is reserved for companies with extensive budgets and sufficient staff [24].

Filling in spreadsheets with answers to questionnaires is subject to manipulation because it is not a closed loop. Spreadsheet data is limited to subjective opinions and there is little room for reflection. Spreadsheet data cannot always be gathered from the original sources, which reduces authenticity and integrity [25]. Intersubjective aspects were missing from past timeframes, unless companies used third parties to interpret the data. Objective aspects are not covered, since the various objects (operational processes and data) are not interconnected. Objectivity can be achieved with GRC tools that connect operations to strategy, properly configured via clearly defined business rules. But GRC tools are expensive to implement and to maintain [24] and reserved for large organisations with deep pockets.

This paper describes a research journey from 2008 to 2016, focusing on the development of a BIS artefact that enables intersubjectivity via a dashboard and reporting function. It presents a set of core artefact functionalities that can assist company boards and managers in identifying organisational gaps, gathering operational factual data and thus increasing awareness. It also helps to prioritise investments and enables decision-making. This paper first presents an ontological model that is the precursor of the artefact, and a Design Science Research (DSR) approach [26] to continuous development, design, engineering and maintenance of the artefact. The artefact is later on compared to another artefact with a similar objective. The artefact was designed to incorporate multiple threat and risk models, such as OCTAVE [35], STRIDE and Information Security frameworks such as ISF, OWASP, Cloud Security Framework and ISO27000 series, to master the problem of security management with one single source of truth. Three cases describe the artefacts working and their practical contribution, finally an in-depth artefact comparison is performed by a panel of experts.

3 Enterprise Ontology

Performing a secure business transaction in a connected digitised world requires a view across the boundaries of the enterprise. To share a common, intersubjective view, risk management "could be integrated throughout the organisation. This made it easier to specify the knowledge and competencies needed to manage risk and to identify blind spots." [27]. This shows that all actors involved in the supply chain, i.e. the extended enterprise of secure transactions, needed to be involved. In 2009, at the start of this research, Electronic Patient Files (EPD in Dutch) were examined from the point of view of a customer with a business requirement. In this case, there is treatment by a surgeon and the use of data repositories in order to treat the patient [15].

DEMO – a methodology that is used to design enterprises – is based on several theories, including the ψ theory [28]. This Greek letter PSI stands for Performance in Social Interaction. The ψ theory focuses on the performance of the social interactions of actors. In this paper [15] the DEMO delayering in B-I-D takes into account inter-subjective communication between social actors, the reasoning of subjects and objective data in repositories of facts. The B layers represent *Business* transactions, the I layer the *Information* layers and the D layers the *Data* layer. In this research DEMO is used to provide the design for the BIS artefact and elicit the collaboration and inter-action between parties to gain the required intersubjective assurance. To deal with some core transactions the Securimeter artefact contains business rules for actors. The DEMO model shown in Fig. 2 depicts the artefacts working, per transaction type, including actors and sources per case.

B-A represent the actors and require facts related to production and communication. T represents the transactions related to the handling of this request, whereas B-CA represents composite actors. B-APB represents the data repositories that contain facts such as transaction logs. The outlined area, described as 'Security Performance Meter', represents the BIS artefact. In the three examples below we describe transactions (e.g. business requirements) that were initiated by three different actors: a request from a board member and two requests from a manager. For page limitations we refer to the online dataset (https://easy.dans.knaw.nl/ui/datasets/id/easy-dataset:77502/tab/2) tab Chapter 7 of this research project that captures all the required evidence accompanying each case.

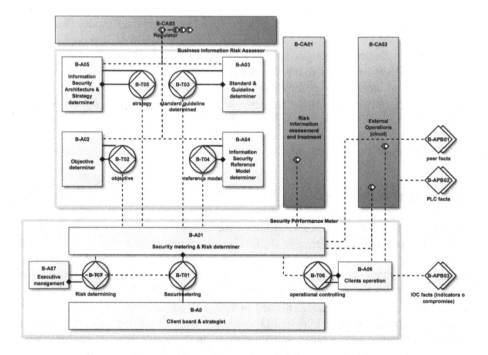

Fig. 2. The DEMO model for the BIS artefact.

4 Establishing the Requirements for the Securimeter Artefact: Three Cases

According to DEMO, a successful transaction is established after the acceptance from the requesting actor. In the context of BIS, we have identified three examples of a request from a board member or manager to deliver an overview of the risk and security level of the organisation. He or she might want to report this information to an audit committee or regulator. We refer to this actor as the 'Client board' (B-A0), since this is an entity who wants to gain or maintain a certain level of information risk assurance. This actor makes a request for a transaction (B-T01) and information is delivered via certain processes and extracted from internal or external data repositories B-APB01/02/03. In this section three examples are presented of a business request that leads to BIS artefact requirements. The first case involves a large government organisation with a broad and complex IT landscape. To maintain a certain level of *BIS* control, they adopted the Baseline Information Security Government (Baseline Informatiebeveiliging Rijksdienst (BIR). The BIR consists of 12 domains which are categorised as people, process and technology controls. These domains were included in the artefact via 133 questions the organisation is required to answer. This case describes the artefact's contribution to effectively measuring, controlling, demonstrating and reporting on this BIR, since the organisation is subject to regulatory supervision. The second case involves a financial firm that wants to gain periodically insight into their critical risks and treatment plans. The third case relates to extracting operational data from a production environment to gain insight into critical assets. This information is necessary to gain control of new or missing assets (e.g. a production plant).

4.1 Government Case

The governmental organisation must comply with the BIR [29]. This norm is based on the ISO 27000 series and the 12 domains match the domains of the ISO such as; Information Security Policy, Information Security management organisation, Asset management, Personnel security, Access management etc. In order to frequently report on the status of BIR maturity, this actor requires a periodical status overview on the effectiveness of controls. This customer request starts a process which extracts the status of the key controls in the organisation within the BIR. These controls are implemented within for example IT operations, via processes and technology. The effectiveness of these controls can be measured and expressed in numbers, for example via maturity models with predefined scales (e.g. ISO 15504). Within this, a 0% score refers to Non-existent (N), everything in between is partially achieved (P) or largely achieved (L), and 100% represents fully achieved (F). This NPLF scoring leaves room for multiple criteria per maturity level of the control. By testing and scoring each control on its design and effectiveness, this can be reflected in a dashboard. In an ideal situation, there is an automated scripted process of proofing the design and effectiveness of most of these controls. The figure below shows a dashboard of the key BIR domains. Every domain reflects multiple controls that are weighted and collectively express, via NPLF scores, into the dashboard with meters per domain. The improvement values per domain are expressed in green or in red, if there is a decrease in maturity level. The overall colour of the meter shows the progression compared to the predefined desired state.

When an organisation is subject to multiple regulators (e.g. Authoriteit Persoonsgegevens) or internal control frameworks (e.g. ISO), it is desirable that all of these baselines are mapped on the existing baseline (BIR). This cross-referencing of models, labelled as 'x-ref' in the upper left in the meta-model, and their controls, is needed in order to establish a collective set of the existing controls in an exhaustive framework, in order to avoid double work on identical controls. In this case, the actor requests only to report on the BIR status via a reflection of control effectiveness via an NPLF score expressed in a dashboard with meters. See Fig. 3 for the Dutch dashboard, the domains mentioned in Dutch match the English translation of 5 = Information Security Policy, 6 = Information Security management organisation, 7 = Asset management, 8 = personnel security, 11 = Access management 12 = Acquisition and development of Systems, 13 = Incident management and 14 = Business Continuity Management.

4.2 Finance Case Study

The second example of a business request shows insight into all information risks, expressed in a score ranging from low to critical. This is needed for executive management (B-A07) to be aware of the risks, the risk owners and the treatment plans, and for regular reporting on the functioning of the information risk assurance. This request kicks off a transaction (B-T07) that extracts information from the information risk determiner, where all risks are identified with a risk indication of low, medium, high or critical, derived from processes and documentation.

(B-CA01) in the repository of the artefact. This risk indication is based on the Business Impact Analysis (BIA) and various predefined treatments (e.g. security controls). Within the BIA, a thorough trade-off is made for the risk treatment plan, based on the risk appetite of the organisation. This is usually determined via policies and procedures stored in a repository (B-CA01). The person responsible for determining the information risk policies and standards is usually the Chief Risk Officer (B-T03). The security controls that might mitigate the risks are predefined in the IS standards and models, and the person responsible for determining this (B-T04) is usually the Chief Information Security Officer (CISO).

Figure 4 displays the result of a business request for an overview of risks and all relevant data needed to enable an intersubjective view. This view is called intersubjective because it involves sharing benchmark data on for example Open Web Application Security Project (OWASP) penetration testing results with other organisations. Capturing penetration testing data in the artefact makes it possible to compare the risk profile with those of peers (e.g. other business units). The information displayed in this dashboard can also be used in interaction with other stakeholders, such as regulators, auditors or committees.

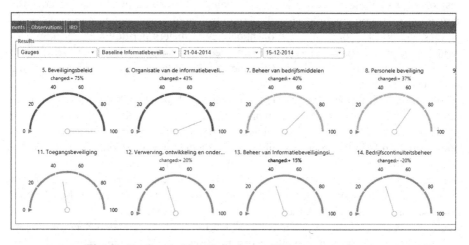

Fig. 3. Artefact dashboard displaying BIR status per domain

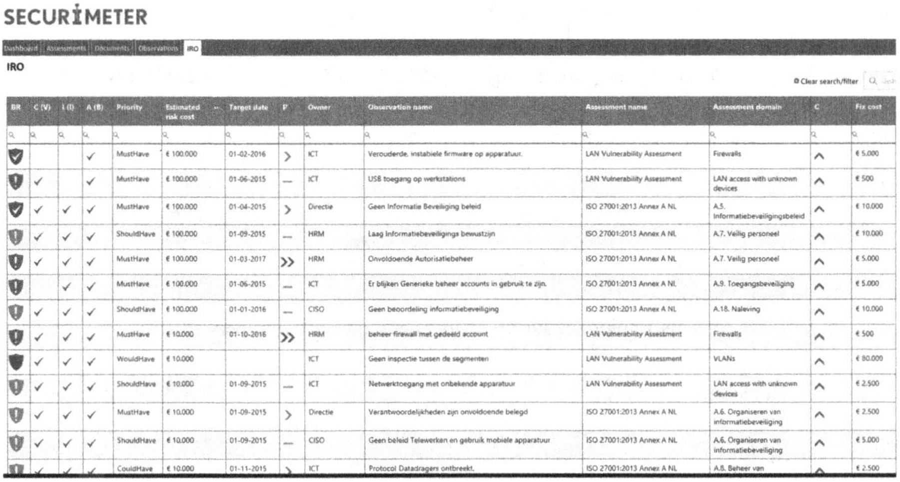

SECURIMETER

Fig. 4. Artefact dashboard displaying all identified risks.

4.3 Utility Company Case

A large utility company requires frequent inventories to be made of their critical IT assets that control the Programmable logic controller (PLC) environments. In this example, the security manager requests operational data to be mapped on one of the key controls "asset inventory" and be reflected in a delta score. The API function is a function in the artefact that makes it possible to import operational data into the artefact via 'Dynamic-link library (DLL) parsing', which enables data from operational sources, in this example QualysGuard vulnerability data, to be processed in the artefact. The API requirement implementation in the artefact resulted in the ability to parse data into the artefact and this reflects the key control effectiveness via the dashboard. In addition, other customer requests were engineered into the artefact. For example, in 2013–2015, core interventions designed to increase BIS governance were distilled into the initial requirements for the SecuriMeter artefact [30].

5 Artefact Requirements that Solve Problems

The objective of DSR research is to establish artefacts that solve real-life problems. The collective set of requirements within the DSR artefact should contribute in this goal. Frequent validation involving stakeholders, such as users, engineers and customers to confirm that the artefact requirements actually help solve the problem at hand is necessary. Wieringa [31] refers to using the regulative cycle to determine the right set of artefact requirements and to validate if it contributes to solving the problem. In Q1 of 2012 five managers participated in a Group Support System (GSS) session. GSS research was used to enable social interaction between stakeholders suffering from the problem of a one-dimensional spreadsheet approach that limits sharing of knowledge and thus intersubjectivity. GSS was used throughout this research project to establish consensus on the artefact requirements [32]. The aim of this GSS session in 2012 was to discuss, select and prioritise the initial dashboard requirements for the artefact. The question was: *Which management information would CIOs and CISOs consider important for managing their business security (from governance to operation)?* The table below shows the top 5 items (out of a total of 22) (Table 1).

Table 1. Top 5 management information items for BIS according to CIOs and CISOs.

Management information for managing BIS	Rating *
1. Risk thermometer	10
2. Policy versus implementation versus checking with numbers	8.8
3. Factual figures (for management presentation purposes)	8.8
4. Hot items	8.3
5. Audits and 'traffic light reports'	8

*Scale from 1 to 10, in which 10 is most important.

These requirements were designed and engineered in the artefact, taking a Design Science Research approach. An important contribution was made by collaborating with experts in the field on extracting operational and process data and processes for use in the artefact. Since 2010 numerous GSS sessions contributed in additional requirements for the artefact such as assessments to capture operational data. Besides our own experience of GSS sessions to co-develop new requirements, De Vreede et al. [33] also revealed that brainstorming groups using GSS "to *generate more unique ideas, and higher quality ideas than groups doing manual brainstorming.*" In the table below we highlight the most relevant and significant contributions that were made on the data level since the establishment of the artefact in 2010 (Table 2).

Table 2. Summary of security assessments in the artefact designed to solve practical problems.

Initiation date	Problem	Requirement to solve the problem	Result # tests at organisations
9-8-2011	Lack of insight into virtualisation risks (version 4)	Virtualisation Security Assessment	7 assessments on version 4 and 8 assessments on version 5 per 4-7-2013*
12-8-2011	Lack of insight into Web threats and risks	Web application vulnerability assessment	+20 assessments since 2011
12-8-2011	Lack of insight into firewall configuration vulnerabilities	Firewall security assessment	+10 assessments since 2011
9-8-2011	Lack of insight into Wireless networks' vulnerabilities and risks	Wireless vulnerability assessment	+5 assessments since 2011

(*continued*)

Table 2. (*continued*)

Initiation date	Problem	Requirement to solve the problem	Result # tests at organisations
12-8-2011	Lack in insights into LAN vulnerabilities	LAN vulnerability assessment	+40 assessments since 2011
5-6-2012	Lack of insight into social media usage and related risks	Social media vulnerability assessment	5 assessments taken on 4-7-2013*
11-4-2013	Lack of cookie compatibility	Cookie assessment	+2 assessments since 2013
11-4-2013	Lack of DigiD pre-audit requirements	DigID pre-audit	+10 assessments since 2013
9-11-2011	Lack of BYOD vulnerabilities and risks	BYOD assessment	
14-6-2013	Lack of insight into web application vulnerabilities	Web application vulnerability assessment	+20 assessments since 2013
13-10-2013	Lack of database vulnerabilities and risks	Database security assessment	+2 assessments since 2013

*Vulnerability reports in an XML format. This functionality provides the opportunity to import all XML reports into the artefact using the API for DLL parsing functionalities.

6   From Enterprise Ontology to Securimeter Artefact

An artefact comparison against an existing other artefact can bring additional insights on the working and the artefacts' positioning compared to other tools. It can also support the future development process of the artefact. In agreement with the manuscript commission an objective comparison between SecuriMeter and a similar security measurement and reporting tool is proposed. The manuscript commission and then researcher agreed to compare the SecuriMeter Artefact with the tool of the Information Security Forum (ISF), "The ISF Accelerator". By comparing both tools based on the ENISA criteria (1), these criteria were set based on an extensive examination by ENISA into Information Security and Risk management tooling. According to the manuscript commission these criteria are sufficient for the required comparison and will contribute the research project in its' academic contribution. In agreement with the promotors and the manuscript commission it was decided that in addition to the ENISA criteria, both tools also needed to be compared based on the scientific claim (e.g. functionalities) that were derived from this research work and as presented in this paper (2). Since this research project is based on Design Science Research, and the control over progress and effects within DSR are typically at the hands of the person designing, i.e., the researcher, the comparison needs to be objective, thus without interference of the researcher, and repeatable. Important note is that during the comparison study no new release of the artefact was made, thus the entire study was executed on the same version.

I have selected GSS as a method for this qualitative comparison of tooling since GSS is also proposed in the entire project as a research method to gain a deeper understanding of the topic and to record intermediate steps. GSS is a research method that can use multiple iterations, with or without group interactions [31] and all steps, scores and arguments are recorded in the GSS software to assure objectivity, controllability, repeatability. With this in mind the following research approach is proposed.

Research Approach for the Artefact Comparison

The risks of objectivity, controllability, repeatability and generalisability are taken into consideration during this comparison study. Therefor the following objective criteria and controllable steps are embedded. The criteria that form a "Frame of Reference" are:

- 1. ENISA Criteria, and
- 2. Additional criteria derived from the deliverables in this PhD research project:

The following controllable research steps and goals are proposed;

First Step:

- The researcher submits the criteria proposed by the commission, being ENISA criteria, and the presented functionalities of the SecuriMeter artefact to the promotors. The entire list of criteria is also attached in the appendices. The goal is to have clear predefined criteria which can be compared in the next steps (Table 3).

After this the 100 + criteria are delivered to co-promotor professor Mulder who processed the criteria in an online survey tool so a group of experts can prioritize the criteria on relevance for comparison. Before submitting it in final version to the experts Mulder requested a group of nine people to test the set-up, in this pre-test the criteria, the listing and the online tooling. This is called step 1a. According to Recker [34] Page 78, "*a pre-test is a tryout, and its purpose is to help produce a survey form that is more usable and reliable. Pre-testing helps refine the instrument and ensure executability of the survey*". Recker describes on page 80 of his book to perform an instrument pre-test three objectives to pursue when doing pre-tests of survey instruments:

- *Evaluate the authenticity of the questions,*
- *Evaluate the survey interface and layout, and*
- *Establish validity and reliability of the survey instrument.*

Table 3. List of participant characteristics of the online survey test step 1a.

Participant	Role	Industry	Submitted
1	Project manager security	Financial services	Y
2	Director	HR services	Y
3	Director	Educational services	N
4	Manager SOC	Telecom	Y
5	Manager call center	Financial services	Y
6	Director	Risk & security company	Y
7	Security architect	Government	Y
8	Teacher security	Educational services	Y
9	Security officer	Government	Y
10	Project manager security	Airport/Aviation	Y

After the test feedback is gained to improve the tool, listing and prepare the real sessions. Also potential ambiguous terms or vague items can be detected and anticipated on. After this a large heterogeneous group from multiple business domains can score the provided criteria based on relevance for comparison and on the validity for the risk and security field. In this initial step the participants are not able to influence each other [35] nor are they influenced by the session operator professor Mulder (Table 4).

Table 4. Participant characteristics in the comparison study step 1b.

Participant	Role	Industry	Submitted online	Present at 6 July session
1	CISO	Media	Y	N
2	CISO	Financial services	Y	N
3	Software security specialist	Software testing	Y	Y
4	Manager	Accountancy	Y	Y
5	Consultant	Security services	Y	Y
6	Consultant	Security advisory	Y	N
7	Director/Professor	Research institute	Y	Y
8	Partner at consulting firm	Security and risk advisory	Y	Y
9	Director EMEA	Security and risk advisory	Y	N
10	Director security services	Security and risk advisory	Y	N
11	Consultant	Security and risk advisory	Y	Y
12	Auditor	Financial services	Y	N
13	Information security officer	Government	Y	Y
14	Auditor	Financial services/Auditing	Y	N
15	Consultant in education	Educational services	Y	N

With this step all scores are recorded per participant and analytical motivations are submitted in the system. This is to assure the objectivity, controllability and repeatability during and after the research project.

An additional GSS session is held based on the online pre-submitted data. This so called "Relay Group method" increases the productivity of the group and enables a double loop learning which increase the quality of the outcome [33]. To address the large deviations between the individual scores and to discuss this in the group a better qualified core set of criteria is established which has been validated by experts from the field. Also a prioritisation of all the criteria is done based on the relevance for a comparison study.

All steps, scores and arguments are submitted in the GSS system to assure the objectivity, controllability and repeatability. The sessions are moderated by an experienced session moderator, which is required according to the ground rules of group moderation published by Hengst [36] and addressed in multiple other publications [37–39]. The objective of this first step is to selectively narrow down the 100 + list of criteria to eventually establish a core set of criteria that can be considered relevant according to experts opinion and to do a further thorough comparison analysis on in the next steps.

Second Step

The second step is to record the two tools in a video demonstration on their performance with regard to the selected criteria.

1. SecuriMeter tool is presented in a demo to present the previous derived criteria (origin; 1 (ENISA) and 2 (Additional)). This demonstration is recorded on film to assure objectivity, controllability, repeatability.
2. ISF "Accelerator" tool is presented in a demo to present the previous derived criteria (origin; 1 (ENISA) and 2 (Additional)). This demonstration is recorded on film to assure objectivity, controllability and repeatability.

The objective of this second step is to deliver two tool demonstrations on video about the core functionalities/criteria of both tools.

Third Step

In this third step eleven other participants from a heterogeneous group participate in a GSS session which will be moderated by co-promotor professor Mulder. A predefined agenda is set and shared prior to the meeting so the participants can individually prepare the GSS session. The GSS session is introduced by the two video demonstrations of the artefacts. According to Recker video films increase the credibility (e.g. internal validity) (page 94), this method was chosen to assure the objectivity and controllability of the comparison study [34]. All 11 participants are asked to compare the presented functionalities and score the functionalities. All steps, scores and arguments are recorded in the GSS system to assure the objectivity, controllability and repeatability of the research. The objective here is to deliver an in-depth analysis on the predefined selected criteria and an analysis on the deviations given by the expert respondents (Table 5).

The Final Deliverables of These 3 Steps Are:

– Clearly defined criteria for the tool comparison.
– Two demonstrations of both tools recorded on film.
– An in-depth comparison analysis of both tools based on predefined criteria.

Deliverables

The first an online pre-test to test the working of the meeting wizard tool was executed among 9 participants. After that step an online survey (blind, different time different place) was executed to get the initial input on all the comparison criteria. The objective

Table 5. List of participant's characteristics of the GSS expert panel held on 10th August 2017 (step 3).

Participant	Title	Role	Industry	Invited	Present at 10th Aug
1	Dr.	Security consultant	Information security services	Y	Y
2	Drs, MA	Advisor	Government	Y	Y
3	Dr. RE	Auditor/lecturer	Government	Y	Y
4	MSc CISA	Consultant	Information security services	Y	Y
8	Drs, CISM, CISA	Auditor/ISACA Chair	Financial services	Y	Y
6	MSc, RE	Auditor	Financial services	Y	Y
7	Prof. Dr. ir.	Professor	Education	Y	Y
8	MSc	Consultant	Security services	Y	Y
9	MSc MISM	Information security officer	Transportation	Y	Y
10	BC, RE	Auditor	Financial services	Y	Y
11	MSc	Information security officer	Government	Y	Y

Table 6. Type of test during the comparison including dates.

Type of test	Date	Step
Online survey test	20 June 2017	1a
Blind test	2 July 2017	1b
Criteria selection session	6 July 2017	1b
Video demonstration	2 Augustus 2017	2
Comparison session	10 August 2017	3

is to have the participants of this session get to know the items and prepare their own session. The answers that are submitted by the participants via the online tool are captured in the GSS database and presented to the group based on the largest variance (above 40% non-consensus). The objective in this stage is to get a better understanding on the items that have a large variety. All participants that scored high are asked to provide their feedback. The feedback on all 29 discussed items is captured in the GSS Meeting tool and later on visible in the report. Below are the most relevant comments and learnings and the related decisions are highlighted (Table 6).

- On the criteria "pricing" the remark was made about the fact it can be two folded; price of the product and the pricing model (e.g. user based, processor based, fixed fee, pay per use?)
- It doesn't matter how big the company is, that's only relevant for the scaling. Not relevant for the importance. Small companies can process large amounts of money or sensitive data.
- According to two participants a trail license is key. This is the only way, "seeing is believing". You need to get your hands on the product. One participant scored this low in his first online submission but wants to revise his answer based on the discussion; he thinks it is really relevant.
- The view point on how to look at items is determined by the role you fulfil in the organisation. For example a manager weighs his criteria different than for example the subject matter expert (auditor).
- Initially language seems not relevant by the group but after the discussion that tools in other languages (e.g. Hebrew, Chinese) are limiting in use of acceptance. For example government in Netherlands demands tools in Dutch.
- One participant mentioned: "Some criteria are scored completely different before the session than after the group discussion within the group"
- Another participant raised: "Important is to determine the objective of the tool (doel van de tool) before selection"
- Some of the criteria are not smart was a remark of most of the participants. The ENISA list seems outdated.
- Setting the criteria and the relevance of criteria is also determined based on the level of maturity of the organisation. A less mature organisation requires more guidance.

Comparison Criteria

In the final round it is the objective to have the participants selects the core criteria which they think are relevant for the eventual tool comparison. With the knowledge they have gained from the previous rounds and discussions (double loop learning [40]). All criteria are presented via the Meeting Wizard iPad interface and all participants were asked to answer Yes = useful for the comparison, No = not useful for the comparison. A complete list of all comparison criteria arose, ranked based on the score of the group. Below is a list of all criteria with +85% consent, thus 6 out of 6 scored yes.

Videos with Artefact Demonstrations

Based on these criteria two video demonstrations are recorded and delivered:

- Securimeter video, accessible via: https://youtu.be/wBNg2oyK4c4. Recorded on 1 August 2017 in Ede
- ISF Accelerator video, accessible via: https://youtu.be/EXLyGUFDwu0. Recorded on 18 July 2017 in Nieuwegein

SecuriMeter   **ISF Accelerator**

As a final deliverable the objective of the last research step 3 is to collectively compare the core functionalities of a Business Information Security (BIS) artefact. The prepared video clips of two consultants presenting the predefined criteria in the two artefacts, being the "ISF accelerator" and the "SecuriMeter" are required to be watched by the participants prior to the GSS session. The two movies are also shown during the session and will collectively - through group discussion – being used to assess the tools on the availability of the functionalities and thereby compare the two tools.

Prior to the meeting the experts need to prepare this session by looking into the list of predefined functionalities (comparison criteria) and the video script that is used to record the presentations. By looking into this list prior to watching the video the experts will be better prepared for the group session. The entire list of all 37 criteria items including the video demonstrations of the two artefacts were shared one week prior to the session. In the table below the scores of both tools are presented. The variance represents the deviation of the scores of the experts. The deviations above 40% are discussed in the group and further detailed in the analysis section.

Additional Insights after Demonstrating, Evaluating and Comparing the Artefact
In 2000 de Vreede et al. [33] stated that discussion groups working on outcomes of others have better results than groups that start from scratch. De Vreede et al. refer to Decathlon Groups when Groups need to start from scratch and Relay Groups when they work on previous collected data. De Vreede stated: *"Relay groups appeared to be more productive than Decathlon groups, in particular in terms of elaborations to previous contributions" Relay groups also produced slightly more unique ideas, but not significantly. Hence, we may conclude that overall a Relay method is preferable in terms of productivity than a Decathlon method.* In this research project the last expert group used the data of the previous group in order to enable productivity of the group, since rating such an amount of criteria *and* compare the tools based on these criteria may take multiple hours and may be a mental stretch. This might have an impact on the participant's satisfaction. As De Vreede et al. continue in their research *"Relay groups were also found to be more satisfied"*, in terms of interest accommodation.

With this knowledge an additional step was added to the GSS meeting. In addition to the comparison of the two artefacts the experts were also asked, based on their prior gained and shared knowledge, to brainstorm on the research question *"Which parameters that influence the Maturing Business Information Security (MBIS) process can be considered as requirements for an artefact designed to capture, measure and report the MBIS process?*

The objective of this question was to gain a qualified insight through discussion and listing of parameters via experts' opinions. This seems specifically interesting for me as a researcher to see if the experts perceive the same artefact requirements compared to the ones I have gained via this research project. From all 98 answers given by the experts I will highlight the most relevant one that are "already part of the SecuriMeter" artefact, marked as AP, "not yet in the artefact" marked as NP, or are a "part of the analysis method", marked as PAM. PAM refers to the analysis method which enables knowledge sharing, consensus building on priorities, decision-making, stakeholder engagement, increasing the awareness and enables reflection. PAM encompasses two artefacts:

One being the collaborative analysis method that enables team collaboration to define the parameters for analysis of the BIS maturity and two the SecuriMeter tool that supports the administrative work (for measuring and reporting purposes), which can be used to report insights into the state of BIS maturity on multiple levels (strategic, tactical and operational).

A subset of the list that was derived via experts is displayed in the table below. The relevant –new - items that gave new/or inspiring insights on the topic, are listed including my reflection (as a researcher).

Interesting finding from the expert participants is that most of the submitted answers relate to either "preconditions" or "enablers" of the BIS improvement process such as; tone at the top, culture, enable lower in the organisation decision-making, knowledge, education etcetera. These items are most of the time collectively determined based on strategic objectives, regulatory requirements or the type of industry an organisation is in. Therefor the majority, 55 of the total 98, of the items were marked as "part of the analysis method". This means that the majority of the parameters raised by the experts are subject to some form of –team- collaboration.

21 items of the total 98 are already functionalities present within the SecuriMeter aretfact.

10 items are both subject to PAM as well as a future requirement since these are not present in SecuriMeter yet. These items are interesting and reflected below since they can serve as future artefact requirements. 18 items are not yet present but can well be considered as a requirement and are potential backlog items that the developers can take into consideration for the next sprints. Therefor this additional comparison was a meaningful exercise (Table 7).

Table 7. Abstract of the 98 requirement suggested by the experts on multiple levels.

Organisational level	Artefact requirement suggestion submitted by the experts	AP = Already Present in SecuriMeter	NP = Not Present in SecuriMeter	PAM = Part of the Analysis Method	Researchers reflection on suggestions
Governance					
G	Needed: governance structure in which interconnectivity exits between stakeholder on several layers			PAM	Collectively fill in the questionnaires via GSS
G	Link to business objectives			PAM	Can be done via referencing the domains of a standard towards a strategic objective
G	Country of operation		NP		Very relevant functionality for a multinational dealing with multiple foreign regulatory requirements
G	Awareness of what the desired level of maturity is: compliance-driven or self-imposed goals?	AP		PAM	Defining the desired level can be done in SecuriMeter, and how the organisation is engineered in its processes (control oriented, self-imposed, or threat oriented) can also be defined. Stating this is always subject to debate on interpretation for example via GSS
Management					
M	Freedom for taking action			PAM	Needs to be set and mandated by management, for example by working in small Agile teams (DevOps way of working)

(continued)

Table 7. (*continued*)

Organisational level	Artefact requirement suggestion submitted by the experts	AP = Already Present in SecuriMeter	NP = Not Present in SecuriMeter	PAM = Part of the Analysis Method	Researchers reflection on suggestions
M	Support prioritizing specific risks and measures: best value for your money.	AP		PAM	This is partly present but can be improved via the IRO. Making the IRO part of a collaborative process to prioritize risk treatments tuned to the value for money
M	Translate known risks into costs of business discontinuity or lost opportunities		NP	PAM	This is partly present but can be improved via the IRO. Making the IRO part of a collaborative process to link risks to lost opportunities
M	Security as part of KPIs, yearplan of employees		NP	PAM	Integrate with HR rewarding mechanisms
M	Tone at the bottom			PAM	
M	Available budget		NP		
M	Look outside the organisation and learn from others their mistakes		NP		
M	Trustworthyness or (un)certainty of data. Data regarding the maturity of a control deteriorates over time.		NP		
M	Different mitigation options incl pro's and con's		NP	PAM	
M	Reliability of management information		NP		Reliability can be improved via sign off process and retention policies on the information submitted in SecuriMeter

(*continued*)

Table 7. (*continued*)

Organisational level	Artefact requirement suggestion submitted by the experts	AP = Already Present in SecuriMeter	NP = Not Present in SecuriMeter	PAM = Part of the Analysis Method	Researchers reflection on suggestions
M	Management approach/type		NP	PAM	Increasingly important due to agile way of working were decision making is delegated more down in the organisation and teams
M	Level of knowledge and expertise of management		NP	PAM	Current knowledge and expertise of management can be assessed via SecuriMeter (e.g. via number of certifications or taken courses), defining the gap can also be done by setting clear knowledge requirements per maturity level per domain. Improvement is needed in explicating the expertise gap
Operations					
O	Every 4 years: review all operations for usefulness and lean		NP		
O	All security operations must have a purpose. if not, DELETE		NP		Enforce alignment of controls towards business objectives. Mandatory functionality to reference a control towards an objective
O	Security data must be an integral part of operational data		NP	PAM	Therefor requires the same BIA process as regular data

(*continued*)

Table 7. (*continued*)

Organisational level	Artefact requirement suggestion submitted by the experts	AP = Already Present in SecuriMeter	NP = Not Present in SecuriMeter	PAM = Part of the Analysis Method	Researchers reflection on suggestions
O	Make improvements visible to employees	AP		PAM	
O	Include operations as active component in improvement of security, not just as only serving for execution of what is decided at other levels		NP	PAM	
O	Skilled employee		NP	PAM	Current skills level can be assessed via SecuriMeter (e.g. via number of certifications or taken -online- courses), defining the gap can also be done by setting clear knowledge requirements per maturity level per domain. Improvement is needed in explicating the expertise gap

7   Conclusions

A key finding of this research is that BIS frameworks and tools mainly focus on subjective opinions, gathered via questionnaires and processed in spreadsheets. In recent years, such opinions have being shared, discussed and evaluated by teams in organisations, making subjective questionnaires intersubjective. However, the structure of these questionnaires is not well suited to scale up within an organisation or in an industry as a whole. The main reason for these limitations of scalability is the need for a unifying ontological model and centralised tool that supports intersubjectivity.

Another finding is that technological monitoring using objective data (e.g. log files, technical state compliance monitoring, etc.) isn't combined with an intersubjective organisational approach, such as SIEM, where data is linked to the ontological layer of transactions. The research on this BIS artefact combines ontological, infological and data logical layers of information. In the artefact a combination of subjective, inter-subjective and objective data is collected, monitored, evaluated and used as a steering mechanism. The first step in this research project (in 2010) was to carry out a literature review and prioritise parameters to be used in the artefact. This was supported by expert views gathered using the 'decathlon' [33] approach to meetings. These were supported by technology that enables many meetings on the same data and with the same outcome requirements to be linked together. In this case, the outcome was to define the functionalities of the experimental artefact. Examples include the ISO 27000 mapping in the research published in 2011 and core interventions designed to improve the maturity of BIS [41]. Study outcomes were all included in the artefact according to this DSR method [26]. Besides these scientific steps, a great deal of empirical data was collected during thousands of development hours in collaboration with individual scholars, universities of applied science, companies and the Dutch Ministry of Economic Affairs.

As shown in this paper, the artefact consists of numerous subjective, and, when shared and discussed, intersubjective questionnaires, import log data collected with the XML parser (objective data) and checklists with weighing that deliver mandatory proof of control effectiveness (intersubjective). Capturing data from multiple security devices (e.g. firewalls), combined with checklists that require evidence, e.g. from DigiD (a Dutch identification method used by the Government) audits, BIC (baseline for Information Security for housing corporations) and BIWA (baseline for Information Security for water companies) audits, virtualisation and cloud audits, is not feasible with spreadsheets. Data showing evidence can be captured in the artefact using the document management function. Combining data and comparing it across industries (benchmarking) is limited, but necessary according to the latest Antwerp Management School validation [42] and numerous studies. Industry measurements e.g. BIWA and Baseline Informatiebeveiliging Gemeente (BIG) are examples of a growing body of valuable benchmarking data in the artefact. Numerous other measurements on for example OWASP (software vulnerability scans) and DigiD, offer other perspectives which provide factual insights into the operations of organisations and enable bench-marking. This contributes to the assurance that boards, senior management, regulators etc. are increasingly demanding in order to achieve more visibility and control.

The discussion during the paper presentation at the Enterprise Engineering Working Conference on 30th of May 2018 in Luxembourg focused on the comparison of two types of Security artefacts showed from the video. Namely the differences between the adoption in organizations spreadsheet based tool 'ISF Accelerator' and the collaborative tool 'Securimeter'. In essence this discussion reflected the relevance of the problem statement and rigour of the artefact requirements.

For page limitations we refer to the online dataset (https://easy.dans.knaw.nl/ui/datasets/id/easy-dataset:77502/tab/2).

Appendix

See Fig. 5.

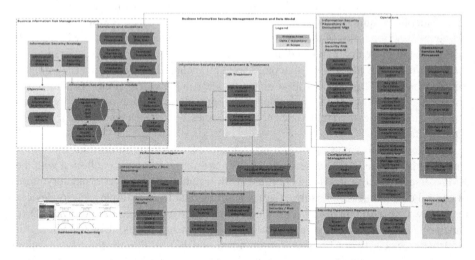

Fig. 5. Meta-model for the BIS processes and data. The grey areas represent the scope of the artefact (dashboard tool).

References

1. Ponemone: Cost of Data Breach Study: Global Analysis, Ponemon Institute LLC, United States (2016)
2. Ponemon Institute: Business Case for Data Protection, Ponemon Institute LLC (2009)
3. Cashell, B., Jackson, W., Jickling, M., Webel, B.: The Economic Impact of Cyber-Attacks, Congressional Research Service, The Library of Congress, United States (2004)
4. ITGI: Information Risks: Who's Business are they?, United States: IT Governance Institute (2005)
5. Alberts, C.J., Dorofee, A.: OCTAVE Method Implementation Guide version 2.0, Carnegie Mellon University Software Engineering Institute, Pittsburgh, Pennsylvania, (2001)
6. Stonenburner, G., Goguen, A., Feringa, A.: NIST Special publications 800-27 Risk Management Guide for Information Technology Systems, National Institute of Standards and Technology, Gaithersburg (2002)
7. ISF, IRAM: Information Risk Assessment Methodology 2, Information Security Forum (2016). https://www.securityforum.org/tool/information-risk-assessment-methodology-iram2/
8. Hubbard, D.: The Failure of Risk Management. Wiley, Hoboken (2009)
9. ENISA: Principles and Inventories for Risk Management/Risk Assessment methods and tools, Brussel: European Network and information Security Agency (ENISA) (2006)

10. Yaokumah, W., Brown, S.: An empirical examination of the relationship between information security/business strategic alignment and information security governance. J. Bus. Syst., Governance Ethics 2(9), 50–65 (2014)
11. Zitting, D.: Are You Still Auditing in Excel?. Sarbanes Oxley Compliance Journal (2015). http://www.s-ox.com/dsp_getFeaturesDetails.cfm?CID=4156
12. Flores, W., Antonsen, E., Ekstedt, M.: Information security knowledge sharing in organizations: Investigating the effect of behavioral information security governance and national culture. Comput. Secur. 2014–43, 90–110 (2014)
13. Van Niekerk, J., Von Solms, R.: Information security culture; A management perspective. Comput. Secur. 29, 476–486 (2010)
14. Seale, C.: Researching Society and Culture, 2nd edn. Sage Publications, Thousand Oaks (2004). ISBN 978-0-7619-4197-2
15. Bobbert, Y.: Use of DEMO as a methodology for business and security alignment. Platform for Information Security, pp. 22–26 (2009). www.ee-institute.org/download.php?id=133&type=doc
16. ISO/IEC27001:2013, ISO/IEC 27001:2013: Information technology – Security techniques – Information security management systems – Requirements, ISO/IEC, Geneva (2013)
17. Cherdantseva, Y., Hilton, J.: A reference model of information assurance & security. In: IEEE proceedings of ARES, vol. SecOnt workshop, Regensburg, Germany (2013)
18. GOV.UK: The Security Policy Framework (SPF), Statement of Assurance questionnaire in Excel - Gov.uk
19. Halkyn, ISO27001 Self Assessment Checklist hits record downloads, 19 February 2015
20. von Solms, S., von Solms, R.: Information Security Governance. Springer, New York (2009). https://doi.org/10.1007/978-0-387-79984-1. ISBN 978-0-387-79983-4
21. ITGI: COBIT Mapping: Mapping of CMMI for Development V1.2 With COBIT. IT Governance Institute, United States of America (2007). ISBN 1-933284-80-3
22. Koning, E.: Assessment Framework for DNB Information Security Examination, De Nederlandsche Bank, Amsterdam (2014)
23. Volchkov, A.: How to measure security rom a governance perspective. ISACA J. 5, 44–51 (2013)
24. Papazafeiropoulou, A.: Understanding governance, risk and compliance information systems the experts view. Inf. Syst. Front. 18, 1251–1263 (2016)
25. Deloitte: Spreadsheet Management, Not what you figured (2009)
26. Bobbert, Y.: Defining a research method for engineering a Business Information Security artefact. In: Proceedings of the Enterprise Engineering Working Conference (EEWC) Forum, Antwerp (2017)
27. Bobbert, Y.: Porters' elements for a business information security strategy. ISACA J. 1, 1–4 (2015)
28. Dietz, J.: Enterprise Ontology. Springer, Heidelberg (2006). https://doi.org/10.1007/3-540-33149-2
29. MBZK: Baseline Informatiebeveiliging Rijksdienst 2017, Den haag: Ministerie van Binnenlandse Zaken en Koninkrijksrelaties (2017)
30. Bobbert, Y., Mulder, J.: Governance practices and critical success factors suitable for business information security. In: International Conference on Computational Intelligence and Communication Networks, India (2015)
31. Wieringa, R.: Design Science Methodology for Information Systems and Software Engineering. Springer, Heidelberg (2014). https://doi.org/10.1007/978-3-662-43839-8
32. Bobbert, Y., Mulder, J.: Group support systems research in the field of business information security; a practitioners view. In: 46th Hawaii International Conference on System Science, Hawaii US (2013)

33. De Vreede, G., Briggs, R.O., Van Duin, R., Enserink, B.: Athletics in electronic brainstorming; asynchronous electronic brainstorming in very large groups. In: Proceedings of the 33rd Hawaii International Conference on System Sciences (2000)

34. Recker, J.: Scientific Research in Information Systems. Springer, Australia (2013). https://doi.org/10.1007/978-3-642-30048-6

35. Asch, S.: Effects of group pressure upon the modification and distortion of judgment. In: Guetzkow, H. (ed.) Groups, Leadership and Men, Carnegie Press, Pittsburgh (1951)

36. den Hengst, M., Adkins, M., Keeken, S., Lim, A.: Which facilitation functions are most challenging: a global survey of facilitators, Delft University of Technology, Delft (2005)

37. Vreede, G., Boonstra, J., Niederman, F.: What is effective GSS facilitation? A qualitative inquiry into participants' perceptions. In: Proceedings of the 35th Hawaii International Conference on System Sciences, Delft University of Technology, Netherlands (2002)

38. Vreede, G., Vogel, D., Kolfschoten, G., Wien, J.: Fifteen years of GSS in the field: a comparison across time and national boundaries. In: Proceedings of the 36th Hawaii International Conference on System Sciences, HICSS 2003 (2003)

39. Kolfschoten, G., Mulder, J., Proper, H.: De fata morgana van Group Support Systemen. Informatie 4(5), 10–14 (2016)

40. Argyris, C.: Double-loop learning, teaching, and research. Acad. Manag. 1(2), 206–218 (2002)

41. Bobbert, Y., Mulder, J.: A research journey into maturing the business information security of mid market organizations. Int. J. IT/Bus. Align. Gov. 1(4), 18–39 (2010)

42. Mari, G.: Cyber Security; Facts or Fiction, Antwerp Management School, 14 November 2016. http://blog.antwerpmanagementschool.be/

Exploring a Role of Blockchain Smart Contracts in Enterprise Engineering

Barbora Hornáčková, Marek Skotnica$^{(\boxtimes)}$, and Robert Pergl

Faculty of Information Technology, Czech Technical University,
Prague, Czech Republic
{skotnmar,robert.pergl}@fit.cvut.cz

Abstract. Blockchain (BC) is a technology that introduces a decentralized, replicated, autonomous and secure databases. Smart contract (SC) is a transaction embedded to blockchain that contains executable code and its own internal storage, offering immutable execution and record keeping. Enterprise Engineering (EE) examines all aspects of organizations from business processes, informational and technical resources, to organizational structure. Therefore, blockchain and smart contracts have been subject of interest concerning the discipline of Enterprise Engineering (EE) and how they can be used together.

In this paper, principles for creating smart contracts from DEMO models are described and a software architecture of an IT system based on EE integrating smart contracts is proposed. Finally, a proof-of-concept implementation of a smart contract of a mortgage process using a DEMO methodology was developed, to demonstrate the feasibility of the proposed concepts.

Keywords: Enterprise Engineering · DEMO · DEMO methodology
Blockchain · Blockchain 2.0 · Smart contract

1 Introduction

The blockchain is mostly known as the underlying technology of Bitcoin, but since its introduction, there has been a wide variety of applications. The blockchain is a decentralized, replicated, and secure database running on a peer-to-peer network. Due to the solutions, it brings to problems such as the double-spending and Byzantine Generals' Problem, blockchain has been called a breakthrough in the computer science [27]. Blockchain 2.0 enhances the application of blockchain beyond cryptocurrencies and introduces concepts for flexible and programmable transactions referred to as smart contracts. Smart contracts enable the creation of more complex decentralized applications (Dapps) and even decentralized autonomous organizations (DAOs) on the blockchain.

The automation of SC creation could be a great benefit, as it would bring a level of security. As explained in the paper by Alex Norta [18] referencing a

© Springer Nature Switzerland AG 2019
D. Aveiro et al. (Eds.): EEWC 2018, LNBIP 334, pp. 113–127, 2019.
https://doi.org/10.1007/978-3-030-06097-8_7

crowdfunding project that was hacked because it contained security flaws, resulting in a \$50 million loss. "The incident shows it is not enough to merely equip the protocol layer on top of a blockchain with a Turing-complete language such as Solidity to realize secure smart-contract management. Instead, we propose in this keynote paper that it is crucial to address a gap for secure smart-contract management pertaining to the currently ignored application-layer development" [18].

Therefore, the blockchain and smart contracts have been subject of interest concerning the discipline of Enterprise Engineering (EE) and the usage of smart contracts in the DEMO methodology, enhancing the creation of Dapps.

The paper is organized as follows: In Sect. 2, the research question is summarized. In Sect. 3, the underlying scientific foundations are briefly discussed. In Sect. 4, a compatibility of BC and EE is evaluated. In Sect. 5, principles to devise smart contracts from DEMO models is proposed. A proof of concept case is provided in Sect. 6. The related work is discussed in Sect. 7. In Sect. 8, the current results are summarized and further research is proposed.

2   Research Question

The main goal of this paper is to formulate principles of using blockchain smart contracts in the DEMO methodology. The DEMO methodology is an enterprise modelling methodology for transaction modelling, and analysing and representing business processes [5]. The blockchain presents a new technology that can be used for implementation of processes. The underlying intention is to determine a possible cooperation between them in an IT system. Based on the goal of the paper, the research question was defined as: **How can blockchain smart contracts be used in the implementation of an enterprise information system (EIS) based on DEMO methodology?**

3   Theories Used

3.1   Enterprise Engineering

Enterprise Engineering (EE) is the scientific discipline focused on designing whole or a part of an enterprise. It examines all aspect of the enterprise from business processes, informational and technical resources to organizational structure. EE is built on four pillars: Enterprise Ontology, Enterprise Architecture, Enterprise Governance, which all together form Enterprise Design [6].

3.2   DEMO Methodology

DEMO means "Design and Engineering Methodology for Organizations". It is an enterprise modeling methodology for designing organizations developed by Jan Dietz and others. DEMO is based on the Organization Essence Revealing (OER) paradigm and the ψ-Theory (PSI, Performance in Social Interaction) of organizations [5].

DEMO Transactions. In DEMO, the basic pattern of a business transaction is composed of the following three phases [13]: (i) An actagenic phase during which a client requests a fact from the supplier agent. (ii) The action execution which will generate the required fact. (iii) A factagenic phase, which leads the client to accept the results reported.

Basic transactions can be composed to account for complex transactions. The DEMO methodology provides an method for understanding of the business processes of the organization, as well as the agents involved, but is less clear about pragmatics aspects of the transaction, such as the conversation structure and the intentions generated in each agents mind [13].

3.3   DEMO Machine

The DEMO Machine [24, 25] is a theoretical computational concept that formalizes a simulation of DEMO models. The underlying ontology also serves as a guide to implement information systems based on DEMO models.

3.4   Blockchain

Blockchain (BC) is a technology introduced [16] by Satoshi Nakamoto[1]. It is mostly known for its use with Bitcoin as it is its underlying technology. It is a new way of looking at transactions, assets exchange or even whole organizations. It introduces decentralized, autonomous, replicated and secure database. Based on cryptography offers trustless [21] network with no need of intermediary, resulting in major resource and also time saving. The possibilities of applying this technology are very broad and it could be effectively used in most of the parts of our world.

Private and Public Blockchain. The original intention of blockchain and bitcoin-like implementation was to create a public network, but due to some limitations it brings, private blockchains have been developed as well. The main disadvantage of public blockchain is the amount of computational power it needs in order to maintain the ledger, when used at a large scale. The second issue is an openness of the system and a consequent lack of privacy of transactions and its content. The difference between public and private blockchain is based on controlling who can be part of the network, in more detail, it means who can participate in the network and in which parts, who can execute the consensus protocol and manage the ledger. It is also refereed to as a permissioned blockchain, in contrast to the public blockchain, which is permissionless. It requires an invitation to join a private blockchain, where the access control mechanism may vary [28]. This means that in private blockchain, there is a control over the extent to which it is decentralized and anonymous [20]. Private blockchains are faster,

---

[1] Satoshi Nakamoto is probably a pseudonym for either one person or a group of people, the identity is currently unknown.

as there is a reduced number of processing nodes, and the transaction costs might be lower [20]. On the other hand, this access control brings extra costs and complexity to the process of maintaining or joining the blockchain. There are also hybrid solutions combining private and public blockchains refereed to as "consortium blockchains" [20].

3.5   Smart Contracts

The idea of smart contracts (SC) [29] is to offer more complex solutions than just a sell/buy transactions. Smart contract is a transaction embedded in blockchain that contains enhanced logic – a contract that is executable, has its own data storage and can access other resources to evaluate its current state and perform actions – a contract made of code. "A smart contract is a set of commitments that are defined in digital form, including the agreement on how contract participants shall fulfill these commitments" [17].

The main characteristic of a programmable smart contract is, that it does not require trust between parties, as after its creation in blockchain, it would be able to execute itself immutably. The parties would not need to be in a further contact or use an intermediary, it would be autonomous instead. Smart contracts are not doing something that was not possible before, however they reduce the complexity of common problems and they help with automation [27].

Ethereum. Ethereum is an open-source platform for blockchain applications with its own blockchain and cryptocurrency ether. This platform offers an environment to run decentralized applications based on smart contracts. As they claim "applications that run exactly as programmed without any possibility of downtime, censorship, fraud or third party interference." [8] Unlike bitcoin it offers much more than one kind of transaction, it allows users to create custom operations of any complexity and, more importantly, save the state. It is stateful, it can detect changes to data and remember them [3].

3.6   Dapps, DAOs and DACs

Smart contracts have a potential not just to be simple contracts between several parties, but over time they could become very complex systems involving many parties and resources. The definition of decentralized applications (Dapps) can vary, but in general it refers to open source autonomous applications that use decentralized network and executes across decentralized network nodes [3].

When further enhancing Dapps and creating applications that handle complicated functionality, they interconnect between each other and this all happens in an autonomous decentralized manner, we may create a decentralized autonomous organizations (DAOs) and even decentralized autonomous corporations (DACs). DAOs and DACs are "a concept derived from artificial intelligence. Here, a decentralized network of autonomous agents perform tasks, which can be conceived in the model of a corporation running without any human involvement under the control of a set of business rules. In a DAO/DAC, there are smart contracts as agents running on blockchains that execute ranges of pre-specified or pre-approved tasks based on events and changing conditions" [27].

4   Evaluation of BC and EE Compatibility

The first important thing to realize is that Enterprise Engineering [4] is a scientific discipline with an underlying enterprise modelling methodology for transaction modelling, and analysing and representing business processes (DEMO) [5]. On the other hand, blockchain and smart contracts are a technology. But from the nature of the problems they are both addressing and even from the underlying terminology they use, it seems like they could be used together. This is a more challenging question and a thorough understanding of both of them is required to bring about a correct way of using them together.

4.1   Smart Contract Misconceptions

Autonomous Smart Contracts. An idea that smart contracts can operate fully autonomously is partly true, but more in sense of immutably following a stated logic, rather than performing actions independently. Smart contracts are not programs that are active all the time, they are pieces of code that are run only when invoked. In Ethereum, this is possible either by sending a transaction or a message to the contract's address. So, the idea often presented, that smart contract actively waits for some event (a certain date) and then executes itself is a misconception [23].

External Services. One of very common attributes we find when researching smart contracts, is that they are designed to use external data. But this is not that easy to achieve and it is given by the very principle of determinism, which is an essential feature of a blockchain. When running a smart contract, all nodes must come to the same result, therefore they must operate on the same data. Using external data sources to gather data for a smart contract's execution is impossible, as we cannot be sure that the same data will be served to all nodes. Secondly, smart contracts cannot be self-initiated.

All data used must be determined at the invocation of a smart contract. Data must be sent to the contract as a parameter of the invoked function, or produced by so-called *oracles* [2]. Oracles are an Ethereum design pattern and they serve as "the interface between contracts and the outside. Technically, they are just contracts, and as such their state can be updated by sending them transactions. In practice, instead of querying an external service, a contract queries an oracle; and when the external service needs to update its data, it sends a suitable transaction to the oracle." [1]. This is a common solution to the need of external data, but the fallback is that we again rely on an centralized external service, that we need to trust.

Furthermore, smart contracts should not initiate any action outside the blockchain. For example, it might be an idea for a smart contract to call an external API when some condition has been met. In this moment, there is at least 23880 [10] active nodes in the Ethereum network. All of these independent nodes are executing the same smart contract code so it would result in 23880 API calls with the same request. Another problem is that the source code of a smart contract is public and it is running on untrusted machine so anyone can fake the API call. That is what smart contract or any blockchain transaction should not be used for. One must understand, it is not an executional system, it is more of a notarization system or controlling system, a trustless database.

Privacy Issues. As a public blockchain is a distributed database, there is no access control to the data and actions it holds. Every node can see everything: a transparency by nature. Therefore, it should be considered thoroughly what to store in a public blockchain and to ensure security of confidential information.

4.2   BC as a Transaction Execution System

BC smart contracts can be used to execute the DEMO models because they are represented by a Turing-complete programming language. There are two options how to do that.

The first option may be to implement the whole DEMO transaction execution on blockchain through smart contracts. With all the limitations and misconceptions introduced earlier, it might not be possible to implement full business logic and, moreover, there is no need to run the exact same transaction execution multiplied on thousands of computers. Furthermore, transaction execution on blockchain is not always without expenses, this may vary based on the platform used. But in general, choosing this approach is questionable because we have applications in "regular" programming languages, which once developed, are free of cost.

The second option may be to choose only some transactions, of which full or partial execution on blockchain would bring benefits. We can make use of blockchain's notarization of SC code and secure a trustless transaction execution when operating with untrusted third parties or multiple organizations. The remaining transactions are executed by a standard EIS. For example, we have a contract that states once a certain amount of money is paid, an asset will be transferred by an external company. This alternative makes use of the primary benefits that BC technology brings.

4.3   BC as a Notarization System

Based on the definition of the Blockchain: "It introduces decentralized, autonomous, replicated and secure database, that based on cryptography offers trustless network without a need of intermediary", another application of BC in

EE could be to serve as a notarization system. Smart contracts can offer notarization of documents, agreements and all information related to transactions, progress and results of transactions. BC could than provide a consistent and reliable source of data, facts and transaction states for all parties involved in the process.

5 Principles to Devise Smart Contracts from DEMO Models

In this section we discuss principles of creating BC smart contracts based on the DEMO methodology. Next, we introduce a software architecture of an enterprise information system based on DEMO that communicates with a smart contract.

5.1 SC Based on DEMO

In the previous section, we introduced what could be a possible usage of smart contract in EE. We explained that there are two possible approaches, that can also be combined:

- *Notarization* of documents, agreements and all information related to transactions, progress and results of transactions.
- *Trustless execution* of transactions or a part of transactions.

As mentioned before, the decision whether to use SC for the process implementation is individual for every case. In general, a good use case could be to use it when operating with untrusted third parties or multiple organizations. There is no such need for notarization or trustless execution within the internal business processes, but the need arises when dealing with transactions on the border of the scope of interest, when communicating with external actors. A BC smart contract can also represent the coordination point between an internal IT system and external actors.

5.2 DEMO Transaction as Contract

A DEMO transaction is represented as a contract in a blockchain. The contract has its own address, internal storage, attributes, methods and it is callable by either an external actor or another contract. This is the functionality needed to represent a DEMO transaction. In this paper, we implemented the execution of DEMO transactions according to the DEMO Machine [24] and associated theories. For mapping contracts to the corresponding DEMO transaction, we use the names defined in the Transaction Product Table. The contract then encapsulates the transaction notarization or execution.

5.3 Notarization

Notarization of a DEMO transaction facts can be divided into two parts:

- Notarization of the transaction P-facts and documents.
- Notarization of the transaction execution C-acts and C-facts.

In the first case, we are looking at using a smart contract as a storage of facts. To construct a smart contract carrying transaction facts, we can combine information from three models: Organization Construction Diagram, Bank Contents Table, Object Fact Diagram and Action Model. From them we can retrieve which object facts are needed for the transaction and where in the transaction execution they arise, we can evaluate the changes of the objects associated with the transaction execution. An object class can be represented as an internal state variable in the contract with the corresponding name from the DEMO model. A smart contract then serves as a storage of facts (database) for the transaction.

In the second case, we want to notarize the transaction execution. We use the complete transaction pattern from where we take all possible C-Facts and add their representation into the contract. The contract then holds its current state as a C-fact. For every C-Act, we create a contract method that changes the contract state to the corresponding C-Fact. Every change of a C-Fact issues an Ethereum system-wide notification (Event), allowing external systems to keep track of their contracts. Once the transaction is completed and the P-fact was created, another event is emitted stating the P-fact.

5.4 Transaction Execution in SC

To implement a transaction execution in the contract, we need to understand the whole DEMO model and the relationships between transactions.

In the PSD model, the response links and wait links are specified and we can see enclosed transactions. Action rules are guidelines for dealing with the events that actors have to respond to. In practice, they are being to referred to as business rules [7] so they can be used to construct the execution logic. If we execute a certain C-act in the contract, we look at the action rules that contain this C-act and we construct the corresponding method accordingly. Depending on the actor roles we define the executor of the method, we define general conditions based on the transaction pattern, such as that to perform a promise, the contract must be requested. Finally, we translate the action rule pseudo-code to a contract code. In this case, we also need to add the notarization of the fact on which the transaction operates. Method to execute a C-act is named after the C-act concatenated with the transaction name e.g. `promiseMortgageCompletion`.

If a transaction encloses other transactions, we have to decide how to handle them. There are three possible solutions. Firstly, the sub-transaction can be implemented as another contract. The enclosing contract then stores the address of the sub-contract. This way, when the action rule contains a response link for the child transaction C-act, we call the corresponding C-act method of the child contract. The sub-transaction can also store a reference to the enclosing transaction to implement the wait links. Secondly, there must not always be a need to create a separate contract for sub-transactions, we can implement the sub-transaction inside the main contract. This can be convenient if we are interested only in a partial execution on BC for the sub-transactions. Finally, the last option is that we do not handle the sub-transactions at all and leave this outside of BC.

5.5   Extending the DEMO Model

Using SC with DEMO is the part of the implementation of the organization. From this point of view, the essential DEMO models should not change when using SC. SCs only implement transactions and, in some cases, an actor role can be assigned to it. In both cases, the underlying essential DEMO models are not affected.

As the implementation of a contract can be derived from the DEMO models, the creation of the contract code could be produced from the DEMO models. In this case, we would define a way to identify the transactions and types of their integration on the BC. A solution could be to introduce Transaction Blockchain Table (Table 1) that maps transactions to their BC implementation. As for the actor roles assigned to SC, this would be defined in the Actor Function Matrix.

Table 1. The transaction blockchain table template

Transaction	Fact notarization	Transaction notarization	Execution
Transaction kind	List of facts to notarize	Yes/No	List of C-Acts to execute

5.6   Software Architecture

An implementation of an IT system consists of two parts:

- Enterprise information system (EIS): An IT system that supports the business processed modelled in DEMO. It executes the transactions that do not need to be available in BC.
- Blockchain: A blockchain that executes desired DEMO transactions. It also serves as an audit log to keep the history of desired C-Facts.

The architecture of an IT system integrating the enterprise information system and blockchain is illustrated in Fig. 1. The EIS contains mainly a business process management (BPM) engine and a blockchain API. The BMP engine is an transaction execution system. The blockchain API is an interface for communication between the BPM engine and the blockchain. The communication with blockchain is carried out through a blockchain node. It contains a transaction processor and a blockchain database, which holds the smart contracts or

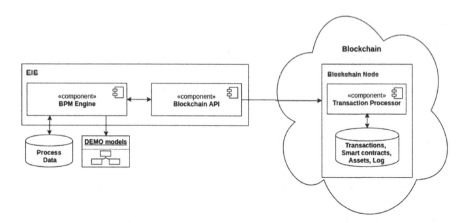

Fig. 1. Architecture of an IT System Based on EE and BC

blockchain logs. The DEMO models and methodology also serves as an orchestrator for the cooperation of the components (BPM engine, blockchain API and smart contract). They all use the transaction patterns, transaction names, facts, etc., as defined by DEMO.

5.7   EIS and BC Communication

The communication between the EIS and SC is a one-way interaction based on the principles described in Sect. 4. As BC cannot return values or call external services directly, all the interaction is handled from the EIS side.

The EIS contains an API for communicating with blockchain, such as web3.js. This API facilitates the contract deployment, sending of transactions to the contract, getting data from the contract. Using the events mechanism, the API monitors the blockchain log and "listens" for certain events. This way the API can watch the change of transaction state or results of contract execution and act on it, mostly if it is a transaction involving external actors.

6   Proof of Concept

In this part, we describe a proof of concept using a financial transaction, the process of a mortgage, implemented in the Ethereum Solidity programming language for smart contracts. Due to space limitation, we only present the conclusions. The whole proof-of-concept description as well as a smart contract source code can be found in a repository https://github.com/MIDNP/DemoBlockchain. The example is based on a presumption that a property ownership record is held in a public blockchain. This is a relevant case for the developing countries where it can bring many benefits as described in [19].

6.1 Technologies Used

Solidity. Solidity [9] is a programming language for implementing smart contracts specially designed for the Ethereum Virtual Machine (EVM). It is a Turing-complete high-level language compiled to the EVM bytecode. Solidity was chosen because it is developed under Ethereum and it is the most used and actively developed language for smart contracts for EVM.

Remix. Remix is a browser-based IDE for creating smart contracts with integrated debugging and testing environment. Remix offers development, compilation and deployment of Solidity contracts, as well as access to already deployed contracts. The testing environment allows running the transactions in a sandboxed blockchain in a browser with JavaScript VM, with a possibility to switch between virtual accounts and spent virtual ethers for full smart contract testing [22].

6.2 Mortgage Process Description

The mortgage contract is a complex process involving several parties, dependent processes, level of trust between parties and a lot of documents proving results of auxiliary processes; Notarization is involved for all parts. These aspects all contribute to overall complexity and costs of the process. Thus it appears as a good use case, where modeling by DEMO would capture the essence of the process and a smart contract could offer an automated notarization, data sharing between parties and payment processing, thus reducing the need of manual processes, as illustrated in Fig. 2.

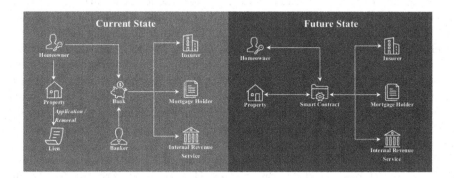

Fig. 2. Mortgage process changed using smart contract [26]

The description of the mortgage process is based on a review of several on-line mortgage guides [12,14] and consultation with a real estate agent. The description of the process was then modeled with DEMO to fully understand and illustrate the process. Here we omit the common pre-approval phase.

6.3 Summary

We have used the DEMO methodology to understand and reveal the essence of a mortgage process. Using the proposed principles of creating a contract introduced in Sect. 5, we were able to create working smart contracts based on the DEMO models.

We created a trustless notarization of the process. The contract ensures immutability of the agreed mortgage conditions, such as the amount of payment and interest rate. Further, it controls the execution of some parts, such as automatic mortgage payment control and automatic lien release request. This way, the Client can be sure that once the mortgage has been paid off, the lien will be released. It also defines a single point of access to the data and coordination for all parties as well as it simplifies some steps, as automatic control can be performed, thus allowing us to carry out some acts tacitly. Using smart contract does not change the essential DEMO model, as they belong to the implementation, which becomes simplified. For example, the Client would not have to bring the confirmation about insurance to the Loaner, because this is done by the smart contract – this reduces the overall process steps behind mortgage and eliminates bureaucracy, lags and errors.

The smart contract implementation uses only a standard transaction pattern. An extension to complete pattern would be analogous. The pattern is implemented as a state machine and the model constraints are implemented by function constraints and require() function.

7 Related Work

7.1 SC Based on BPMN

BPMN is one of the most widely used standard modeling notations and there have been efforts to use BPMN for smart contract implementation. One of them is described in a paper by Weber et al. [30]. The paper elaborates a similar approach to ours of implementing a business process using BPMN on blockchain. It recognizes two alternatives of using blockchain as "a choreography monitor, it stores the process execution" [30] or "as an active mediator among the participants, it coordinates the collaborative process execution." [30]. The approach then introduces a method of translating a BPMN model into a smart contract. This method is mainly addressing collaborative process execution for participants with lack of trust.

To compare, the approach described in this paper may help to prevent possible errors or unwanted states due to the C4-ness quality criteria [5] of demo models. This is very important since the history of a smart contract can't be changed and the code is hard to update once deployed. But in general, both solutions introduce similar findings and principles about the usage of BC and process modeling and a method of translating the models to smart contracts. In the end, it comes down to the comparison of DEMO and BPMN [15] itself and evaluating the appropriateness of their use and ability to cover all possible situations when modeling processes.

7.2   SC Based on Petri Nets

Another interesting solution can be found in the work of García-Bañuelos [11]. This paper focuses on an optimized execution on the blockchain. It defines a method of transformation of BPMN processes (modeled in a subset of the BPMN standard) into smart contracts through the use of optimized Petri nets. "The method takes as input a BPMN process model. The model is first translated into a Petri net. An analysis algorithm is applied to determine, where applicable, the guards that constrain the execution of each task. Next, reduction rules are applied to the Petri net to eliminate invisible transitions and spurious places. The transitions in the reduced net are annotated with the guards gathered by the previous analysis. Finally, the reduced net is compiled into Solidity." [11]. The work focuses on encoding the control-flow and evaluation of data conditions, however it does not discuss how participants would be bound to the contract instance, and access control.

8   Conclusions and Further Research

We have answered the research question defined in Sect. 2 by proposing two ways of using smart contracts in the DEMO methodology in the context of EIS. Such integration would bring blockchain's benefits to process execution, namely secured and trustless storage of data and immutable transaction execution. This might bring a new way of looking at transactions with external actors, where the blockchain can serve as a trustless coordination of the operation and a notarized data source. The application of the DEMO methodology to the business processes behind smart contracts brings insight and overview to the whole operation. This helps to reduce unwanted states, prevent errors and improve security which is crucial for smart contracts, because they are representing valuable assets. Further, it may potentially serve as a basis for creating well-designed Dapps and DAOs.

In the end, a proof of concept was developed based on a mortgage process. We have defined and analysed the process, applied the DEMO methodology and consequently developed an Ethereum Solidity contract using our principles, showing the possible approach of the topic.

8.1   Further Research

In this paper, only a very introductory steps were taken in order to answer the As for future work, a formalization of the described principles of translating DEMO models into contract code could be considered, as well as an automatic creation of contracts by BPMS based on EE such as a DEMO engine. Secondly, possibilities of optimization of the contract code should be explored to reduce costs and enhance effectiveness of a blockchain execution.

Another topic to enhance is assets representation on the blockchain. Consider, how would our proof-of-concept mortgage process change, if the property and its ownership were represented digitally on blockchain instead of cadastre. That way, further automation could be introduced and the importance of smart contract would gain new dimensions. DEMO methodology could also be used for such assets digitalization and creation of their blockchain representations. However, these thoughts are obviously conditioned by changes in society and legislation.

Acknowledgement. This research has been supported by CTU SGS grant No. SGS17/120/OHK3/1T/18.

References

1. Bartoletti, M., Pompianu, L.: An empirical analysis of smart contracts: platforms, applications, and design patterns. In: Brenner, M., et al. (eds.) FC 2017. LNCS, vol. 10323, pp. 494–509. Springer, Cham (2017). https://doi.org/10.1007/978-3-319-70278-0_31
2. Buterin, V.: Ethereum and oracles (2014). https://blog.ethereum.org/2014/07/22/ethereum-and-oracles/
3. Dannen, C.: Introducing Ethereum and Solidity. O'Reilly Media Inc., Brooklyn, New York (2017)
4. Dietz, J.L.G., et al.: The discipline of enterprise engineering. Int. J. Organisational Des. Eng. **3**(1), 86–114 (2013)
5. Dietz, J.: Enterprise Ontology Theory and Methodology. Springer, Heidelberg (2006). https://doi.org/10.1007/3-540-33149-2
6. Dietz, J.: The discipline of enterprise engineering (2014). https://www.alexandria. unisg.ch/export/DL/224477.pdf. Accessed 25 Apr 2014
7. Dietz, J.L.: The Essence of Organization - An Introduction to Enterprise Engineering. Sapio bv (2012)
8. Ethereum: Ethereum project. https://ethereum.org/. Accessed 29 Nov 2017
9. Ethereum Solidity: Solidity documentation. https://solidity.readthedocs.io/en/develop/index.html. Accessed 22 Nov 2017
10. ethernodes.org: The ethereum nodes explorer. https://www.ethernodes.org. Accessed 03 Dec 2017
11. García-Bañuelos, L., Ponomarev, A., Dumas, M., Weber, I.: Optimized execution of business processes on blockchain. In: Carmona, J., Engels, G., Kumar, A. (eds.) BPM 2017. LNCS, vol. 10445, pp. 130–146. Springer, Cham (2017). https://doi.org/10.1007/978-3-319-65000-5_8
12. Hands on Banking: Steps in the lending process. https://handsonbanking.org/adults/buying-home/getting-mortgage/steps-in-the-lending-process/. Accessed 21 Nov 2017
13. Liu, K., Clarke, R.J., Andersen, P.B., Stamper, R.K. (eds.): Information, Organisation and Technology: Studies in Organisational Semiotics. Springer, Heidelberg (2001). https://doi.org/10.1007/978-1-4615-1655-2
14. MGIC for Homebuyers: The mortgage process. https://homebuyers.mgic.com/getting-your-mortgage/mortgage-process.html. Accessed 21 Nov 2017
15. Mráz, O., Náplava, P., Pergl, R., Skotnica, M.: Converting DEMO PSI transaction pattern into BPMN: a complete method. In: Aveiro, D., Pergl, R., Guizzardi, G., Almeida, J.P., Magalhães, R., Lekkerkerk, H. (eds.) EEWC 2017. LNBIP, vol. 284, pp. 85–98. Springer, Cham (2017). https://doi.org/10.1007/978-3-319-57955-9_7

16. Nakamoto, S.: Bitcoin: a peer-to-peer electronic cash system (2009). http://www. bitcoin.org/bitcoin.pdf
17. NEO: Neo smart contract introduction. http://docs.neo.org/en-us/sc/introduc tion.html. Accessed 2 Jan 2018
18. Norta, A.: Designing a smart-contract application layer for transacting decentral- ized autonomous organizations. In: Singh, M., Gupta, P.K., Tyagi, V., Sharma, A., Ören, T., Grosky, W. (eds.) ICACDS 2016. CCIS, vol. 721, pp. 595–604. Springer, Singapore (2017). https://doi.org/10.1007/978-981-10-5427-3_61
19. O'Connor, J.: How cardano can help development in Africa (2018). https:// cardanofoundation.org/press/how-cardano-can-help-development-in-africa/
20. Pilkington, M.: Blockchain technology: principles and applications. In: Olleros, F.X., Zhegu, M. (eds.) Research Handbook on Digital Transformations (2015). https://ssrn.com/abstract=2662660
21. Preethi, K.: Eli5: What do we mean by "blockchains are trustless"? medium. https://medium.com/@preethikasireddy/eli5-what-do-we-mean-by-blockchains- are-trustless-aa420635d5f6
22. Remix: Remix - solidity ide https://remix.readthedocs.io/en/latest/. Accessed 22 Nov 2017
23. Rikken, O.: 3 smart contract misconceptions. https://www.coindesk.com/3-comm on-smart-contract-misconceptions-explored/. Accessed 03 Dec 2017
24. Skotnica, M., van Kervel, S.J.H., Pergl, R.: A DEMO machine - a formal foundation for execution of DEMO models. In: Aveiro, D., Pergl, R., Guizzardi, G., Almeida, J.P., Magalhães, R., Lekkerkerk, H. (eds.) EEWC 2017. LNBIP, vol. 284, pp. 18–32. Springer, Cham (2017). https://doi.org/10.1007/978-3-319-57955-9_2
25. Skotnica, M., van Kervel, S.J.H., Pergl, R.: Towards the ontological foundations for the software executable DEMO action and fact models. In: Aveiro, D., Pergl, R., Gouveia, D. (eds.) EEWC 2016. LNBIP, vol. 252, pp. 151–165. Springer, Cham (2016). https://doi.org/10.1007/978-3-319-39567-8_10
26. Smart Contracts Alliance: Smart contracts: 12 use cases for business & beyond (2016). http://www.the-blockchain.com/docs/Smart%20Contracts%2012%20 Use%20Cases%20for%20Business%20and%20Beyond%20-%20Chamber%20of%20 Digital%20Commerce.pdf. Accessed 08 Oct 2017
27. Swan, M.: Blockchain. O'Reilly Media Inc., Sebastopol (2015)
28. Swanson, T.: Consensus-as-a-service: a brief report on the emergence of per- missioned, distributed ledger systems (2016). http://www.ofnumbers.com/wp- content/uploads/2015/04/Permissioned-distributed-ledgers.pdf
29. Szabo, N.: Smart contracts: building blocks for digital markets (1996). www.fon.hum.uva.nl, http://www.fon.hum.uva.nl/rob/Courses/InformationIn Speech/CDROM/Literature/LOTwinterschool2006/szabo.best.vwh.net/smart _contracts_2.html
30. Weber, I., Xu, X., Riveret, R., Governatori, G., Ponomarev, A., Mendling, J.: Untrusted business process monitoring and execution using blockchain. In: La Rosa, M., Loos, P., Pastor, O. (eds.) BPM 2016. LNCS, vol. 9850, pp. 329–347. Springer, Cham (2016). https://doi.org/10.1007/978-3-319-45348-4_19

On DEMO

Validating the DEMO Specification Language

M. A. T. Mulder[(⊠)]

Leusden, Netherlands
mark@mulderrr.nl

Abstract. The Design and Engineering Method for Organisations (DEMO) is the principal methodology in Enterprise Engineering (EE). The Design and Engineering Method for Organisations Specification Language (DEMOSL) states the rules, legends, and metamodel of DEMO. Therefore, any DEMO model must comply with this specification. Moreover, to enable automation of the DEMO model validation, we need a metamodel that can accurately represent DEMO models. With DEMOSL as the appointed specification language for DEMO, with automation as target, we need to validate the fitness of DEMOSL for modelling DEMO.

Our findings provide insight into the amount of changes and the complexity and direction of change to complete the metamodel and make it usable for automation. We found that some incomplete, inconsistent or inadequate specifications in DEMOSL hinder its use as a prescriptive metamodel. We describe these limitations in DEMOSL as a whole and in the separate Construction Model (CM), Process Model (PM), Action Model (AM) and Fact Model (FM).

Finally, we conclude that the metamodel needs improvement to be able to model all allowed DEMO models.

1 Introduction

The Design and Engineering Method for Organisations (DEMO) [1] is the principal methodology in Enterprise Engineering [2]. This so-called essential model of an organisation is the integrated whole of four aspect models: the Construction Model (CM), the Action Model (AM), the Process Model (PM) and the Fact Model (FM). Each model is expressed in one or more diagrams and one or more cross-model tables.

1.1 Aspect Models

The CM is the first and the most comprehensive model to produce when modelling an organisation in DEMO, applying the Organisational Essence Revealing (OER) method. A CM is a model of the construction of an organisation (or better: of a Scope of Interest), by which is understood the identified transaction kinds and the actor roles that are either executor or initiator of these transaction

© Springer Nature Switzerland AG 2019
D. Aveiro et al. (Eds.): EEWC 2018, LNBIP 334, pp. 131–143, 2019.
https://doi.org/10.1007/978-3-030-06097-8_8

kinds. The resulting 'network' of transaction kinds and actor roles is always a set of tree structures, which arise from the inherent property that every transaction kind has exactly one elementary actor role as its executor (and vice versa), and that every actor role may be initiator of none, one or more transaction kinds.

A CM is expressed in an Organisation Construction Diagram (OCD), a Transaction Product Table (TPT) and a Bank Contents Table (BCT). The OCD is a graphical representation of the identified transaction kinds and actor roles, and the links between them. Apart from initiator and executor links, actor roles may also be connected to transaction kinds through information links. They express that the actor role has (reading) access to the history of all transactions of the transaction kind with which it is connected. Therefore, the transaction kind shape may also be interpreted as a transaction bank.

The AM of a Scope of Interest comprises the guidelines that guide actors in doing their work, i.e. performing their coordination acts and their production acts. An AM is expressed in Action Rules Specifications (ARSs) and Work Instruction Specifications (WISs). Action rules, which are actually (imperative) business rules, guide actors in responding to the coordination events that they have to deal with. They are currently expressed in a semi-structured English-like language. Work instructions guide actors in performing production acts, i.e. in bringing about the products of transactions.

The PM of a Scope of Interest bridges its CM and the coordination part of its AM. To this end, it specifies how the transaction kinds in a tree are related to each other. More precisely, it specifies which transaction steps in an enclosed transaction kind are connected to which steps in the enclosing transaction kind, and by which kind of link (response link or wait link). A PM is expressed in a Process Structure Diagram (PSD), and (optionally) in one or more Transaction Pattern Diagrams (TPDs).

The FM of a Scope of Interest bridges its CM and the production part of its AM. To this end, it specifies the various entity types, property types, attribute types and entity types, as well as their mutual relationships. The current version of DEMO is called DEMO-3. It is published in [3] and in [4].

1.2 Problem Statement

We started this research on the observation of limited automated support of the DEMO modelling. We considered building new automation with the necessary modelling and validation support. To stick as closely as possible to the design of DEMO we chose to adopt the Design and Engineering Method for Organisations Specification Language (DEMOSL) documentation as the backbone of the automation and hoped to have all rules, legends, and the metamodel of DEMO. This first attempt at a metamodel that can accurately represent DEMO models turned out to have omissions. This triggered the investigation of the DEMOSL information. The underlying research question is to find the metamodel that supports the full representation of DEMO models in such a way that the automation and exchange of valid DEMO models is supported.

1.3   Observations

With the partial DEMOSL-metamodels in mind, we tried to project existing DEMO models onto the metamodel using newly developed automation and in doing so we discovered some practical imperfections. In addition, during the project of building a tool to support DEMO modelling the analysis of the meta-model showed some inconsistencies. Not all partial metamodels allowed for modelling correct DEMO models and not all parts of the metamodel were connected. This may have consequences for the usability of DEMO models as a whole. Theoretical benefits might not be usable when the DEMO model is reduced to its aspect models. DEMO claims to be a method that can reveal the essence of the organisation by combining the four partial analysis. A search of the literature did not yield any research or findings on this subject.

1.4   Research Design

The research was conducted using Design Science Research (DSR) [5]. It aims at the design of a complete and automated metamodel of DEMO, facilitating model validation and integration of other technologies. The first step in the research was to validate DEMOSL to check its fitness as metamodel for this purpose. The second step will be the expansion of DEMOSL to support the specification of automated storage and exchange of DEMO by expanding the specification to all model aspects that need to be described. This not only includes the data model and business rules, but also the representation metamodel needed to exchange the representations of a DEMO model. The third step will be the validation of this metamodel with existing DEMO models. Finally, we will investigate the usability of this automation for building new DEMO models together with other technologies.

In the remainder of this paper we will discuss the DEMO metamodel by first defining the notion of Meta Model. We will subsequently report on our findings on the metamodel per aspect model. We end with conclusions and future research.

2   Notion of Metamodel

To be able to validate the metamodel of DEMO, we need a definition to describe the requirements of the metamodel. We will use the following definition of a metamodel [6]: "meta-models define sets of valid models, facilitating their transformation, serialization, and exchange.".

Analysing this definition, we have to define which models are valid. The metamodel of these valid models needs to be sufficiently complete to describe all sets of models that are allowed. Moreover, the metamodel needs to be restrictive enough to reject models that are not valid.

According to this definition, metamodels should facilitate exchange of the models. Following this part of the definition means that all aspects of the model that are drawn, noted, related or specified need to be described in such a way that the same representation can be reproduced with the specification.

The serialisation of a model allows for the exchange of model information with possibly a different syntax than the model is represented itself. This is needed to store and retrieve models and business rules to and from repositories.

Transformation of the models is something that is not included in the base of DEMO but is part of the current research project. Therefore, we must be able to specify the DEMO models in the metamodel well enough to enable the partial transformation of the model (e.g. from ontological to implementation level).

3   DEMOSL Inconsistencies

The consistency of the current metamodel of DEMO, named DEMOSL, was analysed with new tools. Earlier, Gouveia [7] verified the FM and suggested changes in the value type but those did not affect the metamodel. Van Kervel [8] has created his own model to describe specifically the transaction pattern of DEMO models. Other literature research did not yield any results on changes to the metamodel. Furthermore, no documented or published, complete implementation of DEMOSL has been found. In the next paragraphs we will analyse the DEMOSL models. We used the published DEMOSL versions 3.6 [9] and 3.7 [4] to analyse the metamodel. DEMOSL 3.7 has been published and already included some results of this research project.

3.1   Metamodel

We will make three remarks on the model exchange requirement. First, no part of the DEMOSL metamodel is currently capable of registering all needed information to exchange names, formulations or visual information from diagrams, tables or specifications. DEMOSL has never been intended to describe these aspects of the meta model. Secondly, although the name of an object can be seen as the identity of that object, the metamodel must include the name to be able to exchange this identity. Finally, concerning the diagrams and tables used in DEMO, no metamodel is given in DEMOSL. This definition is needed to be able to exchange the same visual information.

3.2   Construction Model

The metamodel of the CM 3.6 (Fig. 1) [9, sl. 27] shows five entity types and represents the meta level to combine actor roles and transaction kinds. In addition, the metamodel of the CM 3.7 (Fig. 2) [4, sl. 31] shows six entity types. The change in the metamodel is a partial result of this research. We will elaborate on the improvements and remaining issues.

The Transaction Kind (TK) entity type models transaction kinds. Aggregate Transaction Kind (ATK) is the aggregation of transaction kinds. With the 'TK is part of ATK' relation, the transactions within a selected set can be replaced

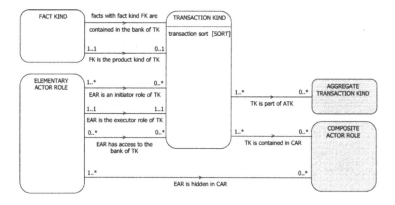

Fig. 1. Meta model 3.6 of the CM [9, sl. 27]

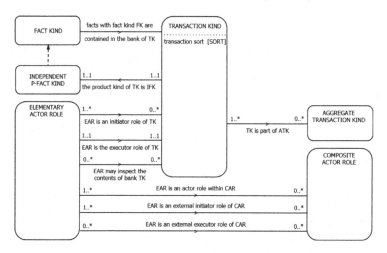

Fig. 2. Meta model 3.7 of the CM [4, sl. 31]

by a single component, an ATK. That is how the transaction kinds stay in the model and are represented in aggregated form. ATK that are out of the Scope of Interest (SoI) have no TK to refer to. The metamodel states that this reference is mandatory (1..*) whereas the example in [3, p. 89] shows several unreferenced instances of ATKs.

The Fact Kind (FK) entity type in DEMOSL 3.6 represents both the coordination fact and production fact of an TK. This notion is not consistent with the FM, therefore, it has been changed in DEMOSL 3.7. The FK and Independent P-Fact Kind (IFK) contain all facts that are created during all transactions. Interstriction between transaction kinds and actor roles is modelled using the 'EAR has access to the bank of TK' that has been rephrased to 'may inspect the contents of bank' relation. Solely inspection of the ATKs cannot be represented in the metamodel.

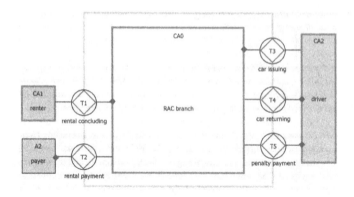

Fig. 3. RAC model from TEoO [3, p. 72]

As can be seen in Fig. 3 the diagram displays a grey boundary. This boundary has been described in 3.6 [9, sl. 7] and 3.7 [4, sl. 7] as the SoI. The DEMO method states that TK can be on the boundary of the SoI to represent a TK communication between the inside and outside of the SoI. The 3.7 metamodel cannot relate any component as being inside or outside any SoI nor can it model the name of the SoI.

The entity types Elementary Actor Role (EAR) and Composite Actor Role (CAR) store the actor roles of the model.

The initiator and executor roles are separately modelled as relations for the elementary and the composite actor roles. This set of
relations has evolved from the 3.6 metamodel
where 'EAR is hidden in CAR' did not suf-
fice for modelling various EAR roles within
a CAR. A collection of actor roles is available through the 'EAR is an actor role within
CAR' relation. This relation requires that
for every CAR at least one EAR is present.

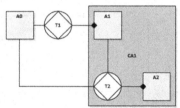

Fig. 4. Transaction kind and CAR

When modelling an actor role outside the SoI, this is not valid.

Although the CAR includes TKs according to note 4 [4, sl. 31], the relation 'TK is contained in CAR' of version 3.6 has been omitted and, therefore, the transaction cannot be explicitly related with a CAR. Moreover, note 4 states that the TKs between the EARs are included within CAR. The situation of CAR2 in Fig. 5 and CA1 in Fig. 4 shows that this situation cannot be modelled. In the latter A0 would initiate CA1. Without this metamodel relation it is not clear whether the transaction kind T2 in Fig. 4 is part of CAR.

In the DEMO method, the first step is creating a CM is to create a CAR and relate it to the border transactions. These CARs with their border transactions cannot be captured by the metamodel. The next step in the DEMO method is to reveal the inner actor roles within the CAR. When these actor roles are too

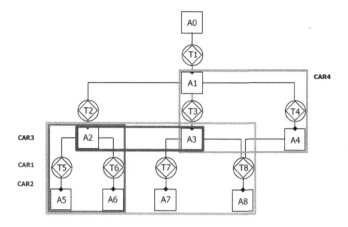

Fig. 5. CAR example [4, sl. 10]

complex to be revealed at once, new CARs can be used. This hierarchical CAR can neither be modelled in metamodel 3.6 nor 3.7. When a EAR is found to be part of multiple CARs, the CAR might relate. This relation is not present in the metamodel and this needs to be resolved. In the metamodel of 3.7, an example (Fig. 5) of multiple CARs within the same CM has been given. CAR1 as well as CAR3 is contained within CAR2[1] but whether this relation is relevant cannot be modelled.

We summarise the issues found in the CM: inconsistent relation to the FM (but fixed in 3.7); mandatory TK for ATKs; mandatory EAR for CARs; missing inspection relation to separate ATKs; missing scope of interest; missing CAR to TK relation; missing CAR hierarchy; missing relation TK in CAR; missing interstriction between ATK and CAR or SoI.

3.3   Process Model

The PM metamodel 3.6 (Fig. 6) shows three entity types. The PM metamodel 3.7 (Fig. 7) shows four entity types. The entity type Transaction Process Step Kind (TPSK) is partially renamed to Transaction Kind Step Kind (TKSK) but we will refer to this entity type with TPSK. The transaction kind entity type represents the same entity type as show in the CM (Fig. 2), making the connection between the CM and the PM.

The Process Step Kind (PSK) entity types in the metamodel 3.6 extends the TK with the process steps using a Cartesian product. This allows for a modelling of the relation between a TPSK of one TK and a PSK in another TK using the 'is initiated from' relation. Moreover, the wait conditions between two process steps can be modelled using 'is a wait condition for' relation.

---

[1] The initiator and executor roles in the example notes are incorrect.

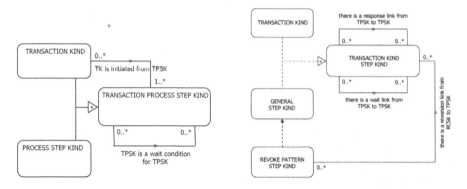

Fig. 6. Process meta model 3.6 [9, sl. 28]   **Fig. 7.** Process meta model 3.7 [4, sl. 32]

The relation 'TK is initiated from TPSK' in metamodel 3.6 did not allow a TPSK to invoke a Revoke Step Kind (RSK) in another TK. Therefore, in metamodel 3.7 the relation has been changed to a self-reference 'there is a response link from TPSK to TPSK'. This relation does not sufficiently restrict the model and needs note 2 [4, sl. 32] that the transaction pattern will limit the possibilities.

The transaction pattern itself has been extended with a reversion link to support the step kinds from Revoke Pattern Step Kind (RPSK) patterns to the General Step Kinds (GSK). The reversion link is part of the transaction pattern. When the internal transaction pattern is added to the metamodel, all steps should be included. However, the metamodel does not allow for modelling the complete transaction pattern.

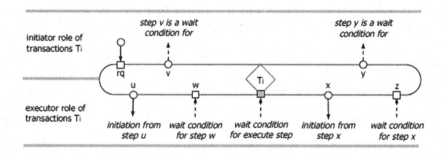

Fig. 8. Process model legend [4, sl. 18]

In the PSD visualisation (Fig. 8), swim lanes are introduced. These are not present in the metamodel.

In summary the issues found in the PM metamodel are: insufficient links between TPSK instances (but fixed in 3.7); partially modelling of transaction pattern; swim lanes.

3.4   Action Model

The AM metamodel (Fig. 9 [4, sl. 33]) has a single entity type representing
action rule information of a specific PSK with a reference to the related TPSK.
In the formal specifications the AM is specified in Extended Backus - Naur
Form (EBNF) [10]. The specification mentions three main parts. The first part
specifies the preconditions to execute the action. The second part specifies the
conditions to be evaluated. The last part specifies the executed actions in case
of a valid or invalid condition. The syntax of the relations to the FM are not
fully specified. In the AM it is not clear whether the relation is about reading,
writing or creating a FK.

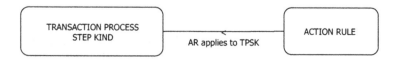

Fig. 9. Action meta model 3.7 [4, sl. 33]

The information in the AM is not sufficiently detailed to validate a model.
The verbalisation used in the ARS can be specified in relations (Fig. 10).

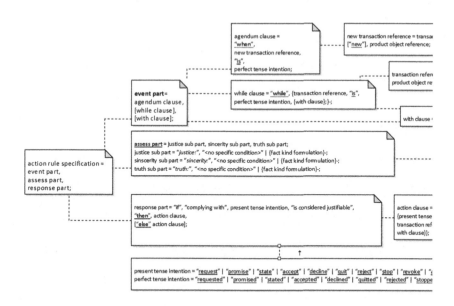

Fig. 10. (Partial) Action rule specification

We analysed the ARS with ANother Tool for Language Recognition
(ANTLR) to validate the completeness of the specifications. Though ANTLR

has a slightly different syntax on EBNF, we translated all rules to be validated. The result is that the following specifications were missing: property kind name; object variable; dimension; perfect tense sentence; product object reference. These specifications need to be defined, or their reference needs to be altered, to be able to use the ARS. Furthermore, we found that some definitions of variables were not distinct enough to be parsed by the ANTLR specifications. This could mean that the specification is ambiguous in variable definition. The attribute variable, abstract variable and product variable are connections to the fact model. These connections should be present in the metamodel in Fig. 11.

A summary of the issues found in the AM metamodel are: specifications need additions and elaborations and variable naming needs addition.

3.5   Fact Model

The model and the metamodel are expressed in the same notation. Therefore, we **bold** for the metamodel of the FM and *italic* for the FM itself. The FM metamodel 3.7 (Fig. 11) contains eight **entity type**s. The difference between the 3.6 and the 3.7 version is the addition of the 'P-' naming prefix. We omit this prefix in this paper for short writing where no ambiguity can be found. This metamodel allows for simple *entity types* and for specialised, generalised or aggregated *entity types*. *Entity types* can contain two types of *property types*: *value type* (i.e. attribute) and *property types* (i.e. relation).

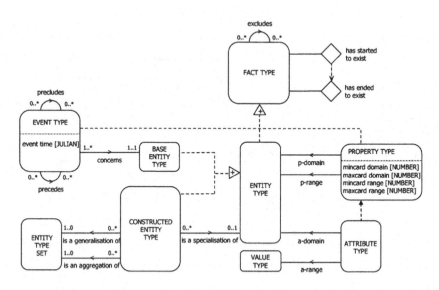

Fig. 11. Fact model 3.7 metamodel [4, sl. 34]

An *entity type* can be modelled using **entity type**. The name of an *entity type* [4, sl. 22] has not been added to the FM metamodel.

The *property type*, or relation, between *entity type*s is expressed as a **property type** that has a domain **entity type** and a range **entity type**.

$$pdomain(x) \iff x \in \textbf{entity type}$$

$$prange(x) \iff x \in \textbf{entity type}$$

$$\exists x : relation(x) \implies x \in \textbf{property type}$$

$$\forall x, y : relation(x, y) \implies pdomain(x) \land prange(y)$$

The name of a *property type* [4, sl. 22] has not been added to the FM metamodel.

The **attribute type** is a specialisation of **property type** and acts the same way as the **property type**. Note 2 [4, sl. 34] states that the relations adomain and arange are also specialisations. An attribute can be formulated in this rule

$$adomain(x) \iff x \in \textbf{entity type}$$

$$arange(x) \iff x \in \textbf{value type}$$

$$\exists x : attribute(x) \implies x \in \textbf{attribute type}$$

$$\forall x, y : attribute(x, y) \implies adomain(x) \land arange(y)$$

The name, dimension and unit of an *attribute type* [4, sl. 22] has not been added to the FM metamodel.

Every **property type** has a minimum and maximum cardinality for domain and range.

The **event type** entity type matches the IFK entity type of the CM. Therefore, it adds two relations to the creation of a *fact kind* in the CM; precedes and precludes. The precedence law [4, sl. 26] states that two **fact kinds** have an order in time. The preclusion law states that the two **fact kinds** cannot occur both. This precedence as well as the preclusion law affect the CM and the PM but are not mentioned in either the metamodel or the diagrams of the CM or the PM. The *property type* event time on the **event type** entity type is probably meant as the moment in time the event occurred. This is also expressed in the 'has started to exist' event type.

The concerns relation links the **event type** to the **base entity type** in such a way that every transaction kind that creates an independent fact kind also has to have a concerning **entity type**. This is expressed on instance level in this rule

$$\forall x : event(x) \implies baseEntity(x)$$

$$\exists x : baseEntity(x) \implies event(x)$$

This notion of concerns to a **base entity type** means that an **event type** can never concern a **constructed entity type**. Therefore, transaction kinds cannot be a concern to specialisations of entity types whereas in the example RAC [3, p. 75] the 'RENT-PAID RENTAL' is a specialisation of 'RENTAL' while 'RENT-PAID RENTAL' is the concern of 'P2 the rent of Rental is paid'.

The **constructed entity type** deals with the specialisation of **entity types** and the generalisation and aggregation of **entity type sets**. The distinction between type and type set is used to keep together the entity types used for the set operation. Note 3 [4, sl. 34] does non visually connect the **entity type set** to the **entity type**. We only found a typo '1..0' in the relations of the **constructed entity type**.

The **fact type** is a generalisation of **entity type** which can start or end to exist. To model the existence of a fact, we need the time it began its existence and the time its existence ended. Occurring production events will be stored as an **event type**, similar to the **property type**, related to an **entity type**.

The exclusion rule on **fact type** [4, sl. 25] can be used to make two disjoint collections of **entity types**, **property types** or even **event types**.

$$\text{entity type1} \cap \text{entity type2} = \varnothing$$

$$property1(x) \iff x \in \text{entity type1}$$

$$property2(x) \iff x \in \text{entity type2}$$

$$\forall x, y : property1(x, y) \implies \neg property2(x, y)$$

$$\forall x, y : property2(x, y) \implies \neg property1(x, y)$$

In summary the issues found in the FM metamodel are: no name on entity type; no name on property type; no name, dimension and unit on attribute type; CM and PM lack precedence and preclusion laws; specialisations cannot be concerned with event type; cardinality on entity type set is incorrect; no time in start and end events.

4   Conclusions and Future Research

When comparing the aspect models with our requirements for automated support we can conclude that the metamodels are incomplete, inconsistent and, moreover, not implementable in their current state. This restricts the possibilities for automating DEMO model validation. Despite the required improvements DEMOSL is a solid base for a metamodel. The CM, PM, FM and AM all have some faults in their metamodels, therefore, we are unable to implement a correct representation of a DEMO model without changes. To validate all models a complete metamodel with all business rules has to be build. This supersedes the current entity type metamodel of the models but requires a complete and restricted mathematical model of all allowed DEMO models.

For automation there is a need to improve the metamodel DEMOSL to be able to model all allowed DEMO models. This metamodel needs all entity types to address the properties and relations between all concepts. In addition, the metamodel needs to be completed with all business rules to create a full DEMO specification.

Post presentation comments on the paper have been addressing the relevance of making a distinction between the concrete and abstract syntax of the metamodel. The discussion on the different concepts of SoI and CAR that essentially are addressing the same problem will be part of the next paper. Relevant is the usage of the metamodel. In future research the intended use of the metamodel needs to be addressed first. Finally, the usage of the DEMOBAKER AM syntax will be studied for usage in the specification of the AM.

References

1. Dietz, J.L.G.: Enterprise Ontology: Theory and Methodology. Springer, Heidelberg (2006). https://doi.org/10.1007/3-540-33149-2
2. Dietz, J.L.G., Hoogervorst, J.A.P.: The discipline of enterprise engineering. Int. J. Org. Des. Eng. **3**, 86–114 (2013)
3. APC Perinforma: The essence of organisation. Sapio Enterprise Engineering (2013)
4. Dietz, J.L.G., Mulder, M.A.T.: Demo specification language 3.7 (2017)
5. van Aken, J., Andriessen, D.: Handboek ontwerpgericht wetenschappelijk onderzoek. (Handbook for Design Science Research). Boom Lemma (2011)
6. Aßmann, U., Zschaler, S., Wagner, G.: Ontologies, meta-models, and the model-driven paradigm. In: Calero, C., Ruiz, F., Piattini, M. (eds.) Ontologies for Software Engineering and Software Technology, pp. 249–273. Springer, Heidelberg (2006). https://doi.org/10.1007/3-540-34518-3_9
7. Gouveia, D., Aveiro, D.: Things, references, connectors, types, variables, relations and attributes – a contribution to the FI and MU theories. In: Aveiro, D., Pergl, R., Gouveia, D. (eds.) EEWC 2016. LNBIP, vol. 252, pp. 181–195. Springer, Cham (2016). https://doi.org/10.1007/978-3-319-39567-8_12
8. Van Kervel, S.J.H.: Ontology driven enterprise information systems engineering. PhD thesis, Delft University of Technology, Delft (2012). ID: urn:NBN:nl:ui:24-uuid:8c42378a-8769-4a48-a7fb-f5457ede0759; ths:Dietz, J.L.G. - org:TU Delft - dgg:TU
9. Dietz, J.L.G.: Demo specification language 3.6 (2017)
10. Feynman, R.: EBNF: a notation to describe syntax (2016)

Modeling the System Described by the EU General Data Protection Regulation with DEMO

Duarte Gouveia$^{(\boxtimes)}$ and David Aveiro$^{(\boxtimes)}$

Madeira Interactive Technologies Institute, University of Madeira,
Caminho da Penteada, 9020-105 Funchal, Portugal
duarte.gouveia@m-iti.org, daveiro@uma.pt

Abstract. In this paper we use Design and Engineering Methodology for Organizations (DEMO) to formally describe the European Union General Data Protection Regulation (2016/679) which entries into force and application on May 25, 2018. This law introduces a paradigm shift in information systems by requiring by design and by default much more control on personal data and its processing. The data subjects can give and remove consent for processing and establish restrictions on what the data is processed for. They can also ask for their information, object to automated decision making based on it, require changes to that information or ask that it be erased ('right to be forgotten'). When they ask for their information, it must be provided in a machine-readable format, which implies data portability and the ability to provide it to another party. This law creates a new role, the data protection officer, and assigns duties to data controllers, data processors, supervisory authorities, national authorities and EU authorities. This work shows how DEMO can present in a simple way the system described by this law, and analyses the challenges and insights provided by using this modeling method.

Keywords: Enterprise engineering · DEMO · Data protection
Modeling

1 Introduction

The object of study for this paper is the European Union (EU) Regulation 2016/679 [1], named "General Data Protection Regulation" (GDPR). This Regulation enters into force and application on May 25, 2018. It is the biggest change in data privacy regulation in Europe in the last 20 years, as it replaces the Data Protection Directive 95/46/EC (1995) [2].

Protection of personal data is a part of the fundamental rights and freedoms of natural persons. The GDPR aims at promoting the free flow of personal data and protecting it at the same time.

The GDPR:

- Gives data subjects the right to be forgotten (erasure of personal data), the right to object to automated decisions, the right to data portability, the right to establish restrictions on processing, and the right to remove previously given consent.

© Springer Nature Switzerland AG 2019
D. Aveiro et al. (Eds.): EEWC 2018, LNBIP 334, pp. 144–158, 2019.
https://doi.org/10.1007/978-3-030-06097-8_9

- Transfers most of the responsibility to the controllers of personal data, relying on self-enforcement, without prior approval and with minimal reporting obligations. At the same time, it also increases applicable fines up to 4% of total worldwide turnover of the preceding fiscal year or 20 000 000 EUR, whichever is higher.
- Creates consistency mechanisms to assure the same ruling across EU, based on national supervisory authorities in EU countries and the European Data Protection Board ("The Board").
- Requires a much higher control on both processing activities and personal data elements by design and by default [1 art. 25], which introduces new challenging requirements on how information systems should be designed and implemented.

Although this law is restricted to the European Union [1 art. 3], it is important to note that it is also applicable for entities of other countries whenever they handle personal data about persons that are in the EU or if their activities aim to offer goods, services or monitor behaviour in the EU. The entities that perform those activities must have a representative within the EU to comply with this regulation. [1 art. 27].

In this paper we model the full system described by GDPR using "Design and Engineering Methodology for Organizations" (DEMO) [3]. At current time we could not found in the literature attempts to model the GDPR with a process/transaction approach. There are a few works, using other approaches, that address more specific domains, like the Open Digital Rights Language (ODRL), typically using semantic frameworks to represent the knowledge expressed by the legal text of GDPR, focusing on the rights of the data subject. Our approach is a process based and includes the full extent of GDPR, from the data subject up to the consistency mechanisms at the European Union level.

In Sect. 2 we briefly introduce DEMO. In Sect. 3 we present the research questions and the research design. In Sect. 4 we summarize the GDPR [1] using the first step of DEMO - Performa, Informa, Forma analysis (PIF analysis) [3, 4]. In Sect. 5 we present the Actor Transaction Diagram (ATD) that summarizes the system described by the GDPR. In Sect. 6 we perform a critical analysis of the result of applying DEMO to the object of study. In Sect. 7 we conclude and present future work.

2 Literature Review

The foundational method of Organizational Engineering is the "Design and Engineering Methodology for Organizations" (DEMO) [3]. A core idea of DEMO is that to model business interactions we should use a communication-centric approach, instead of the data-centric approach which is the dominant approach in the design of information systems.

The communication-centric approach has its roots in the Action Workflow Loop [5] presented in Fig. 1. Being "general and universal", this loop models the core pattern of all successful interactions.

Fig. 1. Action Workflow Loop [5]

According to Denning and Medina-Mora [6], "Incomplete workflows invariably cause breakdowns, and if they persist, they give rise to complaints and bad feelings that interfere with the ultimate purpose of work – to satisfy the customer."

DEMO extends this core loop through the Performance in Social Interactions (PSI) Theory [3, 4]. It describes the world through a model based on transactions, each producing a single result, initiated by a set of actor roles and executed by one actor role. This results in the simplified pattern presented in Figs. 2 and 3 which uses a sequence of coordination acts surrounding a production (execute) act.

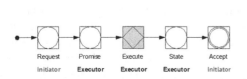

Fig. 2. Simplified pattern for a PSI transaction [3]

Fig. 3. Order, execution and result phases [7]

As depicted in Figs. 2, 3 and 4, the transaction starts with a request (rq) by the initiator which includes the desired outcome in full detail. If the executor can fulfil that request, he will promise (pm) a delivery and then execute, producing the expected result, stating (st) its completion to the initiator. If the delivered result is as requested, the initiator will finish the transaction by accepting (ac) the result, otherwise it can be rejected (rj). It is important to note that this pattern assigns different acts to the initiator and the executor actor roles. The core acts described can be grouped into three phases, as can be seen in Fig. 3: order (O-phase), execution (E-phase) and result (R-phase) [7].

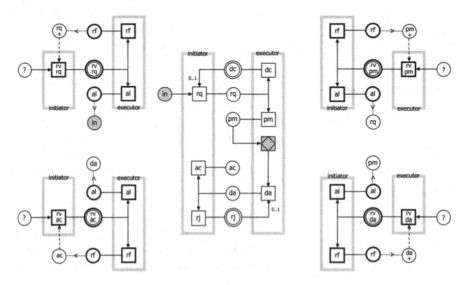

Fig. 4. DEMO 4.3 complete transaction pattern [8]

This simplified description becomes more complex, as can be seen in Fig. 4, as additional revoke acts are needed and so are added to each phase [7]:-

- The *initiator* can change his mind and **revoke** the request (rv rq) at any time.
- The *executor* can **decline** (dc) the initial request if he does not wish, is not able, or can't deliver in the conditions requested by the initiator.
- The *executor* can **revoke** his previous **promise** act (rv pm).
- The *executor* can **revoke** his previous **state** act (rv st).
- The *initiator* may **reject** (rj) the **state**d (st) result.
- The *initiator* may **revoke** a previous **accept** (rv ac).

Revoking acts contradict previously established expectations. They may be initiated by any of parties and the counterparty may allow the revoke or refuse it.

3   Research Questions and Research Design

As a starting point, we establish the following three research questions for this work:

- Can DEMO be used to model the system described by the GDPR?
- Does the resulting DEMO model provide a simpler, more useful, and easier to understand than the text law?
- What parts of the GDPR are hard or challenging to model with DEMO?

To make research design options explicit, we adhered to the extension of the research design pattern presented in [9] and depicted the research process in Fig. 5. This pattern identifies three phases for the research process (Strategic, Tactical, Operational).

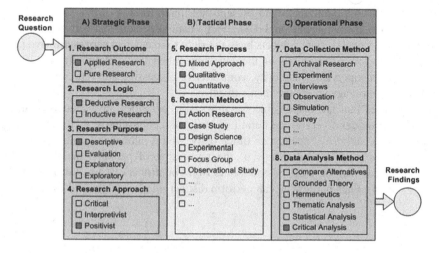

Fig. 5. Research design options using [9] pattern

In this work we aim at applied research (A1), as we use an established method (DEMO) to a specific real-world case (GDPR). The application of DEMO uses a top-down, deductive approach (A2) as research logic. The result of applying DEMO is a model that describes (A3) the system presented by GDPR in a succinct way. DEMO uses a positivist (A4) approach, as it assumes there is one truthful ontological solution and a reliable path that different researchers can follow to reach similar conclusions.

At the tactical phase, GDPR modeled with DEMO is used as a Case Study (B6) provides a result, presented in Sects. 4 and 5, that can then be evaluated by qualitative measures (B5).

The results of applying DEMO to the GDPR will be observed (C7) and critically analyzed (C8) in Sect. 6.

4   Performa Informa Forma (PIF) Analysis on GDPR

The GDPR [1] is a document with 88 pages, 173 preamble topics and 99 law articles. The PIF analysis is the first step of DEMO method and analyzes the text that describes the system, identifying transactions and actor roles. Since the law is so long we summarize it in the following four sub-sections: organizations and organizational roles; processing activities; personal data; consistency mechanism. We reference the article numbers in [1] for future use, as well as the business/ontological transactions, numbered with prefix OT and datalogical transactions numbered with prefix DT. These transactions will be used in Sect. 5.

4.1   Organizations and Organizational Roles

The GDPR references several organizations and several organizational roles within them that take part in this system, as depicted in Fig. 6. To provide a global view on the system we will first name them and present their main roles.

When some entity has personal data about a natural person, that natural person is a **data subject** [1 art. 4]. Data subjects have the right to mandate a **representative** [1 art. 80], namely to lodge complaints on the data subject behalf and claim effective judicial remedy from a supervisory authority, controller or processor. The representative only acts by delegation/agency of the data subject.

The entities that are responsible for processing activities are called **controllers**. The GDPR provides a very broad definition on what a controller is: a "natural or legal person, public authority, agency or other body which, alone or jointly with other, determines the purpose and means of the processing of personal data" [1 art. 4]. A controller can also be a set of controllers (joint controller) [1 art. 26] or an under-taking [1 art. 4]. Each participant can perform distinct roles as established by a contract.

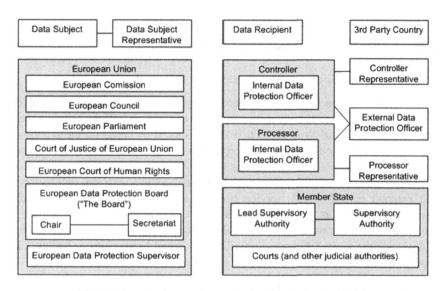

Fig. 6. Organizations and organizational roles in the GDPR

Some controllers are excluded from the scope of this law. For example:

(a) If the controller is a natural person in the course of a purely personal or household activity [1 art. 2];
(b) An official authority handling a record on criminal convictions and offenses [1 art. 10];
(c) A member state or entities within EU acting according to law [1 art. 2].

The controller is responsible for processing activities, that are performed by **processors**, under the direct supervision of the controller.

The GDPR introduces the notion of **processor** as the "natural or legal person, public authority, agency or other body which processes personal data on behalf of the controller" [1 art. 4].

An entity that assumes the role of controller for a processing activity, can also be the processor for that processing activity, or it may delegate its performance to other third party, i.e., another entity "under the direct authority of the controller or processor" [1 art. 4] These delegations have specific rules that will be addressed later on [1 art. 24–31].

Both controller or processor entities might require the designation of a **data protection officer** [1 art. 37–39], and provide the resources to perform its role and maintain its expert knowledge, secrecy or confidentiality, in an independent manner, reporting directly to the highest management level [1 art. 38]. Despite his independence, the data protection officer only acts by delegation/agency of a controller or processor. For public authorities, except courts, the existence of a Data Protection Officer is mandatory [1 art. 37].

For controllers and processors, that role is required if:

(a) there is "regular and systematic monitoring of data subjects on a large scale" [1 art. 37];
(b) "special categories of data" are processed at large scale [1 art. 37].

The Data Protection Officer is the point of contact for the Supervisory Authority and Data Subjects [1 art. 38]. To assure that their tasks [1 art. 39] are fully and timely performed, the choice of Data Protection Officer should be based on the professional qualities and expert knowledge on data protection law and practices [1 art. 37] and in the absence of conflict of interests [1 art. 38].

The role of Data Protection Officer can be performed by an internal staff member or by an external person with a service contract. A body representing categories of controllers or processors may designate a shared data protection officer [1 art. 37]. A group of undertaking may appoint a single data protection officer. A public authority may designate the same data protection officer to several "authorities or bodies, taking account their organizational structure and size" [1 art. 37].

The specific tasks for Data Protection Officers [1 art. 39] are described in Sect. 4.4.

The GDPR defines **recipient** of data as those to which personal data is disclosed, whether they are a third party or not. However, public authorities that receive personal data in accordance to the law should not be considered recipients of personal data.

If a controller or a processor are entities not established in the EU, the GDPR requires that they designate a **representative** in the EU, except if that entity is a public authority, or if the processing is occasional, does not include on a large scale special categories of personal data and "is unlikely to result is risk to the rights and freedoms of natural persons, taking into account nature, context, scope and purpose of the processing" [1 art. 27].

At a different level, the GDPR identifies the organizational and roles that address the consistency mechanism: **EU Member States**, **third party countries** and **EU institutions** and **bodies**.

The institutions referenced in the GDPR regarding EU Member States are: (a) **lead supervisory authority** [1 art. 51–59]; (b) **supervisory authorities** [1 art. 51–59] and (c) **courts** (and other judicial authorities) [1 art. 78–79]. A member state may have more than one supervisory authority, but one of them assumes the leading role for participating in the consistency mechanism.

Third party countries are referenced in general and no specific institutions within them are mentioned.

The EU institutions referenced by the GDPR are: (a) **European Commission**; (b) **European Council**; (c) **European Parliament**; (d) **Court of Justice of European Union**; (e) **European Court of Human Rights**; (f) European Data Protection Board ("**The Board**") [1 art. 68–76]; (g) **European Data Protection Supervisor** [1 art. 68].

4.2 Processing Activity

A processing activity "means any operation or set of operations which is performed on personal data or on sets of personal data, whether or not by automated means, such as collection, recording, organization, structuring, storage, adaptation or alteration, retrieval, consultation, use, disclosure by transmission, dissemination or otherwise making available, alignment or combination, restriction, erasure or destruction" [1 art. 4]. A processing activity should be lawful, fair and transparent [1 art. 5].

A processing activity may be performed by human actors or can be wholly or partly automated. The GDPR grants data subjects the right to object a processing, including profiling [1 art. 21, art. 22].

Every time a controller wishes to "introduce a processing activity" (OT1), it must identify for that processing:

(a) An explicit and legitimate purpose [1 art. 13–14];
(b) Its legal basis [1 art. 13–14];
(c) The required data to perform it and its categories [1 art. 13–14] based on the Data Minimization principle, i.e., the minimum set of data required to perform the processing activity [1 art. 5];
d) The recipient(s) or category of recipients of that personal data [1 art. 13–14];
e) In the case of intention to transfer data to a third party country, assure the appropriate safeguards and that the decisions by the EU Commission about that country are met.

The GDPR considers as legitimate purpose- that does not require consent, public interest; scientific or historical research and statistical purposes. These purposes should ensure the principle of data minimization, may include technical and organizational measures, like pseudonymization, and should favor further processing to no longer permit the identification of data subjects, if possible.

The legal basis of a processing activity can be one or more of the following:

(a) Consent
(b) Contract
(c) Legal obligation
(d) Legitimate interest.

The explicit consent must be given by the data subject for each specific processing activity [1 art. 6], in the context of a easily accessible written form, with clear and plain language, clearly distinguishable from other matters [1 art. 7]. The data subject may remove consent at any time, and it should be as easy to withdraw consent as it was to give it. The burden of proof for the explicit consent is on the controller.

If the data subject is a child (by default, under 16 years old), the consent must be given by the holder of parental responsibility [1 art. 8].

When the legal basis is established by a legal contract, consent is assumed [1 art. 6].

The legal basis can be established by law, either from a EU member state, from EU, when the controller is subject to it, or when the task is "carried out in public interest or in the exercise of official authority vested in the controller" [1 art. 6].

The legal basis can be established by legitimate interest when there are vital interests of the data subject or another natural person, or the legitimate interests by the controller or by a third party [1 art. 6, 13, 14];

Before executing a processing activity, the data subject must be informed about the processing activity information and about its rights, but this only needs to be done once [1 art. 13–14].

Regarding the processing activity, the controller must provide the information from "introduction of processing activity" (OT1), as well as the controller identity and contact details, or of data protection officer, if applicable.

The data subject must be informed of the right to rectification, erasure and restriction of processing, right to data portability, right of removal of previously given consent, and the right to lodge a complaint with the supervisory authority. The data subject must also be informed of what data is needed by contractual requirement and of the existence of automated decision making. Among that needed data is profiling, as well as the logic involved and the significance and the envisaged consequences of such processing for the data subject [1 art. 13–14].

If the controller intends to use the personal data to further processing, it must inform the data subject beforehand [1 art. 13–14].

The controller must keep a record of all its processing activities (DT58) [1 art. 30].

4.3   Data Element - Personal Data

Personal data is any information related to a natural person (data subject), that allows direct or indirect identification. That information can be "a name, an identification number, location data, an online identifier, or to one or more factors specific to the physical, physiological, genetic, mental, economic, cultural or social identity of that natural person" [1 art. 4].

There are special categories of personal data that require special consideration. For example:

(a) Genetic data, that can provide unique information about a person, and enable identification with a biological sample [1 art. 4];
(b) Biometric data, means personal data from specific technical processing relating to the physical, physiological or behavioral characteristics of a natural person [1 art. 4];
(c) Data concerning health of a natural person (physical or mental), including the provision of health care services, which reveals the health status [1 art. 4];
(d) Criminal convictions can only be hold by an official authority. [1 art. 10].
(e) Personal Data in the context of churches and religious associations, may have the supervision of an independent supervisory authority [1 art. 91].

Another special category of personal data is "profiling data", when personal data is used "to analyze or predict aspects concerning that natural person's performance at work, economic situation, health, personal preferences, interests, reliability, behavior, location or movement" [1 art. 4].

In doubt about personal data classification in the impact assessment, the controller might ask the supervisory authority for a "Prior consultation" (BT3).

Every time new data elements are collected relating a data subject, the provenance of that information should be registered [1 art. 14], as well as the period for which the personal data will be stored, or if that is not possible, the criteria to determine that period [1 art. 13–14]. If the origin of those data elements is not the data subject, a "Notification" (DT52) must be sent to the Data Subject within a reasonable period, at least at the time of first communication with the data subject or of the disclosure to another recipient, but always within one month of collecting data.

4.4   Consistency Mechanism

The consistency mechanism is a set of transactions between **supervisory authorities** and **The Board** to define and apply consistent rules across the EU. When a new processing is being introduced (BT1) the controller may request for a prior consultation (BT3) [1 art. 35, 36] with a supervisory authority regarding doubts about special categories of personal data and the recommended procedures to handle them. The supervisory authority may also ask for an opinion of The Board (BT27) [1 art. 64, 70]. If The Board considers it appropriate, it may also collectively agree on a binding decision (BT24) [1 art. 65], as well as guidelines (BT23) [1 art. 64, 70].

The existence of certifications (BT29) [1 art. 42] and codes of conduct is promoted by the GDPR. The Board performs the accreditation of certification bodies (BT28) [1 art. 43, 70], that will certify controllers and processors.

Both controller and processor may need to perform impact (BT2) (BT15) [1 art. 35] and compliance (BT7) (BT14) assessments [1 art. 39]. The controller may perform data accuracy verifications (BT5), as well as take measures to reduce risk (BT6).

The Board and the supervisory authorities perform periodic revision for monitoring compliance (BT26) [1 art. 70] and analysis and report on activities (BT25) [1 art. 71]. Additionally, the supervisory authorities might review certification (BT21) [1 art. 57, 58]and conduct investigations (BT20) [1 art. 57, 58].

We were able to identify many datalogical transactions regarding notifications. The controller may notify the data subject (DT52) [1 art. 34], the processor (DT59) and the supervisory authority (DT62) [1 art. 31, 33]. The processor may notify the controller (DT56). The supervisory authority may notify the processor (DT55) [1 art. 58], the controller (DT59) [1 art. 58] and The Board (DT65), and can advise the member state (DT68). The Board may notify the supervisory authority (DT63) and advise (DT66) [1 art. 70] the EU Commission. The EU Commission keeps a status list of third party countries [1 art. 44–50] regarding their data protection laws and procedures. If a country is blacklisted, additional contractual measures may be required between the controller and the processor.

The controller (DT53), supervisory authority (DT61) [1 art. 60] and The Board (DT64) [1 art. 70] must perform public communications under certain conditions established by the GDPR. If everything else fails, the supervisory authority may impose remedies and fines (BT10, BT16) on the controller and/or the processor [1 art 58, 78, 79, 82–84].

The supervisory authorities of different countries can establish cooperation each other (BT17) and make notifications (DT60) to each other. These transactions be initiated at any time by any supervisory authority, with other specific supervisory authority as executor, except for the one that took the initiator role in that transaction.

5   Actor Transaction Diagram (ATD)

As the second DEMO step, the ATD, depicted in Fig. 7 was developed. It shows 8 scopes of interest (data subject, controller, processor, supervisory authority, The Board, certification body, EU Commission and EU Member State) and two additional actors (data recipient and parental right holder) with only one transaction.

Also interesting is the fact that several of the organizations and organizational roles identified in Fig. 6, Sect. 4.1 do not appear in the ATD in Fig. 7. The omitted roles are the ones that do not perform ontological transactions, like the chair and secretariat of The Board, or third-party countries. The courts were out of scope because summarizing it to a single transaction would be an oversimplification. The courts are described by other laws, not the GDPR.

The representatives, for data subject, controller and processor, are all actors by agency/delegation, and therefore may exist and get the proper authorization to be able to take the roles. The same happens with the data protection officer, although the GDPR appears to give many attributions to that functional role. According to DEMO, those attributions are for the controller and processor, who may perform them with or without the data protection officer functional role.

We modeled datalogical transactions in the ATD as in this case they are essential to this business model. Therefore, are promoted to the ontological level and included in the ATD presented in Fig. 7. We kept their identifiers as datalogical transactions (DT#) to distinguish them from the original ontological business transactions (BT#). Actor Roles are numbered (AR#) mapping the executer actor role with the transaction identifier number.

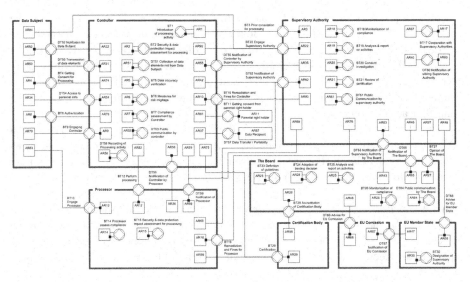

Fig. 7. Actor transaction diagram for the GDPR (high resolution image available at https://sites. google.com/view/gdprwithdemo/)

In total, there are 49 transactions, including 30 Business/Ontological transactions (BT) and 19 Datalogical transactions (DT), as can be seen in Table 1 and in Fig. 7. Due to lack of space the transaction result for each of these transactions was not included.

Table 1. Ontological/business transactions (BT) and data transactions (DT) for the GDPR

ID	Transaction Name	ID	Transaction Name
BT1	Introduction of processing activity	DT50	Transmission of data elements
BT2	Security & data protection impact assessment for processing	DT51	Collection of data elements not from Data Subject
BT3	Prior consultation for processing	DT52	Notification of Data Subject
BT4	Getting consent for processing	DT53	Public communication by controller
BT5	Data accuracy verification	DT54	Access to personal data
BT6	Measures for risk mitigation	DT55	Notification of Controller by Supervisory Authority
BT7	Compliance assessment by controller	DT56	Notification of Controller by Processor
BT8	Authentication	DT57	Data transfer / protability
BT9	Engage Controller	DT58	Recording of processing activity
BT10	Remediation and Fines for Controller	DT59	Notification of Processor
BT11	Getting consent from parental right holder	DT60	Notification of sibling Supervisory Authority
BT12	Perform processing	DT61	Public communication by Supervisory Authority
BT13	Engage Processor	DT62	Notification of Supervisory Authority
BT14	Processor assess compliance	DT63	Notification of Supervisory Authority by The Board
BT15	Security & data protection impact assessment for processing	DT64	Public communication by The Board
BT16	Remediation and fines for Processor	DT65	Notification of The Board
BT17	Cooperation with Supervisory Authorities	DT66	Advise for EU Comission
BT18	Monitorization of compliance	DT67	Notification of EU Comission
BT19	Analysis & report on activities	DT68	Advise for EU Member State
BT20	Conduct investigation		
BT21	Review of certification		
BT22	Engage Supervisory Authority		
BT23	Definition of guidelines		
BT24	Adoption of binding decision		
BT25	Analysis & report on activities		
BT26	Monitorization of compliance		
BT27	Opinion of the Board		
BT28	Accreditation of Certification Body		
BT29	Certification		
BT30	Designation of Supervisory Authority		

6   Critical Analysis

The result of applying DEMO to the GDPR resulted in a total of 48 island of trans-actions that do not connect to other transactions, with a single exception of dependency between transactions BT1 and BT3. This answers positively the first research question – applicability of DEMO to the GDPR.

There are several transactions that appear to be repeated in several scopes of interest. If we did not split the transactions in several scopes of interest, we could have reduced the number of transactions, namely less 5 ontological transactions. Transactions BT7, BT14 and BT26 could be reduced to a single one, as well as BT2, 15; BT10, 16; BT19, 25; and 2 datalogical transactions DT55, 56; DT62, 63. We believe it is not realistic to implement all these scopes of interest in a single technological implementation. It is likely, however, that one organization might want to include the controller, the processor and data subjects (for internal clients) into the same technological implementation.

We got 8 scopes of interest, with an average of 9 actor roles per scope of interest, which is a quite complex system. The existence of so many transactions that do not logically connect to each other in any way, makes the description of this system in the GDPR harder to understand and a global picture to summarize it harder to conceive. For that reason, we believe the most important finding by this work is the ATD in Fig. 7. At full resolution, Fig. 7 fits on an A3 sheet of paper, which is a simpler global view of the GDPR. This answers positively the second research question.

The DEMO notion of actor roles, and the flexibility of assigning them to organizational roles, and of using delegation, provided a significant reduction in complexity. This is especially relevant for the data protection officer roles and the representative's roles.

Another important finding by this work is the lead importance of introduction of the processing activity (BT1), that was neither clear from the GDPR text law, nor its data requirements summarized in Sect. 4.2.

Regarding the third research question – what parts were challenging to model with DEMO – we found two difficult issues: modelling cooperation between supervisory authorities (BT17) and the inclusion of so many datalogic transactions in the ATD.

Regarding cooperation, the DEMO/PSI transaction pattern handles transactions where one actor role is the unique executor. A cooperation transaction is of a different nature, where two or more participants provide value to the transaction when agreed upon. That is not properly handled by the existing transaction patterns in DEMO.

Regarding the datalogical transactions, the typical DEMO diagrams do not include datalogical transactions as they are not at the core modeling of the system. In this case, if we only presented the ontological transaction, the diagrams would not be as useful, as it would not be a comprehensive model. In the case of the GDPR datalogical transactions are essential to the system, and therefore should be considered at ontological level. Also noticeable is that we don't have any infological transaction. Also, we found that the datalogical transactions in this case would not naturally be enclosed in infological and ontological more general transactions.

We believe this work can be used as a solid base for developing technological solutions that comply "by design and by default" [1 art. 25] with the GDPR.

This document does not include the State Model due to lack of space. Apart from transactions, the elements that would appear on diagram would be: the processing activity; the data element; and the legal basis. The data for these elements was summarized in Sects. 4.2 and 4.3.

Also due to lack of space, the list of transactions in Table 1 does not include the transaction result, as we would expect in a Transaction Result Table.

Due to the limited number of dependencies between transactions, the Process Structure Diagram was not included.

7 Conclusion and Future Work

The GDPR is a demanding and challenging object of study, that is currently requiring many efforts across UE due to its entry into force by May 25, 2018. Although the extent and complexity of the text law, we were able to model the GDPR with DEMO to its full extend. The only challenging part was the cooperation transaction (BT17). DEMO showed to be an adequate method for modeling this system.

The most important findings by this work were:

- The ability of DEMO to model the entire system and represent it in a single figure that fits an A4 paper sheet (best viewed on A3).
- The ability of DEMO to reduce complexity, namely through the existence of actor roles, organizational roles and delegation/agency.
- The identification of a lead transaction for introduction of processing activity (BT1) that puts the focus on the core elements of the State Model: the Processing Activity and the Data Elements.

This work provides a compelling example on the ability of DEMO to synthesize complex systems into a comprehensive, simpler and correct model.

We believe this work is a solid base for the future development of technological solutions that comply "by design and by default" [1 art. 25] with the GDPR.

In the future it would be interesting to use this work as starting point for developing the technical system that encompasses the scopes of interest of: data subject, controller, processor, data recipient and parental right holder, as well as the transactions that interface these scopes with the remaining scopes of interest (supervisory authority and certification body).

Acknowledgments. This work was partially funded by FCT/MCTES LARSyS (UID/EEA/50009/2013 (2015-2017)).

 This work was developed with financial support from ARDITI (Agência Regional para o Desenvolvimento da Investigação, Tecnologia e Inovação), in the context of project M14-20 09–5369-FSE-000001 - Bolsa de Doutoramento.

References

1. European Union Regulation 2016/679, General Data Protection Regulation. http://eur-lex. europa.eu/legal-content/EN/TXT/PDF/?uri=CELEX:32016R0679
2. European Union Directive 95/46/EC, Data Protection Directive. https://eur-lex.europa.eu/ legal-content/EN/TXT/PDF/?uri=CELEX:31995L0046
3. Dietz, J.L.G.: Enterprise Ontology – Theory and Methodology. Springer, Heidelberg (2006). https://doi.org/10.1007/3-540-33149-2
4. Dietz, J.L.G.: DEMO-3 Way of Working, 1 September 2009 (2009)
5. Medina-Mora, R., Winograd, T., Flores, R., Flores, F.: The action workflow approach to workflow management technology. In: Proceedings of the 1992 ACM Conference on Computer-Supported Cooperative Work, pp. 281–288. ACM, December 1992
6. Denning, P.J., Medina-Mora, R.: Completing the loops. Interfaces **25**(3), 42–57 (1995)
7. Van Reijswoud, V.E., Mulder, H.B., Dietz, J.L.: Communicative action-based business process and information systems modelling with DEMO. Inf. Syst. J. **9**(2), 117–138 (1999)
8. Dietz, J.L.G.: The PSI theory – understanding human collaboration (v4.3) (2017). https:// www.researchgate.net/publication/320298882_The_PSI_theory_-_understanding_human_ collaboration. Accessed 25 May 2018
9. Wohlin, C., Aurum, A.: Towards a decision-making structure for selecting a research design in empirical software engineering. Empir. Softw. Eng. **20**(6), 1427–1455 (2015)

DEMO as a Tool of Value Co-creation Strategy Realization

Eduard Babkin and Pavel Malyzhenkov(✉)

Department of Information Systems and Technologies,
National Research University – Higher School of Economics,
Bol. Pecherskaya 25, 603155 Nizhny Novgorod, Russia
{eababkin, pmalyzhenkov}@hse.ru

Abstract. Value co-creation is a new notion in contemporary business practice, which is now also becoming one of the key marketing concepts. The success of the value co-creation strategy is based on the DART (dialogue, access, risk-benefits and transparency) concept which is emerging as the basis for interaction between the consumer and the firm. Still, the lack of a formalized approach towards the representation of the DART mechanism remains an issue. Thus, the purpose of the present paper is to describe a formal approach based on DEMO methodology tools as an attempt aimed at value co-creation process modelling.

Keywords: Service-dominant logics · DEMO · Value co-creation
Transaction patterns

1 Introduction

For organizations of all sizes that seek to be innovative and improve their overall customer experience and engagement, value creation offers a powerful tool to characterize, achieve and develop these targets. Value creation is recognized by the American Marketing Association as one of the key marketing concepts [13]. Traditionally value creation is treated as something that a firm creates and that is usually linked to tangible goods. Service logic challenges this traditional microeconomic model and reverses thinking towards an intangible, knowledge- and resource-based exchange [1, 4, 6, 10–13]. Changes in the marketing environment have provided the consumers with the opportunity to participate in processes that used to be the prerogative of companies only. Nowadays, more and more companies acquire the understanding of necessity of value co-creation integration [6, 11, 12, 15, 16].

Multiple researchers state that the main problem in co-creation strategy realization may be expressed as lack of compliance with a particular high-level architectural framework. Recently, the DART (Dialogue, Access, Risks-benefits and Transparency) scheme [9, 10] was proposed to play the role of such framework. Our contribution is ultimately two-fold. First of all, we demonstrate the appropriateness of DEMO for analyzing the enterprise architecture through the prism of the DART scheme. Second, we propose an initial version of a set of reusable patterns for reengineering of existing DEMO enterprise models following the principles of value co-creation.

© Springer Nature Switzerland AG 2019
D. Aveiro et al. (Eds.): EEWC 2018, LNBIP 334, pp. 159–167, 2019.
https://doi.org/10.1007/978-3-030-06097-8_10

The paper is structured in the following way: Introduction delivers the general overview of the research field and sets the research objectives; Sect. 2 describes the evolution of value co-creation and service-dominant logics and provides the description and analysis of practical issues of the DART approach; Sect. 3 describes the possibilities of DEMO application to the value co-creation process design and introduces the transaction patterns for every block in the DART model on the classical example of pizzeria from [3]; Sect. 4 concludes the paper and describes the future prospects for its development.

2 Value Co-creation: Main Concepts

Value co-creation is a relatively new notion in contemporary business practice. Several points of view regarding value creation and value co-creation exist, and, in fact, the first scholars who started to develop the idea of co-creation were Prahalad and Ramaswamy. In their article [10] they compare and somehow oppose the traditional concept of value creation and the new one – through value co-creation. Generally speaking, consumer-centric firms oblige their potential consumers to contribute to companies' development and research, because only up-to-date information enables the firm to stay on top of the market and address the latest customer needs [4, 9, 10]. Another research [6] displays that value for customers is created throughout the relationship by the customer, partly in interaction between the customer and the supplier or service provider.

The main idea of value co-creation practices, which extension in the modern business permits us to define it as a real strategy, is that the organization seeks efficiency by extending the reach of a business process to a broader class of stakeholders. This general objective articulates into different parameters described in [2] which constitute the motivation of the socialization process effort.

The reflexive relationship between customers and suppliers has also been a hot topic in the elaborations of service-dominant logic (SDL) [13]. SDL is a mind-set through which social and economic exchange phenomena are looked at so that they can potentially be seen more clearly.

In the original premises of SDL [11] the customers were viewed as co-producers to re-evaluate the idea of value being embedded in tangible goods and to redefine the process of value creation. Later this view turned customers into co-creators of value, and recently the co-creation model has been extended to all actors tied together in shared systems of exchange. SDL holds that each party reciprocally creates value and brings its own unique resource accessibility and integrability into the process. SDL stresses a process where providers can offer their applied resources for value creation (value propositions) and collaboratively create value but cannot create and/or deliver value independently.

Still, the utilization of SDL principles and the integration of value co-creation processes into an already existing company structure can neither be absolutely safe, nor give any guarantees of immediate success.

The success of the co-creation value strategy is based on the DART (dialogue, access, risk-benefits and transparency) concept (Fig. 1) described in [10]. DART are emerging as the basis for interaction between the consumer and the firm.

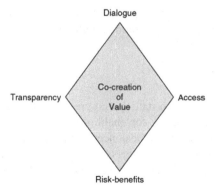

Fig. 1. DART conceptual scheme

As specified in [8], the main characteristics of these blocks are:

1. Dialogue represents interactivity between two equal problem solvers, eager to act and to learn.
2. Access implies facilitating co-creation by offering the right tools for communication between customers and suppliers; it also entails those marketing solutions that result in increased freedom of choice for customers.
3. Risk assessment refers to the customers' right to be fully informed of the risks they face when accepting the value proposition.
4. Transparency represents removal of information asymmetry between the customer and the supplier and practicing the openness of information.

Actually, the value co-creation process can be analyzed and designed as a typical social activity, namely the activity executed by multiple actors [2], where an attempt was made to realize it by the means of BPMN. Social tasks specify the BPMN task concept to denote a process action with a social semantics. Other processes which are modelled within the framework of social activities can be:

- broadcasting of messages/contents from a task to the entire social network;
- posting of messages/contents to one member of the network;
- invitation of people from the social network to perform a specific task;
- invitation to comment or vote on a task or on its outcomes;
- logging-in by users in the BPM system using credentials from a social network;
- search for user skills or reputation within a social network (e.g., for checking recommendations before assigning tasks to users).

The control of social tasks exploits standard BPMN sequence flows, either within a social pool, or between a social and a normal pool. A generic social event concept represents any kind of occurrence within a social network; this can be specialized to express more detailed event types like addition of a new user to the community; establishment of a new social relationship; notification of acceptance/rejection of a social request (e.g., for friendship, invitation to groups or applications), and so on. Social pools, actor categories, social tasks and events are the linguistic building blocks for expressing social design patterns that are archetypal process model fragments representing recurrent process socialization solutions.

3 DEMO Realization

The previous overview leads us to state that co-creation has emerged, in recent years, as an important management strategy for enabling firms to be innovative. However, in spite of the burgeoning literature on the conceptualization of co-creation, little has been done to formalize the co-creation process and to assess methodologies that apply techniques for involving customers in co-creation and the corresponding problems related to risk facing [4, 5, 7, 14]. For the purpose of our research we suppose that the transactions "responsible" for the value co-creation procedure are focused on the knowledge of the characteristics of customer needs, knowledge acquired from supplier and customer learning during encounters, knowledge of links between the characteristics of existing customer needs, customer involvement and co-creation technique selection, and knowledge of the existing and co-created value.

So, the present work wants to investigate the main ways of DEMO models application to the value co-creation process formalization and, possibly, reduction of its critical points. Below the advantages of different DEMO models and their application to co-creation critical points are presented (Table 1):

Table 1. DEMO models contribution to the value co-creation process

Critical points	DEMO model application
Dialogue	The Construction Model, by means of its Interaction Model, shows the boundary of the co-creation value process and the interface transactions with actor roles in the environment [3]. This makes the IAM suitable for objectives individuation. The IAM clearly presents units of collaboration (complete transactions) and shows the ontological units of competence, authorization and responsibility delivering a way for the optimal identification and classification of organizational functions. To assure the quality of the interaction the apparatus of ontological maps based on DEMO [11, 12] can be used
Access Transparency	The State Model becomes particularly useful because of its capacity to detail a part of the CM, namely, the contents of the information banks (coordination and production banks)
Risk-benefits	The Process Model facilitates these decisions considerably because it clearly shows that these side paths are either full-fledged transactions (in which original facts are created), or not. It gives the opportunity to understand what transaction is mostly engaged in the value creation process

Consequently, the analysis of the literature permits us to define the following characteristics of the DART processes which constitute the basis for the transaction patterns design (Table 2):

Table 2. DART blocks and corresponding transactions

DART blocks	Description	Results
Dialogue	It represents interactivity between two equal problem solvers, eager to act and to learn. So, the enterprise invites and adds new actors to the value creation process. Internal business actors generate an invitation by sending a message to a customer (or some social group) starting a dialogue process	A shared list of requirements to product or service
Access	Access implies facilitating co-creation by offering the right tools for communication between customers and suppliers. The internal business actors collect the contributions and use them to produce a decision, which can also be published on a shared electronic resource or distributed in some other way. It is also important to have the possibility to enrich the already created content	Formation of a decision about product/service realization
Risk assessment	Risk-benefits assessment refers to the customers' right to be fully informed of the risks and benefits they face when accepting the value proposition	The right to be informed of risks and benefits deriving from results
Transparency	Transparency removes information asymmetry between the customer and the supplier and is aimed to reach the openness of information. Social contribution to the process can be fostered by delivering timely information on the progress status of activities. The platform will also give the possibility to keep users updated on the views making the process execution more transparent. This design pattern lets an internal performer mark an activity as socially notified in order to generate automatic progress messages to selected social networks	A public-access model of cooperation

Therefore, we propose to introduce the basic patterns of DART-transactions for the value co-creation process modelling. Let us define them as D-transaction, A-transaction, R-transaction and T-transaction. The table below (Table 3) demonstrates the general scheme (initiators, executors and results) of these transactions.

Table 3. General scheme of DART-transactions

DART-transaction	Initiator	Executor	Result
D-transaction	Service company	Customer	Definition of service characteristics
A-transaction	Service company	Customer	A decision about service formation
R-transaction	Customer	Service company	The right to be informed of the risks and benefits deriving from service delivery
T-transaction	Service company	Customer	The public-access model of cooperation

The value co-creation is a choice, a strategy that some enterprises may adopt and some of them may not. But, if an enterprise adopts it, it must follow the DART scheme and that's why we consider D-, A-, R- and T-transactions ontological: they represent the essence of the enterprises which follow the co-creation value strategy. Besides, from the formal point of view the production facts of DART-transactions represent the judgments of actors and also for this reason they can be seen as ontological transactions.

Every DART-transaction will be realized in compliance with the basic pattern of a transaction [3] and the transaction results from Table 4 may be used in the Transaction Result Table. The particularity of these transactions stands in the fact that they will be used only in case the enterprise adopts the value co-creation strategy. We illustrate the application of the proposed DART-transactions in the canonical case of pizzeria and the essential elements of DEMO for our case will be the following:

Table 4. Transaction-result table for a pizzeria in case of value co-creation

Transaction type	Result type
T01 completion	R01 purchase P has been completed
T02 preparation	R02 purchase P has been prepared
T03 payment	R03 purchase P has been paid
T04 D-transaction	R04 pizza characteristics have been defined
T05 A-transaction	R05 the decision about pizza cooking has been formed
T06 R-transaction	R06 the right to be informed of the risks and benefits deriving from pizza cooking has been fixed
T07 T-transaction	R07 the public-access model of cooperation has been created

Despite the apparent simplicity, from the ontological point of view this model has all essential elements of modern enterprises: interaction with the customer, production processes, financial procedures. That's why the demonstration of how a business ontological model is reorganized in case the enterprise adopts the value co-creation strategy (by means of ontological D-, A-, R- and T-transactions introduction into the model) can be seen as a reference model for other cases too.

Besides, even for that well-known model incorporating value co-creation transactions leads to modification of ontological enterprise properties toward active customer engagement to the production and service fulfillment activities. We analyze the pizzeria case because the value co-creation processes take place here too. For example, the pizza-maker and the customer may discuss about the ingredients to put into the pizza. This process, realized in full compliance to DART model has as a result the value for both involved sides: the customer satisfies its need to eat the pizza according to his personal tastes and preferences and the pizza-maker gets the new receipt of pizza which can potentially be used for other customers too.

The Fig. 2 describes the DEMO Process model with the usage of newly introduced DART-transactions. In the D-transaction we consider the enterprise its initiator because after it receives the request of the customer to complete the pizza, it starts the process of value co-creation, activating the dialogue with the customer.

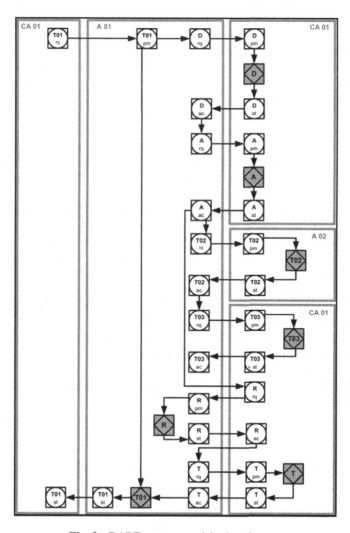

Fig. 2. DART process model: pizzeria case

The Process Model in our case describes the allocation of DART-transactions inside the pizzeria processes and helps to understand the value co-creation strategy realization. Because of the paper format set we chose the previous version of the DEMO notation graphics: the states presentation is realized in a more condensed form here.

4   Results and Discussion

The ontological approach expressed by means of the DEMO methodology and derivative tools makes it possible to reduce the design costs and can be applied to the modelling of value co-creation at both conceptual and operative phases.

We may conclude that the newly introduced artefacts provide the enterprise with critical elements of the value co-creation mechanism. Thus, the analysis of DEMO models provides decision makers with particular means of organizational transformations. Such choice unavoidably deals with information system management, and from such positions the use of the DEMO methodology for both enterprise structure modelling and individuation of the most suitable information system use is quite advantageous. DEMO is easily reproducible and can be applied regardless of the business segment of the enterprise.

So, the future research could include further extension of DEMO models application to the value co-creation critical sides and its broader application to the practical cases. Besides, it is also possible to extend the value co-creation analysis to cover a broader set of cases, for example, in case of pizza delivery. It will possibly enlarge the set of situations involved in this process revealing new particularities of the co-creation process.

Another direction of future research may be represented by the more detailed analysis of DART-transactions, because some of them (like D-transaction, for example) represent not a single transaction, but the sequence of them. Besides, the risk assessment expressed by R-transaction could be analyzed from the point of view of the presence of different social institutions regulating different categories of such risk.

One of the future directions of the research could be the analysis of the process aimed to find personnel with required expertise. The process usually starts with publishing a call for people, to which internal/external observers respond. The internal performer selects the right candidate(s) and publishes the final decision. For such analysis the tool of competence maps can be used.

Acknowledgments. The reported study was funded by Russian Fund of Basic Research according to the research project № 16-06-00300-a.

References

1. Babkin, E., Malyzhenkov, P.: Assessment of brand competences in a family business: a methodological proposal. In: Pergl, R., Molhanec, M., Babkin, E., Fosso Wamba, S. (eds.) EOMAS 2016. LNBIP, vol. 272, pp. 129–138. Springer, Cham (2016). https://doi.org/10.1007/978-3-319-49454-8_9
2. Brambilla, M., Fraternali, P., Vaca, C.: BPMN and design patterns for engineering social BPM solutions. In: Daniel, F., Barkaoui, K., Dustdar, S. (eds.) BPM 2011. LNBIP, vol. 99, pp. 219–230. Springer, Heidelberg (2012). https://doi.org/10.1007/978-3-642-28108-2_22
3. Dietz, J.L.G.: Enterprise Ontology: Theory and Methodology. Springer, Heidelberg (2006). https://doi.org/10.1007/3-540-33149-2
4. Durugbo, C., Pawar, K.: A unified model of the co-creation process. Exp. Syst. Appl. **41**, 4373–4387 (2014)
5. Feltus, C., Proper, E.: Conceptualization of an abstract language to support value co-creation. In: Federated Conference on Computer Science and Information Systems Proceedings. IEEE (2017)
6. Gronroos, C., Ravald, A.: Service as business logic: implications for value creation and marketing. J. Serv. Manag. **22**(1), 5–22 (2011)
7. Hunka, F., van Kervel, S.J.H.: The REA model expressed in a generic DEMO model for co-creation and co-production. In: Aveiro, D., Pergl, R., Guizzardi, G., Almeida, J.P., Magalhães, R., Lekkerkerk, H. (eds.) EEWC 2017. LNBIP, vol. 284, pp. 151–165. Springer, Cham (2017). https://doi.org/10.1007/978-3-319-57955-9_12
8. Mazur, J., Zaborek, P.: Validating DART model. Int. J. Manag. Econ. **44**, 106–125 (2014)
9. Payne, A., Storbacka, K., Frow, P.: Managing the co-creation of value. J. Acad. Mark. Sci. **36**, 83–96 (2007)
10. Prahalad, C., Ramaswamy, V.: Co-creation experiences: the next practice in value creation. J. Interact. Mark. **18**(3), 5–14 (2004)
11. Vargo, S., Lusch, S.: Evolving to a new dominant logic for marketing. J. Mark. **68**(1), 1–17 (2004)
12. Von Maltzahn, C.-F.: Co-creating individuals: a roadmap to value creation in fashion retailing. Amsterdam University of Applied Sciences (2016)

E-resources

13. https://www.ama.org/AboutAMA/Pages/Definition-of-Marketing.aspx
14. Guerreiro, S.: Optimizing Business Processes Compliance Using an Evolvable Risk-Based Approach. https://www.researchgate.net/publication/290122993_Optimizing_Business_Processes_Compliance_Using_an_Evolvable_Risk-Based_Approach
15. Pombinho, J.: Customer Experience-based Value Network Design & Engineering. https://www.researchgate.net/project/Customer-Experience-based-Value-Network-Design-Engineering
16. Pombinho, J.: Objectifying Value Co-creation – An Exploratory Study. https://www.researchgate.net/publication/303513100_Objectifying_Value_Co-creation_-_An_Exploratory_Study

Colored Petri-Net for Implementing DEMO/PSI Transactions for N Actor Roles (N >= 2)

Duarte Gouveia[(⊠)] and David Aveiro[(⊠)]

University of Madeira and Madeira Interactive Technologies Institute,
Caminho da Penteada, 9020-105 Funchal, Portugal
duarte.gouveia@m-iti.org, daveiro@uma.pt

Abstract. This works proposes a colored Petri-Net for implementing DEMO/PSI Transactions. It is based on previous works by the community and on requirement clarifications that happened on a working session on 2017 Enterprise Engineering Working Conference. The solution was designed taking into consideration an asynchronous and distributed system. It also introduces the possibility of using the DEMO/PSI transaction with more than two actor roles. We develop a prototype to validate the proposed solution.

Keywords: Petri-Nets · DEMO · PSI theory · Enterprise engineering

1 Introduction

The purpose of this work is to present a model for implementation of DEMO/PSI transactions using [1, 2] a colored Petri-Net [3]. There have been several previous attempts to model the DEMO/PSI transactions [4–9]. None of these previous works fully complies with what is prescribed by PSI theory, as shown in [7] and as assumed by authors in the case of [8] and [9]. In the 2017's Enterprise Engineering Working Conference (EEWC) there was a PSI Theory Technical Session were several ambiguous issues that discussed, and options chosen. This work does not intend to be the minutes of those discussions in 2017 EEWC. We shall only address the chosen decisions, not to summarize the discussion on the proposals that were discussed but not approved.

2 Decisions from 2017 EEWC – PSI Theory Technical Session

After debate the following decisions were agreed on 2017 EEWC – PSI Theory Technical Session [8]:

- It should be possible to Cancel an act, by the same actor role that performed that act, if no other subsequent act has been performed. For example, the initiator can Cancel Request if the executor has not yet act to Promise or Decline. One open question that remained in 2017 EEWC was if it would be possible to have Cancel acts for Revoke «Acts», for Allow/Refuse Revoke «Acts», «Declines» and «Rejects». We shall address this topic in Sect. 3.

- Three shortcuts have been accepted to simplify interaction in the DEMO/PSI Transaction Pattern.
  - After the sequence "Request, Decline", it should be possible to perform again "Request" as a shortcut for "Revoke Request, Allow Revoke Request, Request".
  - Likewise, after the sequence "Request, Promise, Declare, Reject", it should be possible to perform a new "Declare" as a shortcut for "Revoke Declare, Allow Revoke Declare, Declare".
  - After the sequence "Request, Promise" it should be possible to perform "Accept" as a shortcut of an "(empty) Declare, Accept". The initiator can Accept a transaction even if no result is declared.
- The Execute Act that usually appears on DEMO/PSI transaction pattern should not be included in the Petri-Net as the moment that the Execute Act can take place introduces unnecessary complexities.
- We should be able to initiate more than one reversiogenic conversations for the same transaction, even if from the same actor role, but for different acts, for example, revoke promise and revoke declare. For the same transactions and the same act there can only be one reversiogenic conversation at the same time.
- One of the conclusions in EEWC2017 is that a model for implementing DEMO/PSI is more complex than the usual simplified model that is used for teaching the Enterprise Engineering discipline [2]. The main goal for the model used for teaching is simplicity. The main goal for implementation is making it useful and directly applicable to a software artifact with all its details. In a software artefact we need to enable shortcuts, configurations, namely for the cancel and revoke acts, and we also need to comply with the requirement where two (or more) participants in the transaction asynchronously and in a distributed system. In a distributed system, acts performed by one actor role do not immediately take effect on the counterparty system. They must be acknowledged by the counterparty to produce a state change.

3   Proposed Solution – Colored Petri-Net

Due to the complexity of the proposed Colored Petri-Net, we choose to first present the two figures, and then present them in a way that makes it easier to understand in its full complexity. Figure 1 addresses the Request-Promise section. Figure 2 addresses the Declare-Accept section. The state Promised is the one that joins the two Figures together. That is the only graphical element that is repeated in both figures.

These Figs. 1 and 2 are available with high resolution at: http://www.duarte-gouveia.info/phd/2018/petri_net1.png and http://www.duarte-gouveia.info/phd/2018/petri_net2.png.

Petri-Nets

A Petri-Net is made up of Acts, States, Arrows and Tokens [3]. In Figs. 1 and 2, States are represented as rectangular boxes and States represented as circles.

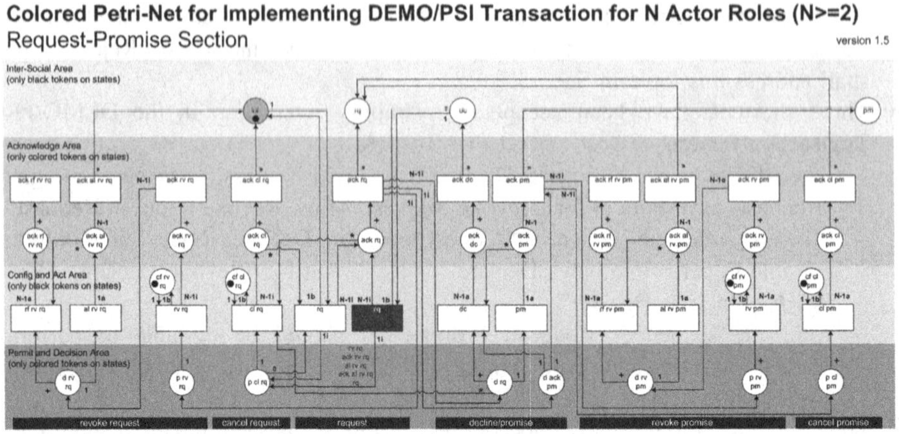

Colored Petri-Net for Implementing DEMO/PSI Transaction for N Actor Roles (N>=2)
Request-Promise Section   version 1.5

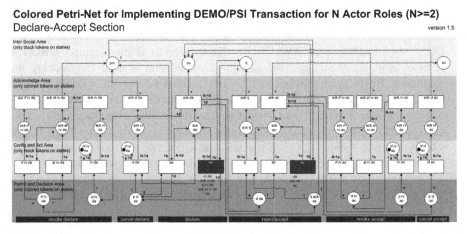

Fig. 1. Request-Promise section of colored Petri-Net for implementing DEMO/PSI transaction for N actor roles (N >= 2) (Color figure online)

Colored Petri-Net for Implementing DEMO/PSI Transaction for N Actor Roles (N>=2)
Declare-Accept Section   version 1.5

Fig. 2. Declare-Accept section of colored Petri-Net for implementing DEMO/PSI transaction for N actor roles (N >= 2) (Color figure online)

For every Act there are inbound Arrows and outbound Arrows. Inbound arrows, linking a State to an Act, are conditions that must be met to allow an Act to occur. Tokens, with its specified cardinality, are consumed when the Act occurs. Outbound arrows, links an Act to a State. Outbound arrows generate tokens that are placed in the target of the arrow.

An Act may have several conditions, from different states. When an Act occurs, it may generate tokens to several states.

At a moment in time, several Acts can satisfy the conditions to be executed. Any of those active Acts can occur unpredictably. This is one of the main features of Petri-Nets that make them good models for asynchronous solutions. When an Act occurs, it consumes and generates Tokens.

Tokens are represented as filled circles that are places inside the States (circles). In Figs. 1 and 2, there are several Token depicted: in the Initial State (in) - in the Inter-Social Area, as well as several tokens in the Config and Act Area. This setting, depicted in Figs. 1 and 2, corresponds to an initial placement of tokens in a transaction that allows all revoke and cancel acts to occur.

Usual Acts in DEMO/PSI Theory Transactions

As depicted in Fig. 1, the usual acts/states in transactions according to DEMO/PSI Theory are: initial state (in); request act/requested state (rq); promise act/promised state (pm); decline act/declined state (dc); declare act/declared state (da); accept act/accepted state (ac) and reject act/rejected state (rj). The execution act, depicted in Fig. 1 is not included in this list. As explained in Sect. 2, the presence of that Act in the Petri-Net, namely when could it occur, introduces many unnecessary complexities and therefore it was remove. The executor can execute whenever he wants. The coordination act of Declare can only occur on the conditions prescribed be the Petri-Net.

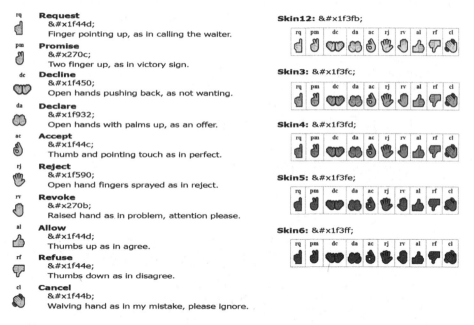

Fig. 3. Proposed graphical characters for representing acts in a DEMO/PSI transaction

Although the shorthand's (rq, pm, dc, da, ac, rj) are familiar to the Enterprise Engineering community, they are a severe barrier to understanding for those outside this research community and even more difficult for users of applications using DEMO/PSI transactions. With the purpose of trying to make the shorthand's more accessible we propose an association between these concepts with a visual representation using Unicode.

We have chosen hand gestures, as depicted if Fig. 3, for each of the acts actor roles can take in a transaction. Using Unicode characters, instead of using images, is a relevant option as it allows all users to use these same characters, as long as they use a font that supports these characters. It also allows some variability as Unicode allows the application of skins to some characters. Applying skins is just putting the skin code immediately after the character code. The code shown in Fig. 3 for each character and for skins is hexadecimal code formatted for HTML display (starts with "&#x", and ends with ";"). For example, for the character Thumbs Up, with Skin 5, 👍, the code would be expressed in HTML as: "&#x 1f44f;&#x 1f3fe;". If used without skin, it will look as the ones presented on the left column of Fig. 3.

The acts Revoke and Cancel are used as prefixes, followed by the corresponding act they are acting upon (rq, pm, da or ac). The Allow and Refuse acts are uses as a second level of prefixes, combined with a Revoke act. For examples, please check Fig. 4.

Software artefacts that use these encodings could tell the history of a transaction by a stream of icons. As examples, please check Fig. 4 where ten histories for distinct transactions. Please notice that acts are ordered by date (from oldest to newest), and acts of the same reversiogenic conversation have the same color.

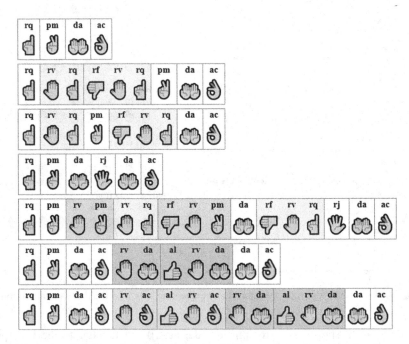

Fig. 4. Seven possible histories of transactions with the sequence of events using the proposed graphical encoding for DEMO/PSI transaction acts.

Multi Actor Role and Color Tokens

The first parameter to configure a transaction is the integer N with the number of actor roles that will take part in it. This Petri-Net does not define an upper limit for the number of actor roles. The rule for moving forward is unanimity, i.e., all participants must agree in the Promise, and all must agree on the Accept. Only one of the participants will do the Request, and likewise only one of the participants will do the Declare. The remaining participants decide on the outcome. If one is against it, it will not move forward. The Petri-Net does not prevent that the same participant performs both the Request and the Declare. We believe this to be an improvement to the existing solutions. All participants, either two or twenty must agree in the Promise and in the Accept to reach the accepted state. The configuration for the transaction may establish constraints on which actor role can do what.

The DEMO/PSI Transaction establishes fixed roles (Initiator; Executor). In previous works [7, 10] we have stated that this lack of flexibility is something that would be beneficial to improve.

The way to distinguish different actors in the Petri-Net is by assigning a different color to each participant. It does not have to be a color. We use the color reference as coloured Petri-Nets is a custom use in the literature. It could just be a distinct number in the tokens according to the actor role identifier. Colored tokens will be used on the Acknowledge Area and the Permit and Decision Area, described below in the Horizontal Area description.

Cardinality Semantics for Inbound Arrows and Outbound Arrows

The proposed Petri-Net requires the use of distinct conditions for inbound arrows and token production rules for the outbound arrows. These alternatives are identified by the labeled used on each arrow. All arrows in the Petri-Net have labels.

For the inbound arrows, those that check conditions and consume tokens the possible labels are:

- "1" – A token of any color must exist to allow the Act to occur, that token will be consumed. It the token color is black any actor can do the act.
- "0" – The Act can only occur if there is no token in the referred State.
- "+" – At least one token of any color must exist so that the Act can occur. Only an Actor Role of a color in that state can Act. All tokens will be consumed.
- "*" – The Act can occur with zero or more tokens, i.e., it can always take place. All tokens, of all colors, if any exist, will be consumed if the Act occurs.
- "N − 1" – Having N as the number of Actor Roles, established for this transaction at configuration time, the Act can occur if there are N − 1 tokens, of any color.

For the outbound arrows, those that produce tokens the possible labels are:

- "1a" – Produce one token of the Actor Role color.
- "1i" – Produce one token of the Actor Role color.
- "1d" – Produce one token of the Actor Role color that performed the Declare act.
- "1b" – Produce one token of color black.
- "N − 1i" – Produce N − 1 tokens, one of each color assigned to the Actor Roles, except for the color assigned to the Actor Role that performed the Request Act.
- "N − 1d" – Produce N − 1 tokens, one of each color assigned to the Actor Roles, except for the color assigned to the Actor Role that performed the Declare Act.
- "N − 1a" – Produce N − 1 tokens, one of each color assigned to the Actor Roles, except for the color assigned to the Actor Role that performed the current Act.

- "N − 1o" – Produce N − 1 tokens, one of each color assigned to the Actor Roles, except for the color assigned to the Actor Role that performed the Request Act.
- "»" – Special powerful semantic with multiple actions to be performed: Remove all tokes from all Inter-Social Area; Remove tokens for Acknowledge Area for posterior acts (in the happy flow sequence); Remove tokens for permit revokes for current and posterior acts (in the happy flow sequence); add permit cancel for antecedent act of the new Inter-Social state.

Horizontal Areas

The Petri-Net presented in Figs. 1 and 2 lays out Stats and Acts in a logical way. There are horizontal areas: Inter-Social Area (in light red); Acknowledge Area (in green); Config and Act Area (in yellow) and Permit and Decision Area (in red).

The Inter-Social Area only contains states – those that establish in which state the transaction is (ini, rq, dc, pm, da, rj, ac). There are two invariants for this area: (a) Only one of these states has a token, but there is always one of those states with a token; (b) That token is a black token. Black tokens can be used by any actor role. The interpretation for the previous invariants is that a transaction is always in one state, even if there are reversiogenic conversations going on.

The Acknowledge Area only contain pairs of state and act with the same name. From each state there is always a condition (inbound arrow) from the state to the act with the same name, although the cardinality is distinct. More on cardinality below. The acknowledge acts are performed immediately before a change of change in the Inter-Social Area. Only these acts lead to changes in the Inter-Social state, except for the shortcut acts, represented by blue boxes, that exist in the Config and Act Area. In the Acknowledge Area we only use colored tokens and never black tokens. Black tokens can be used in Acts by any actor role, while colored tokens restrict the availability of acts for the actor role assigned to a color.

The Config and Act Area contain all other acts that can be performed by the actor roles. There are eight configuration states in this area, two for each of the acts in the happy flow (rq, pm, da, ac). The two options config the availability of Cancel and Revoke for each of the acts in the happy flow. These configuration states contain black tokens that are placed in these configuration states at startup. Although they may be consumed when an act occurs, it is immediately replaced on the outbound arrows. If in the configuration of the transaction a token is not placed in the Config Cancel «Act» or Config Revoke «Act», then those acts will never become available to occur.

The Permit and Decision Area only contain states, and all states contain colored tokens.

Vertical Lanes

The horizontal areas are quite visible due to background color. The vertical lanes are much less visible. At the bottom of Figs. 1 and 2, there are dark boxes with white text that identify the corresponding vertical lane with a pattern for the three areas above (acknowledge, config and act, and permit and decision). The Inter-Social Area is not considered to be part of the pattern.

There are twelve vertical lanes corresponding to four patterns. If you look the vertical lanes of the same pattern you will notice that the states and acts are placed in same positions. Only the cardinality semantics change for each case.

The first pattern for vertical lanes groups the Request vertical lane and the Declare vertical lane.

The second pattern for vertical lanes groups the Decline/Promise and the Reject/Accept vertical lanes.

The third pattern, with four vertical lanes corresponds to the Revoke «Act», for each of the acts in the happy flow (rq, pm, da, ac).

The fourth and last pattern for vertical lanes is the Cancel «Act». There is an instance of the pattern for each of the acts on the happy flow (rq, pm, da, ac).

Network – Several Instances

In a distributed system there can always be races. Races occur when two acts happen at a very close time and due to propagation time through the networks can reach destination in a different order that it occurred. In this model, races are only relevant for changing state in the Inter-Social Area. If a race occurs, i.e. if two state changes occur within, for example 30 s, it should take precedence the state that is prior in the happy flow path (in $<$ rq $<$ dc $<$ pm $<$ da $<$ rj $<$ ac).

Acknowledge

The chosen visual Character for Acknowledge is the hexadecimal code for HTML "&#x 1f44f;" 👏, that is similar to clapping hands, or holding something, depicted with Skin12. As stated previously, the Acknowledge for Acts is what makes the Act take place, therefore we do not need to depict the Acknowledge in history sequences, like the ones shown on Fig. 4, because they should only be part of history when the Acknowledge happens.

A Social Act can only be assumed to exist in the Inter-Social Area when more than one Actor Role acknowledge its existence. Otherwise it wouldn't be social, but private.

Configure Cancel and Revoke

There have been found cases that remove the option to Cancel or Revoke or both as a requirement by law. The difference between the Cancel and the Revoke is that the Cancel is unilateral, while the Revoke requires agreement. The configuration allows to establish for each act which is available.

It would be possible to change this configuration, allowing or removing the token from the configuration for the Act, during the execution of the Petri-Net. This would allow to implement situations where an Actor Role has the right to unilaterally Cancel an act for a period of time, and after than time it is only possible to do so through agreement. The current solution does not provide full flexibility, as it only allows to Cancel «Act» until a subsequent act takes place. However this was what was agreed on 2017 EEWC.

Shortcuts

There are three shortcuts depicted on Figs. 1 and 2. They are presented in blue boxes, and the Acts they shortcut are presented in blue next to those boxes. These shortcuts follow the requirements established in 2017 EEWC. The only difference to what was said on Sect. 2 is that there are now acknowledge acts in the sequence.

4 Critical Analysis

We perform validation for ensuring the correctness of the proposed Petri-Net through the implementation of a prototype available at: http://www.duarte-gouveia.info/phd/ 2018/. We did not found tools that could accept the complex semantic we have used for our inbound and outbound arrows. Having a tested tool could help us on the validation of reachability, liveliness and other properties for Petri-Nets. Building our own validation tool would not give us enough validation as that tool would have to be tested with other Petri-Nets first.

We are aware that some researchers in this community do not "like" the idea that some transactions could have more than two participants. Some argument that they are not needed, others that there is no theory to support that claim, others that the same effect can be achieved with sub-transactions or with collectively fulfilling an actor role. We have shown in previous works [11, 12], based on the law and on real world examples, that although most transactions are among two actor role, there are cases where we need transactions with more actor roles. The researchers that do not agree with the need of more than can benefit from this work by setting $N = 2$ in configuration and keep their beliefs intact.

In several examples DEMO/PSI transactions have shown lack of flexibility on which actor role performs, when reality shows that the actor role Requesting or Declaring is not the one prescribed by the theory. The typical answer for that problem is stating that the actor role is performing that act through delegation, but the model does not provide any hint on how that can be brought to real world implementation of software artefacts. The proposed solution is more flexible, allowing any of the participants to take the initiative, but if requiring unanimity. If one of the participants Declines or Rejects, the transaction gets into Declined or Rejected mode independently of the decision of others.

The proposed solution only works for unanimity decisions, further work could be done to have more flexible voting systems.

The proposed solution does not address the problem of some participants dropping during execution, or new participants coming in. It assumes the number of participants is stable across the execution. Further research is needed to find out when can those changes can happen. We think it is possible to change the number of participants during the transaction without any problem if we do not have any token is the states in the Acknowledge Area and in the Permit and Decision Area. Further research is needed.

5 Conclusion and Future Work

We believe that this work is a substantial contribution for bringing the full DEMO/PSI transaction pattern closer to a software artefact. It complies with the requirements settled in the 2017 EEWC PSI Theory Technical Session.

This work introduces novel contributions like the flexibility of the Actor Roles performing the acts and the ability to handle more than two actor roles. It introduces configuration issues to make the DEMO/PSI transaction pattern more adaptable to software artefacts for real organizations.

The validation for proposed Petri-Net was validated through a prototype. Several other short comings for this research were addressed in the critical analysis and several topics for future research were presented.

Acknowledgments. This work was partially funded by FCT/MCTES LARSyS (UID/EEA/ 50009/2013 (2015–2017)).

 This work was developed with financial support from ARDITI (Agência Regional para o Desenvolvimento da Investigação, Tecnologia e Inovação), in the context of project M14-20 09-5369-FSE-000001- Bolsa de Doutoramento.

References

1. Dietz, J.L.G.: Enterprise Ontology – Theory and Methodology. Springer, Heidelberg (2006). https://doi.org/10.1007/3-540-33149-2
2. Dietz, J.L.G.: The PSI theory – understanding human collaboration (v4.3) (2017). https:// www.researchgate.net/publication/320298882_The_PSI_theory_-_understanding_human_ collaboration/citations. Accessed 25 May 2018
3. https://en.wikipedia.org/wiki/Petri_net. Accessed 23 Apr 2018
4. Van Kervel, S.J.H.: Ontology driven enterprise information systems engineering. Doctoral dissertation, TU Delft, Delft University of Technology (2012)
5. Op't Land, M., Krouwel, Marien R., van Dipten, E., Verelst, J.: Exploring normalized systems potential for Dutch MoD's agility. In: Harmsen, F., Grahlmann, K., Proper, E. (eds.) PRET 2011. LNBIP, vol. 89, pp. 110–121. Springer, Heidelberg (2011). https://doi.org/10. 1007/978-3-642-23388-3_5
6. Krouwel, M.R., Op't Land, M.: Combining DEMO and normalized systems for developing agile enterprise information systems. In: Albani, A., Dietz, Jan L.G., Verelst, J. (eds.) EEWC 2011. LNBIP, vol. 79, pp. 31–45. Springer, Heidelberg (2011). https://doi.org/10.1007/978-3-642-21058-7_3
7. Gouveia, D., Aveiro, D.: Two protocols for DEMO engines: PSI or Tell&Agree. In: CIAO DC (2015)
8. Gouveia, D.: EEWC PSI Theory Technical Session (2017)
9. Skotnica, M., van Kervel, Steven J.H., Pergl, R.: A DEMO machine - a formal foundation for execution of demo models. In: Aveiro, D., Pergl, R., Guizzardi, G., Almeida, J.P., Magalhães, R., Lekkerkerk, H. (eds.) EEWC 2017. LNBIP, vol. 284, pp. 18–32. Springer, Cham (2017). https://doi.org/10.1007/978-3-319-57955-9_2
10. Gouveia, D., Aveiro, D.: Core component of communication. In: Enterprise Engineering Working Conference (2016)
11. Gouveia, D., Aveiro, D.: DEMO/PSI theory and the law of the land. In: Aveiro, D., Pergl, R., Guizzardi, G., Almeida, J.P., Magalhães, R., Lekkerkerk, H. (eds.) EEWC 2017. LNBIP, vol. 284, pp. 50–65. Springer, Cham (2017). https://doi.org/10.1007/978-3-319-57955-9_4
12. Gouveia, D., Aveiro, D.: Modeling exchange agreements with DEMO/PSI and core component of communication. In: Reinhartz-Berger, I., Gulden, J., Nurcan, S., Guédria, W., Bera, P. (eds.) BPMDS/EMMSAD-2017. LNBIP, vol. 287, pp. 220–236. Springer, Cham (2017). https://doi.org/10.1007/978-3-319-59466-8_14

On Teaching

Towards a Multi-stage Strategy to Teach Enterprise Modelling

Henderik A. Proper[1,3](✉) , Marija Bjeković[1], Bas van Gils[2],
and Stijn J. B. A. Hoppenbrouwers[4]

[1] Luxembourg Institute of Science and Technology (LIST), Belval, Luxembourg
e.proper@acm.org, marija.bjekovic@list.lu
[2] Strategy Alliance, Lelystad, The Netherlands
bas.vangils@strategy-alliance.com
[3] University of Luxembourg, Belval, Luxembourg
[4] HAN University of Applied Sciences, Arnhem, The Netherlands
stijn.hoppenbrouwers@han.nl

Abstract. This paper is concerned with the teaching of enterprise modelling. Enterprise models play an increasingly important role in society. In general, such models are not created as mere "one off" artefacts. They rather have a life of their own, covering a broad range of uses (from analysis and understanding, via simulation and design, to execution and monitoring), while involving an even broader variety of stakeholders/audiences. In our view, this increased use of, and even increased dependence on, enterprise models, also makes it important to teach people how to model well.

The aim of this paper is therefore twofold. Firstly, it aims to identify key challenges in teaching enterprise modelling. Secondly, it also aims to provide the humble beginnings of a multi-stage strategy to teach enterprise modelling, meeting these challenges. Both are rooted on a theoretical perspective of modelling, as well as practical experiences. We also reflect on the need for future experimentation and theoretical underpinning of the suggested teaching strategy.

Keywords: Enterprise modelling · Teaching enterprise modelling

1 Introduction

Enterprise models play an increasingly important role in society. In general, such models are not created as mere "one off" artefacts. They rather have a life of their own, covering a broad range of uses (from analysis and understanding, via simulation and design, to execution and monitoring), while involving an even broader variety of stakeholders/audiences. In our view, this increased use of,

This work has been partially sponsored by the *Fonds National de la Recherche Luxembourg* (www.fnr.lu), via the ValCoLa and CoBALab projects.

and even increased dependence on, enterprise models, also makes it important to teach people how to model well.

In line with this, the aim of this paper is twofold. Firstly, it aims to identify some of the key challenges in teaching enterprise modelling. Secondly, it also aims to provide the humble beginnings of a multi-stage strategy to teach enterprise modelling, (at least partially) meeting these challenges. Both will be rooted on a theoretical perspective of modelling, as well as taking on board practical experiences.

The theoretical perspective concerns a fundamental understanding of (enterprise) models, modelling, and (domain specific) modelling languages, also involving earlier work by the authors. The practical experiences involve the experiences of the authors[1] in both teaching enterprise modelling, and real-world experiences in enterprise modelling.

The remainder of this paper is structured as follows. Section 2 will discuss the aforementioned theoretical perspective on enterprise modelling, while also relating this to our experiences in teaching and modelling in practice. This results in some of the key challenges we see towards the teaching of enterprise modelling, that inspired us in designing the suggested teaching strategy. In moving towards this suggested strategy, Sect. 3 builds on this by introducing the concept of grounded enterprise modelling. This involves the idea of considering an enterprise model in a purpose/domain specific modelling language as being *grounded* on a conceptual model in a more generic modelling language. In doing so, we will also integrate our experiences [35,36] in co-designing the ArchiMate enterprise (architecture) modelling language [31]. Based on these inputs, Sect. 4 then provides the outline of an initial multi-stage strategy to teach enterprise modelling. Before concluding, Sect. 5 reflects on the need for future experimentation with, and theoretical underpinning of, the suggested teaching strategy.

2   A Fundamental View on Enterprise Modelling

When discussing strategies on teaching enterprise modelling, it is important to first establish our fundamental view on conceptual modelling, and enterprise modelling in particular.

2.1   Models and Modelling

We understand *models* as essentially being means of communication about some domain of interest, and the *process of modelling* as a communication-driven process led by a pragmatic focus [23]. This view is inspired by different related research tackling the fundamental modelling aspects such as [19,47,54–56], as well as our own earlier work [27,30,36]. In line with this, we consider a model to

---

[1] All authors have, next to their work in research, also worked in industry, doing different assignments involving modelling, and/or have been teaching conceptual modelling to students and/or practitioners.

be: *"an artefact acknowledged by an observer as representing some domain for a particular purpose"* [8].

The *observer* in this definition refers to the group of people involving both the model creators as well as the model's audience. On one extreme, it can refer to the entire society, while on the other extreme, it can refer to an individual. Though it may not be the general rule, in an enterprise modelling context it is very often the case that model creators are at the same time its audience.

Similarly to [19], we define *domain* as any "part" or "aspect" of the world *considered relevant by the observer*. The notions of *world* and *domain* are construed in the constructivist sense, allowing for actual, past, future and possible worlds. This emphasis is in particular relevant when considering domains outside of physically observable objects, which is typical for enterprise modelling.

The *purpose* of a model is often considered as the main discriminant of the added value of a model [47,54,55]. We understand *purpose* as aggregating two interrelated dimensions: (1) the *domain* that the model (should) pertain to, and (2) the intended *usage* of the model by its intended *audience*. The purpose thus provides the basis for identifying required qualities of the specific model [12, 15] (whereby the qualities may be defined in terms of e.g. Krogstie's SEQUAL framework [32,33]).

The purpose of a model does not only define requirements on the scoping of the represented domain, but also on the actual representation in relation to its intended use and audience. In practice, we observe that when the purpose of a model is not explicitly considered and/or not made clear in the modelling process, modellers also lack clear criteria to scope the domain/model. Especially novice modellers, then run the risk of getting "out of control". To ensure one remains focussed on the purpose of the model, it seems relevant to teach learners about agile principles [5], in particular when applied to modelling [2]. This leads to a first challenge in teaching learners how to model:

Challenge 1: *Learners should become aware of the (guiding) role of a model's purpose.*

By stating that a model is an *artefact*, we have chosen to exclude *conceptions* [19], or so-called mental models, from the scope of our definition. Conceptions are *abstractions* of the world under consideration, adopted from a certain perspective, and indeed share this property with models. However, a conception resides in the mind of a person holding it, and as such is not directly accessible to another human being. To communicate the conception, it has to be externalised. While conceptions reside in mental space, models are necessarily *represented* in physical/digital space.

The resulting situation is depicted in Fig. 1. Given a purpose P, an observer will have a *conception* C_D (in their mind) of the modelled domain D, while some model M is intended to be a *representation* of the domain D, and as such should be the digital/physical *manifestation* of the conception. The purpose P influences the conception of the observer, as well as the needed *representation* and *manifestation*.

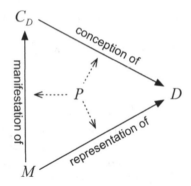

Fig. 1. Fundamental understanding of modelling

Figure 2 refines this, by making explicit that the observer not only has a conception C_D of the modelled domain in their mind, but also of the created model C_M, as well as the purpose C_P. This is an important point, as it underlines the fact that while modelling, multiple observers need to align their conceptions of the domain being modelling, the purpose for which the model is (to be) created, and the actual model itself. This is of particular relevance in the context of collaborative modelling [4, 25, 41, 49].

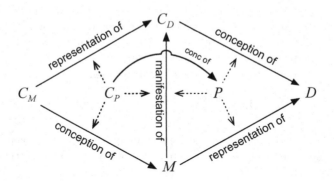

Fig. 2. Conceptions in modelling

Building on the above definition of models, we define a conceptual model to be: *a model where its purpose involves a need to capture knowledge about the represented domain.* In other words, a model answering a need to understand and/or articulate the workings and/or structure of a domain. Such a model needs to reflect human cognition in that it concerns concepts, their relationships, and relevant properties, which makes it a *concept*ual model. An *enterprise model* can be now be defined as a *conceptual model that represent some part and/or aspect of an organisation/enterprise.*

2.2   The Role of a Modelling Language

With this understanding of enterprise models in place, we can turn our attention to modelling languages. As defined in [6,7], we regard a modelling language as having a *linguistic function* and a *representational function*.

The *linguistic function* refers to the ability of a modelling language to frame the discourse about a domain and shaping the observer's conception of a domain [44]. In this regard, a modelling language should provide a *linguistic structure*, involving a specific classification of concepts to be used in the discourse about the world (the embodied *world view*, or *Weltanschauung*). This linguistic structure will differ between e.g. a modelling language for value modelling and one for process modelling.

The *representational function* refers to the ability of the language to express the conceived domain in a purposeful model. This generally involves a *representation system* involving both an abstract and a concrete syntax of the modelling language.

As discussed above, the purpose of a model is often considered as the main discriminant of the added value of a model [47,54,55]. This also entails that if a model, in line with its purpose, needs to be represented in some modelling language, then there has to be an alignment between this purpose, and both the *linguistic structure* and the *representation system* of the chosen modelling language. For example, when the purpose of a given model is to provide senior management with insights into the value exchanges between partners in a business network, then the linguistic function should allow for the expression of concepts such as value, value exchange, and partners. At the same time, the representational function should allow for a representation of a model that is suitable towards the target audience (e.g. senior management).

When learning a modelling language, learners have to master both functions of the language. This means, they have to learn both the *linguistic structure* and the *representation function*. In addition, learners need to learn to judge, for a given modelling language, the aptness of these functions to a modelling purpose at hand.

It is important to acknowledge that the *linguistic structure*, being its essential world view (*Weltanschauung*), may not only limit the freedom of what can be expressed in a model. It may even limit, or at least influence, the way in which modellers observe the domain. This may lead to situations where a modelling language may "feel unnatural", in the sense that the linguistic structure puts to much restriction on a modeller's "freedom of expression". At an anecdotical level, this corresponds to the *hammer* and *nail* paradigm. At a more fundamental level, it corresponds to the notion of linguistic relativity [57][2], which states that the structure of a language determines, or greatly influences, the modes of thought and behaviour characteristic of the culture/context in which it is spoken. As underlying challenges for teaching modelling, we see:

---

[2] More colloquially also known as the Sapir-Whorf hypothesis.

Challenge 2: *Make modellers aware of the role of the modelling language, and its possible costs and benefits towards the purpose of a given model.*

In our experience, learners of an enterprise modelling languages tend to struggle, in parallel, with both the complexities of the (targeted) enterprise modelling language, and getting to grips with the modelling problems that they are asked to solve as part of the learning. This entails figuring out what the main elements in the domain to be modelled are, and then trying to convert those insights into a model conform the modelling language that is used [18]. As such, it seems relevant to distinguish between: (1) learning to conceptualise a domain, in line with a given purpose for the model, and (2) learning how to represent this conceptualisation in terms of the (linguistic structure and representation system of the) target enterprise modelling language.

Challenge 3: *Separation of concerns in learning how to conceptualise a domain, and learning how to represent this in the target modelling language.*

We also find that at the start of the learning process, computer-based tooling tends to get in the way of the learning process. This suggests the need to make a distinction between learning to model, in the given enterprise modelling language, and the use of a supporting modelling tool.

Challenge 4: *Separation of concerns in learning to model using the target modelling language, and the use of an associated modelling tool.*

We certainly do not claim that the above challenges are all challenges facing the learners of enterprise modelling. First of all, they certainly do not include the challenges of e.g. collaborative modelling [4,25,41,49], or the challenges of eliciting knowledge from domain experts and/or stakeholders. However, we do see the above challenges as being at the core of the basic skills needed for (enterprise) modelling.

3   Grounded Enterprise Modelling

In this Section, we introduce the notion of *grounded enterprise modelling*. We suggest this notion as a way to meet Challenge 3, i.e. the need to separate: (1) learning to conceptualise a domain, and (2) learning how to represent this conceptualisation in the target enterprise modelling language. It also will, in our view, *help* meet Challenge 2 on making modellers aware of the role of the modelling language, as well as Challenge 1 regarding the awareness of the purpose of a model.

Inspired by (1) earlier experiences with the need to better manage domain concepts during software and/or information system development [9,28,43] (2) work on explicitly identifying the need to introduce modelling concepts into a modelling language [30,44], as well as (3) the way in which the ArchiMate language was designed in terms of a series of layers with increasingly more specific modelling concepts [35,36], we developed the idea to use generic conceptual models to ground other, more specific, models on top of a semantically rich understanding of the domain in terms of a fact-based model [42,46]. In developing this approach, we also conducted some initial experiments in grounding enterprise models, involving (1) activity models [14,16], (2) system dynamics models [58,59], and (3) architecture principles [10].

Grounding enterprise models starts with the observation that enterprise models, being conceptual models, involve *concepts* and their *relations*, as well as a *typing* of these in terms of modelling constructs offered by the modelling language. Consider, as an example, the ArchiMate [31] model as shown in Fig. 3. It contains, a.o., the concepts Patient, Doctor, Form, Examine and Diagnose. The icons in the boxes indicate wether a concept is a *role* (e.g. Patient), *activity* (e.g. Examine) or a passive *object* (e.g. Form). The line with the double dots is a so-called *assignment* relation. For example, Doctor and Patient are assigned to the Examine activity. The arrows correspond to triggering rules, so e.g. the Examine activity is triggered by the Register activity.

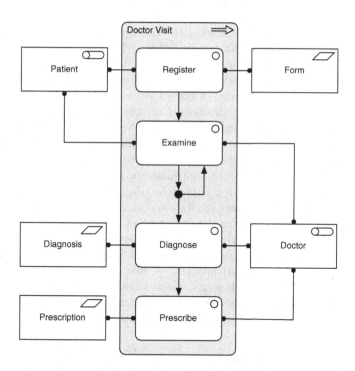

Fig. 3. Example ArchiMate model of a Doctor Visit

In line with Challenge 3, the key idea is to separate learning how to conceptualise a domain, from learning how to represent this in the target modelling language. We propose to do this by first teaching leaners how to create a conceptual model of a domain in terms of *concepts* and *relations*, and then teaching them how to "interpret" such a conceptual model in terms of the modelling concepts offered by the target language.

Towards the first step, i.e. learning to create a conceptual (domain) model, we have found that using a fact-based modelling approach [3, 20, 39] brings four key advantages, as well as two possible disadvantages.

Firstly, fact-based modelling approaches tend to use a simple (and generic) linguistic structure involving (1) a distinction between *types* and *instances*, (2) three kinds of *objects*: *entities*, *labels* and *facts*, as well as (3) *roles* played by *objects* in *facts*. In addition, generalisation and specialisation of types is possible in terms of sub/super types. The *objects* are used to express the concepts of a domain, while *roles* represent the relationships between concepts, in particular between objects playing a role in facts. This means that initially, learners only need to work with a small set of constructs.

Secondly, some of the fact based approaches provide a detailed procedure for modelling [3, 20], which starts by verbalising examples in natural language, and then proceeds with the identification of types, and finally involves the identification of constraints/rules governing the population of the identified types. This provides learners with guidance during the conceptualisation of domains.

Thirdly, fact-based modelling approaches, with their orientation towards facts, are strongly rooted in natural language. Verbalisations in natural language of concrete facts observed in/about the domain to be modelled are used as a starting point for modelling. In our experience, this also helps learners in their efforts to master conceptualisation. Learners and practitioners indeed find the verbalisation of examples rather laborious. Nevertheless, as argued by [20], and supported by our own observations in teaching and modelling in practice, these verbalisations really bring essential conceptualisation decisions to the fore. For learners, this step is, therefore, quite important.

Fourthly, fact-based modelling approaches do not require modellers to make an immediate distinction between entities and attributes. This allows modellers, in particular learners, to explore the structure of a domain first, before having to make a decision on the relative importance between object types.

Using a fact-based modelling approach as a general conceptual modelling approach may also entail disadvantages. A first possible disadvantage is the fact that, similar to ER [17], these approaches have initially been developed for the purpose of conceptual database design. However, as reported in e.g. [26, 43, 53], fact-based modelling can indeed also be used for general domain/ontology modelling.

A second possible disadvantage is the fact that the graphical notation, i.e. the *representation system*, of fact-based approaches tends to be rather elaborate. In the example we give below (see e.g. Fig. 5), one can indeed observe how the graphical representation of constraints result in diagrams with a high visual complexity. Firstly, the constraints themselves, in terms of the dotted lines (see e.g. (c) and (d) in Fig. 5) used, arrows, etc., add complexity. Secondly, since graphically expressed constraints need to be "anchored" unambiguously to the roles within fact types, it becomes necessary to include an explicit graphical representation of roles (e.g. by the so-called "role boxes").

At the same time, however, as argued by Moody [38], it is important to realise that a graphical model needs to reflect the complexities of the domain being modelled. Moody motivates this point in terms of Shannon and Weaver's information theory [52], in the sense that a model will need to reflect all information one wants to capture from a domain (given a modelling purpose). As such, one can only aim to avoid unnecessary complexity in the graphical model, where the necessity of complexity depends on the domain being modelled as well as the purpose for modelling. In this sense, the potential disadvantage of the graphical notation of fact-based approaches can be turned into an advantage, by making learners explicitly reflect about the *purpose* of the model, and the needed level of detail (and complexity) of the model and its graphical representation, and showing how (the graphical constructs/abbreviations) of higher level enterprise modelling languages enable them to more clearly focus the key "message" of the model in line with its purpose.

One could, of course, also choose to "hide" the (necessary) graphical complexity by using simpler graphical models and formulating the constraints in a (structured) textual format. This would be the approach as suggested by the SBVR [39] standard for business rules. This, however, would only transfer the inherent complexity of the constraints from the graphical representation of the model to the textual representation.

As part of the learning process, it could be beneficial to confront learners with different *concrete syntaxes* for the same *abstract syntax* in the context of basically the same representation system.

In the remainder of this Section, we will highlight the notion of grounded enterprise modelling, by grounding the example of Fig. 3 using an ORM [20] fact-based model. Of course, enterprise modelling in general involves many more different models, including goal models, value models, organisational structures, etc, that can be expressed in even so many different enterprise modelling languages. In this sense, the example below only provides an illustration of the concept of grounded enterprise modelling.

In Fig. 4, we see an ORM model[3] dealing with patients visiting a doctor. Patients fill out forms in order to register, they can be examined by a doctor, doctors produce diagnoses, as well as prescribe possibly prescriptions.

What is missing in Fig. 4 is the temporal order in which these facts occur, as well as the fact that these activities take place in the context of a Doctor Visit. Adding these aspects, will of course increase the complexity of the graphical model, and as such, prepare learners for the need to use a more purpose-oriented notation. This leads to the situation as shown in Fig. 5.

In adding a temporal semantics to ORM [11,45] we assume that the regular ORM constraints (cardinality, etc.) need to apply at each individual moment in time. So, a mandatory role constraint, such as the one marked with (a), should

---

[3] To keep the diagram clean, we have omitted all of the so-called reference schemes, which identify how e.g. a Doctor or a Patient is referred to in this domain.

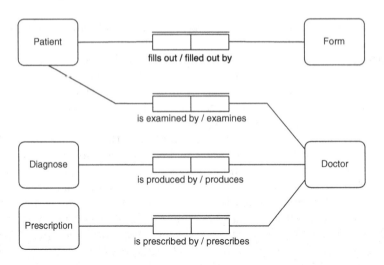

Fig. 4. Doctor Visit example; ORM grounding

apply at each individual moment in time. In other words, if a Register occurence takes place at some moment in time, then (also during that period in time), it must take place in the context of some Doctor Visit.

Normally, ORM uniqueness constraints are represented with a single bar over the involved roles. Now, consider the uniqueness constraint marked with (b). If this one would have been marked with only a single bar, it would have signified that at each moment in time, a Register occurence can only be for one Doctor Visit. This would still make it possible for one Register occurence during some time period T to be assigned to two different Doctor Visits, but at non coinciding intervals in time T_1 and T_2, with $T_1, T_2 \subset T$. The double bar, therefore, signifies that the Registrer occurence can be part of a Doctor Visit once, ever. The patient can of course register for *an other* Doctor Visit by filling out *an other* form.

The required temporal order of events is depicted with an open arrow connecting the involved roles. See, for example, the one marked with (c). This states that for Doctor Visit, we cannot see a Register occurrence after we have started to see (an) Examine occurence(s). We also see (the open arrow further below) that (the way it is modelled in the *example*) after a Diagnose occurence has taken place, for a given Doctor Visit, we can no longer see further Examine occurrences in the context of *this* Doctor Visit. Note also, that a Doctor Visit is only allowed to have one Diagnose occurence, but multiple Examine occurrences, as signified by the double bars.

The constraint pattern marked (d) is also of interest. It insures that the Patient filling out the Form is also the Patient who is to be examined (in the context of one Doctor Visit). Similarly the Doctor doing the diagnosing is also required to be the Doctor writing the prescription.

The process flow as depicted in Fig. 5 does not involve split/join junctions. Such structures could, however, also be modelled using similar temporal

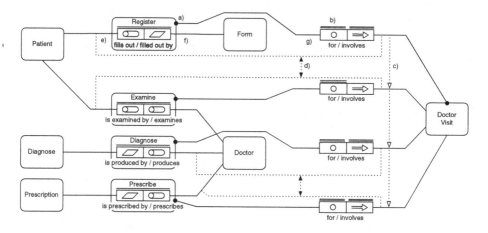

Fig. 5. Doctor Visit example with temporal ordering and ArchiMate mapping

constraints. However, advanced workflow/temporal-ordering patterns, are probably best left to a dedicated modelling language [1]. In grounding enterprise models, we think it is wisest to focus on grounding the main conceptual structure of the domain.

Figure 5 also shows a classification, by means of icons, of roles in terms of the modelling concepts from the ArchiMate language [31]. Doing the latter, provides a transition from capturing the domain in a conceptual model, and mapping the concepts and relations to the modelling constructs offered by the targeted enterprise modelling language. Consider, for instance, the role marked with (e). When a Patient fills out a form, then they are, in terms of ArchiMate enacting a *business role*. The form, see (f), then plays the passive role of a *business object*. The Register occurrence, see (g), plays the role of a *business activity* in the context of a composed *business process* Doctor Visit.

In the case of larger examples, even when limited to educational settings, diagrams in the style of Fig. 5 can easily become rather large. Therefore, we would suggest to also use a graphical abbreviation in the ORM diagrams, in terms of a State Sequence (complex) object type, as used on the left hand side of Fig. 6. Using such a graphical abbreviation, would also "prepare" learners for the need to switch to a more dedicated graphical notation for the modelling purpose at hand. The version represented on the right hand side, would actually result in a more ArchiMate-alike notation, while maintaining the more explicit verbalisation of the original ORM diagram, as well as the addition of the more specific constraints on role participations of Doctors and Patients

4   A Strategy to Teach Enterprise Modelling

In this Section, we highlight the suggested teaching strategy. As mentioned before, it is to be regarded as the first humble beginnings of such a strategy.

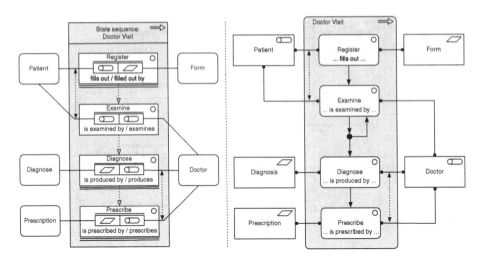

Fig. 6. Doctor Visit example, notational variations

As such, we certainly do not (cl)aim it to be a complete teaching method, including suggested teaching materials, evaluation points, etc. The suggested strategy involves five stages, the first four of which cover the four steps in which we also introduced the Doctor Visit example in Sect. 3. The first two stages focus on learning conceptual modelling in its basic form, while the next two stages work towards the target enterprise modelling language. The final stage aims to increase the awareness of the role of purpose in modelling.

Stage 1: Time-Agnostic Domain Modelling
At this stage, learners should learn basic conceptualisation skills. To this end, it is important for them to use a modelling approach that has a lightweight linguistic structure. As argued before, we consider fact-based modelling quite suitable for to purpose.

Most fact based approaches provide an elaborate procedure for conceptual modelling [3, 20]. In our teaching activities, we usually use the conceptual schema design procedure (CSDP) from ORM [20]. As its name suggest, this procedure was initially designed for the conceptual design of databases. However, the procedure can also be used when developing general domain models/ontologies. In its original form, the outline of this procedure reads:

1. Transform familiar examples into elementary facts, and apply quality checks.
2. Draw the fact types, and apply a population check.
3. Check for entity types that should be combined, and note any arithmetic derivations.
4. Add uniqueness constraints, and check arity of fact types.
5. Add mandatory role constraints, and check for logical derivations.
6. Add label, set comparison and subtyping constraints.
7. Add other constraints and perform final checks.

Step 1 may seem laborious. Nevertheless, as argued by [20], and supported by our own observations in teaching and modelling in practice, these verbalisations really bring essential conceptualisation decisions to the fore, also aiding in learning to model.

In the context of general domain modelling, one has to take specific care in step 3. Towards database design, one might want to combine entity types for "optimisation" [21] purposes, that, for general domain modelling purposes, might better be kept as individual entity types. Furthermore, steps 4 and 5 also involve the selection of "reference schemes" that define how instances of entity types are to be identified in terms of values/labels. While this, indeed, makes sense in the context of database design, this is not always strictly necessary for general domain modelling [26,43,53].

During this stage of teaching, it makes sense to have learners first do assignments on the conceptualisation of basic examples, and then move on to assignments involving examples of the domains that will (later) be modelled in the target enterprise modelling language (such as ArchiMate). However, at this first stage, it is advisable for learners to not yet (have to) concern themselves too much with temporal aspects.

Stage 2: Time-Aware Domain Modelling

At the second stage, it is advised that learners become aware of the role of time, in particular towards the modelling of behaviour in a domain. This means that learners should learn about the concept of time in conceptual modelling, as well as constraints (see Fig. 5) dealing with temporal ordering and cardinality over time.

During this stage, learners should apply the procedure as learned in the previous stage to examples involving behaviour, while then also taking temporal constraints into consideration, in particular an initial understanding of e.g. process flows.

We suggest that learners start by focussing on the basic activities in such a domain, and apply the ORM procedure for these first. This would result in models as shown in Fig. 4. After this, they can apply the ORM procedure again to complement this model with more complex process aggregations, such as it is shown at the top of Fig. 5. This may also lead to modifications of the first model.

Stage 3: Attribute Roles with Concepts from the Target Modelling Language

At this stage, learners should start to think in terms of the modelling constructs of the "target" enterprise modelling language. With a larger (in terms of number of modelling concepts) language, such as ArchiMate, it makes sense to split this into several levels of specificity. For ArchiMate, following its anatomy [35], this could be:

1. *The layer (Business/Information/Technology) at which a modelling element can be positioned.* In other words, ask learners to mark which object types and in the ORM model belong at which of the three layers.

2. *The involvement of concepts in activities: the actual behaviour, a passive involvement (patiens), or an active involvement (aegens).* This means learners should be able to mark which object types pertain to behaviour, and then identify the kind of involvement by marking the associated roles.
3. *The marking of systemic borders in terms of internal concepts, and interfacing concepts (i.e. interface and service).* This involves learners marking which roles/object types are internal, and which ones are external.
4. *The full set of concepts of the ArchiMate language.* This entails a further specialisation of the marking so far towards the actual concepts of the ArchiMate language.

Note that the above process may lead learners to further refine their conceptual model of the domain, as it may (and for didactic purposes should) also lead to further conceptual insight into the domains being modelled.

The suggested overall process would now be: (1) create basic domain model, (2) add temporal aspects in terms of additional object types and constraints, (3) label the resulting model with a mapping to the constructs of the target language.

Stage 4: Convert Model to Target Language, and Complete

This stage requires the learners to express the models in the target enterprise modelling language. Initially, assignments should ask learners to go through the entire process from a basic domain model to the final result in the target language.

As a next step, learners can be asked to further complete the model as formulated in the target enterprise modelling language. For example, as already mentioned in Sect. 3, it would certainly go too far for teaching purpose to be able to e.g. "mimic" advanced workflow patterns at a generic conceptual modelling. These can now be added at the level of the target enterprise modelling language.

Stage 5: Awareness of Modelling Purpose and the Influence of Language

At this stage, learners can be confronted with more contextual considerations regarding the context of modelling, and the purpose for modelling.

As discussed in Sect. 2, when the purpose for the creation of an enterprise model is not clear, modellers not always have good criteria to decide on scoping and the needed level of detail. At this stage, we therefore suggest to teach learners about the agile principles [5] and agile modelling [2] on the one hand, and different relevant qualities of models on the other hand [32,33]. Furthermore, using assignments, learners can be asked to reflect on the purpose of a model at hand, and the consequences for scoping of the model the needed modelling strategy, and even the requirements on the modelling language.

With regard to the latter, this would also be a good moment to confront learners with different *concrete syntaxes* for the same *abstract syntax* in the context of basically the same representation system, e.g. with regards to the earlier (Sect. 3) mentioned considerations on the (necessary) complexity in graphical models. This could be supported by assignments, where learners are invited to produce different representations for the same underlying conceptual structures, while reflecting on the suitability of these towards different purposes.

In teaching enterprise modelling, we also have good experiences with learners working in groups. It makes sense for learners to work alone during stage 1 and 2, but once they have acquired a basic level of modelling skils, the interactions involved when working in groups on larger assignments is likely to drive the exploration and learning process, as different views of the group members need to be reconciled.

Especially stages 4 and 5 can really benefit from group based assignments, preferably in combination with some role playing. It is suggested to ensure that the groups jointly articulate the purpose of the model, and the overall modelling strategy to follow.

Within the groups, discussions can be stimulated (e.g. by means of extra questions in the assignments, or by interventions of a lecturer) regarding scoping, purpose of the model, modelling strategy used, concepts of the language, etc. These discussions may take time, but they are likely to prove the joint understanding. See Fig. 7 for an example taken from a recent lecture on ArchiMate modelling.

In general, it is also wise to ask the groups to capture their decisions. On the one hand, this invites the groups to be more explicit in their considerations. It, on the other hand, makes it easier for the lecturers/coaches to give feedback.

Fig. 7. Groups in action

Stage 6: Tooling

Challenge 4 suggests to separate learning to model in the target modelling language, and learning to use an associated modelling tool. During stage 1 to 4, we therefore suggest to avoid the use of such tools, and rather use pen-and-paper based "tooling". This allows learners to focus on first learning to conceptualise (stage 1 and 2), and then focus on getting acquainted with the target enterprise modelling language (stage 3 and 4). We, therefore, suggest to introduce tooling as the last stage of the learning strategy.

Once modellers have gained basic modelling skills (i.e. stages 1 to 5), it would probably be wisest to first use tools that provide modellers with feedback during modelling tasks [48,50,51].

5   Reflection

In this section, we reflect on the validity of the teaching strategy as outlined in Sect. 4, as well as identify required future work. We will do so from four different angles: (1) foundations of modelling, (2) elaboration of the teaching strategy, (3) utilisation of modelling tools that provide feedback during (learning of) modelling, (4) integration with theories of learning, and (5) empirical validation of the proposed learning strategy.

Foundations: Even though Sect. 2 provided a theoretical base for the presented strategy, more theoretical underpinnings of the concepts and ideas would be welcome. Three streams of thought that we would like to combine and/or confront with are (1) the notion of basic level categorisation from Lakoff [34] and (2) earlier work on conceptualisation as a linguistic [24] and cognitive phenomenon [37,60]. Lakoff's notion of basic categories suggest that by the way we have come to experience the world around us, we develop a basic level of categories, that can then be specialised into more refined categories, or generalised towards more abstracted concepts. The underlying mechanics can be useful to provide more fundamental guidance during the initial conceptualisation of domains (stage 1 and 2), in particular to learners. In the same vain, stages 1 and 2 can benefit from fundamental insights into the process of conceptualisation.

Elaboration: As mentioned in Sect. 4, the strategy as outlined in this paper only provides the humble beginnings towards a more elaborate strategy to learn enterprise modelling. As such, more elaboration of the strategy is needed, possibly even resulting in concrete suggestions for teaching materials and tests.

Feedback: In the discussion of Stage 6 of the proposed (overall) learning strategy, we also suggested that, when starting to use software-based modelling tools, it would be wisest to use tools that provide modellers with feedback during modelling tasks. Experiences by other researchers [48,50,51] suggest this may be rather beneficial. This might be combined with strategies to also utilise explicitly captured modelling strategies [13,29], together with additional explanations and feedback.

Theories of Learning: Although the presented strategy, is based on a theoretical underpinning from the perspective of conceptual/enterprise modelling, a theoretical underpinning from a *theories of learning* [22, 40] is lacking. We would expect this to certainly strengthen the theoretical underpinning of the presented strategy

Empirical Validation: The presented strategy is based on the collective experiences of the authors in teaching and practicing enterprise modelling. However, more controlled experiments are certainly called for to test if the suggested strategy provides repeatable benefits in teaching enterprise modelling to learners. *Does it really aid learners in their learning process? Does it lead to better modellers?*

In moving towards such experiments, we foresee two strategies. Firstly, during and after the learning process, learners can be asked to fill out a survey. This will allow us to validate if the suggested learning strategy results in the desired insights and effects with the learners, in particular when these data are combined with the results of the assignments and/or exams. Ideally, these surveys should continue once the learners have started to model in practice. Secondly, it would of course be ideal to have control groups. This would enable comparative experiments (across the learning stages) of two groups of similar learners, whereby one group learns a new enterprise modelling language "the traditional way", and one group using the suggested strategy.

6   Conclusion

In this paper we presented the humble beginnings for a multi-stage strategy to teach enterprise modelling. This strategy is both rooted on a theoretical perspective of enterprise modelling, and conceptual modelling in general, as well as the practical experiences of the authors in teaching and practicing modelling.

The paper briefly discussed our theoretical perspective on conceptual modelling, as well as the basic idea to use generic fact-based conceptual models to underpin more specific enterprise models. Based on these, we then discussed the suggested strategy to teach enterprise modelling, involving five stages, that takes learners from learning basic conceptualisation skills, to gradually being able to interpret the domain in terms of the target enterprise modelling language. The last stage of the strategy involves more advanced topics concerning the purpose of the model, and the modelling context.

Before concluding, we also reflected on the need for further theoretical and empirical underpinning, towards the further validation and elaboration of the presented learning strategy.

As a first next step, we aim to develop tool support for the idea of grounding enterprise models, as discussed in Sect. 3. More specifically, a modelling environment that allows for a gradual "interpretation" [46] of a "flat" conceptual model in terms of a more specific modelling language (such as ArchiMate). This will also enable us to conduct experiments with novice modellers, to validate the expected positive effects of the suggested learning strategy.

References

1. van der Aalst, W.M.P., ter Hofstede, A.H.M., Kiepuszewski, B., Barros, A.P.: Workflow patterns. Distrib. Parallel Databases **14**(1), 5–51 (2003). https://doi.org/10.1023/A:1022883727209
2. Ambler, S.W., Jeffries, R.: Agile Modeling: Effective Practices for Extreme Programming and the Unified Process. Wiley, New York (2002)
3. Bakema, G.P., Zwart, J.P.C., Van der Lek, H.: Fully communication oriented NIAM. In: Proceedings of NIAM-ISDM, vol. 2, pp. 1–35, August 1994
4. Barjis, J.: Collaborative, participative and interactive enterprise modeling. In: Filipe, J., Cordeiro, J. (eds.) ICEIS 2009. LNBIP, vol. 24, pp. 651–662. Springer, Heidelberg (2009). https://doi.org/10.1007/978-3-642-01347-8_54
5. Beck, K., et al.: Manifesto for Agile Software Development (2001). http://www.agilemanifesto.org. Accessed 14 June 2013
6. Bjeković, M., Proper, H.A., Sottet, J.-S.: Embracing pragmatics. In: Yu, E., Dobbie, G., Jarke, M., Purao, S. (eds.) ER 2014. LNCS, vol. 8824, pp. 431–444. Springer, Cham (2014). https://doi.org/10.1007/978-3-319-12206-9_37
7. Bjeković, M., Proper, H.A., Sottet, J.-S.: Enterprise modelling languages. In: Shishkov, B. (ed.) BMSD 2013. LNBIP, vol. 173, pp. 1–23. Springer, Cham (2014). https://doi.org/10.1007/978-3-319-06671-4_1
8. Bjeković, M., Sottet, J.S., Favre, J.M., Proper, H.A.: A framework for natural enterprise modelling. In: Proceedings of the 15th IEEE Conference on Business Informatics (CBI 2013), Vienna, Austria, pp. 79–84. IEEE Computer Society Press, Los Alamitos (2013). https://doi.org/10.1109/CBI.2013.20
9. Bleeker, A.I., Proper, H.A., Hoppenbrouwers, S.J.B.A.: The role of concept management in system development - a practical and a theoretical perspective. In: Grabis, J., Persson, A., Stirna, J. (eds.) Forum Proceedings of the 16th Conference on Advanced Information Systems 2004 (CAiSE 2004), Riga, Latvia, pp. 73–82. Faculty of Computer Science and Information Technology, Riga, Latvia, June 2004
10. van Bommel, P., Buitenhuis, P.G., Hoppenbrouwers, S.J.B.A., Proper, H.A.: Architecture principles - a regulative perspective on enterprise architecture. In: Reichert, M., Strecker, S., Turowski, K. (eds.) Proceedings of the 2nd International Workshop on Enterprise Modelling and Information Systems Architectures (EMISA 2007). Lecture Notes in Informatics, St. Goar am Rhein, Germany, no. 119, pp. 47–60. Gesellschaft für Informatik, Bonn, Germany (2007)
11. van Bommel, P., Frederiks, P.J.M., van der Weide, T.P.: Object-oriented modeling based on logbooks. Comput. J. **39**(9), 793–799 (1996)
12. van Bommel, P., Hoppenbrouwers, S.J.B.A., Proper, H.A., Roelofs, J.: Concepts and strategies for quality of modeling, chap. 9. In: Halpin, T.A., Krogstie, J., Proper, H.A. (eds.) Innovations in Information Systems Modeling. IGI Publishing, Hershey (2008)
13. van Bommel, P., Hoppenbrouwers, S.J.B.A., Proper, H.A.E., van der Weide, T.P.: Exploring modelling strategies in a meta-modelling context. In: Meersman, R., Tari, Z., Herrero, P. (eds.) OTM 2006. LNCS, vol. 4278, pp. 1128–1137. Springer, Heidelberg (2006). https://doi.org/10.1007/11915072_16
14. van Bommel, P., Hoppenbrouwers, S.J.B.A., Proper, H.A., van der Weide, T.P.: On the use of object-role modeling for modeling active domains. In: Research Issues in System Analysis and Design, Databases and Software Development, pp. 123–145. IGI Publishing, Hershey (2007)

15. van Bommel, P., Hoppenbrouwers, S.J.B.A., Proper, H.A., van der Weide, T.P.: QoMo: a modelling process quality framework based on SEQUAL. In: Proper, H.A., Halpin, T.A., Krogstie, J. (eds.) Proceedings of the 12th Workshop on Exploring Modeling Methods for Systems Analysis and Design (EMMSAD 2007), held in conjunction with the 19th Conference on Advanced Information Systems (CAiSE 2007), Trondheim, Norway, pp. 118–127. CEUR-WS.org (2007)
16. van Bommel, P., Hoppenbrouwers, S.J.B.A., Proper, H.A., van der Weide, T.P.: On the use of object-role modelling to model active domains. In: Halpin, T.A., Krogstie, J., Proper, H.A. (eds.) Proceedings of the 13th Workshop on Exploring Modeling Methods for Systems Analysis and Design (EMMSAD 2008), held in conjunction with the 20th Conference on Advanced Information Systems Engineering (CAiSE 2008), Montpellier, France, vol. 337, pp. 473–484. CEUR-WS.org, June 2008
17. Chen, P.P.: The entity-relationship model: towards a unified view of data. ACM Trans. Database Syst. 1(1), 9–36 (1976)
18. Coenen, A., van Gils, B., Bouvy, C., Kerkhofs, R., Meijer, S.: Business modeling experience for a state pension voluntary insurance case. In: van Bommel, P., Hoppenbrouwers, S., Overbeek, S., Proper, E., Barjis, J. (eds.) PoEM 2010. LNBIP, vol. 68, pp. 46–60. Springer, Heidelberg (2010). https://doi.org/10.1007/978-3-642-16782-9_4
19. Falkenberg, E.D., et al. (eds.): A Framework of Information Systems Concepts. IFIP WG 8.1 Task Group FRISCO, IFIP, Laxenburg, Austria (1998)
20. Halpin, T.A., Morgan, T.: Information Modeling and Relational Databases. Data Management Systems, 2nd edn. Morgan Kaufman, Burlington (2008)
21. Halpin, T.A., Proper, H.A.: Database schema transformation and optimization. In: Papazoglou, M.P. (ed.) ER 1995. LNCS, vol. 1021, pp. 191–203. Springer, Heidelberg (1995). https://doi.org/10.1007/BFb0020532
22. Hilgard, E.R., Bower, G.H.: Theories of Learning. Prentice Hall, Englewood Cliffs (1975)
23. Hoppenbrouwers, S., Wilmont, I.: Focused conceptualisation: framing questioning and answering in model-oriented dialogue games. In: van Bommel, P., Hoppenbrouwers, S., Overbeek, S., Proper, E., Barjis, J. (eds.) PoEM 2010. LNBIP, vol. 68, pp. 190–204. Springer, Heidelberg (2010). https://doi.org/10.1007/978-3-642-16782-9_14
24. Hoppenbrouwers, S.J.B.A.: A functionalist approach to conceptualisation. In: Proceedings of the Fourth International Workshop on the Language Action Perspective on Communication Modelling (LAP 2000), Aachener Informatik-Berichte, RWTH Aachen, Aachen, Germany (2000)
25. Hoppenbrouwers, S.: Asking questions about asking questions in collaborative enterprise modelling. In: Sandkuhl, K., Seigerroth, U., Stirna, J. (eds.) PoEM 2012. LNBIP, vol. 134, pp. 16–30. Springer, Heidelberg (2012). https://doi.org/10.1007/978-3-642-34549-4_2
26. Hoppenbrouwers, S.J.B.A., Bleeker, A.I., Proper, H.A.: Facing the conceptual complexities in business domain modeling. Comput. Lett. 1(2), 59–68 (2005)
27. Hoppenbrouwers, S.J.B.A., Proper, H.A.E., van der Weide, T.P.: A fundamental view on the process of conceptual modeling. In: Delcambre, L., Kop, C., Mayr, H.C., Mylopoulos, J., Pastor, O. (eds.) ER 2005. LNCS, vol. 3716, pp. 128–143. Springer, Heidelberg (2005). https://doi.org/10.1007/11568322_9
28. Hoppenbrouwers, S.J.B.A., Proper, H.A., van der Weide, T.P.: Formal modelling as a grounded conversation. In: Goldkuhl, G., Lind, M., Haraldson, S. (eds.) Proceedings of the 10th International Working Conference on the Language Action

Perspective on Communication Modelling (LAP 2005), pp. 139–155. Linköpings Universitet and Hogskolan I Boras, Linköping, Sweden, Kiruna, Sweden, June 2005

29. Hoppenbrouwers, S.J.B.A., Proper, H.A., van der Weide, T.P.: Towards explicit strategies for modeling. In: Halpin, T.A., Siau, K., Krogstie, J. (eds.) Proceedings of the 10th Workshop on Evaluating Modeling Methods for Systems Analysis and Design (EMMSAD 2005), held in conjunction with the 17th Conference on Advanced Information Systems (CAiSE 2005), Porto, Portugal, pp. 485–492. FEUP, Porto, Portugal (2005)

30. Hoppenbrouwers, S.J.B.A., Proper, H.A., van der Weide, T.P.: Understanding the requirements on modelling techniques. In: Pastor, O., Falcão e Cunha, J. (eds.) CAiSE 2005. LNCS, vol. 3520, pp. 262–276. Springer, Heidelberg (2005). https://doi.org/10.1007/11431855_19

31. Iacob, M.E., Jonkers, H., Lankhorst, M.M., Proper, H.A., Quartel, D.A.C.: ArchiMate 2.0 Specification. The Open Group (2012)

32. Krogstie, J.: A semiotic approach to quality in requirements specifications. In: Kecheng, L., Clarke, R.J., Andersen, P.B., Stamper, R.K., Abou-Zeid, E.S. (eds.) Proceedings of the IFIP TC8 / WG8.1 Working Conference on Organizational Semiotics: Evolving a Science of Information Systems, pp. 231–250. Kluwer, Deventer (2002)

33. Krogstie, J., Sølvberg, A.: Information Systems Engineering - Conceptual Modeling in a Quality Perspective. The Norwegian University of Science and Technology, Stockholm, Norway (2000)

34. Lakoff, G.: Women, Fire, and Dangerous Things: What Categories Reveal About the Mind. University of Chicago Press, Chicago (1997)

35. Lankhorst, M.M., Proper, H.A., Jonkers, H.: The anatomy of the archimate language. Int. J. Inf. Syst. Model. Des. (IJISMD) 1(1), 1–32 (2010). https://doi.org/10.1007/978-3-642-01862-6_30

36. Lankhorst, M.M., van der Torre, L., Proper, H.A.E., Arbab, F., de Boer, F.S., Bonsangue, M.: Foundations. Enterprise Architecture at Work: Modelling, Communication and Analysis. TEES, pp. 41–58. Springer, Heidelberg (2017). https://doi.org/10.1007/978-3-662-53933-0_3

37. van der Linden, D.J.T., Proper, H.A., Hoppenbrouwers, S.J.B.A.: Conceptual understanding of conceptual modeling concepts: a longitudinal study amongst students learning to model. In: Proceedings of the 2nd International Workshop on Cognitive Aspects of Information Systems Engineering (COGNISE 2014) (2014, To appear)

38. Moody, D.L.: The "Physics" of notations: toward a scientific basis for constructing visual notations in software engineering. IEEE Trans. Softw. Eng. 35(6), 756–779 (2009). https://doi.org/10.1109/TSE.2009.67

39. Semantics of Business Vocabulary and Rules (SBVR). Technical report dtc/06-03-02, Object Management Group, Needham, Massachusetts, March 2006

40. Pask, G.: Conversation, Cognition, and Learning: A Cybernetic Theory and Methodology. Elsevier, Amsterdam (1975)

41. Persson, A.: Enterprise Modelling in Practice: Situational Factors and their Influence on Adopting a Participative Approach. Ph.D. thesis, Department of Computer and Systems Sciences Stockholm University/Royal Institute of Technology, Kista, Sweden (2001)

42. Proper, H.A.: Grounded enterprise modelling. DaVinci Series, Nijmegen Institute for Information and Computing Sciences, Radboud University, Nijmegen, the Netherlands (2008)

43. Proper, H.A., Bleeker, A.I., Hoppenbrouwers, S.J.B.A.: Object-role modelling as a domain modelling approach. In: Grundspenkis, J., Kirikova, M. (eds.) Proceedings of the Workshop on Evaluating Modeling Methods for Systems Analysis and Design (EMMSAD 2004), held in conjunctiun with the 16th Conference on Advanced Information Systems 2004 (CAiSE 2004), vol. 3, pp. 317–328. Faculty of Computer Science and Information Technology, Riga, Latvia, June 2004

44. Proper, H.A., Verrijn-Stuart, A.A., Hoppenbrouwers, S.J.B.A.: Towards utility-based selection of architecture-modelling concepts. In: Hartmann, S., Stumptner, M. (eds.) Proceedings of the Second Asia-Pacific Conference on Conceptual Modelling (APCCM 2005), Newcastle, New South Wales, Australia. Conferences in Research and Practice in Information Technology Series, vol. 42, pp. 25–36. Australian Computer Society, Sydney, January 2005

45. Proper, H.A., van der Weide, T.P.: EVORM - a conceptual modelling technique for evolving application domains. Data Knowl. Eng. **12**, 313–359 (1994)

46. Proper, H.A., van der Weide, T.P.: Modelling as selection of interpretation. In: Mayr, H.C., Breu, H. (eds.) Modellierung 2006. Lecture Notes in Informatics, vol. P82, pp. 223–232. Gesellschaft für Informatik, Bonn, Germany, March 2006

47. Rothenberg, J.: The nature of modeling. Artificial Intelligence. Simulation & Modeling, pp. 75–92. Wiley, New York (1989)

48. Ruiz, J., Serral, E., Snoeck, M.: A fully implemented didactic tool for the teaching of interactive software systems. In: Hammoudi, S., Ferreira Pires, L., Selic, B. (eds.) Proceedings of the 6th International Conference on Model-Driven Engineering and Software Development, MODELSWARD 2018, Funchal, Madeira - Portugal, 22–24 January 2018, pp. 95–105. SciTePress (2018). https://doi.org/10.5220/0006579600950105

49. Sandkuhl, K., Stirna, J., Persson, A., Wißotzki, M.: Enterprise Modeling: Tackling Business Challenges with the 4EM Method. Springer, Heidelberg (2014). https://doi.org/10.1007/978-3-662-43725-4

50. Sedrakyan, G., Snoeck, M., Poelmans, S.: Assessing the effectiveness of feedback enabled simulation in teaching conceptual modeling. Comput. Educ. **78**, 367–382 (2014). https://doi.org/10.1016/j.compedu.2014.06.014

51. Serral, E., De Weerdt, J., Sedrakyan, G., Snoeck, M.: Automating immediate and personalized feedback taking conceptual modelling education to a next level. In: Tenth IEEE International Conference on Research Challenges in Information Science, RCIS 2016, Grenoble, France, 1–3 June 2016, pp. 1–6. IEEE (2016). https://doi.org/10.1109/RCIS.2016.7549293

52. Shannon, C.E., Weaver, W.: The Mathematical Theory of Communication. University of Illinois Press, Chicago (1949)

53. Spyns, P., Meersman, R., Jarrar, M.: Data modelling versus ontology engineering. ACM SIGMOD Rec. **31**(4), 12–17 (2002)

54. Stachowiak, H.: Allgemeine Modelltheorie. Springer, Heidelberg (1973). https://doi.org/10.1007/978-3-7091-8327-4

55. Thalheim, B.: The theory of conceptual models, the theory of conceptual modelling and foundations of conceptual modelling. In: Embley, D., Thalheim, B. (eds.) Handbook of Conceptual Modeling, pp. 543–577. Springer, Heidelberg (2011). https://doi.org/10.1007/978-3-642-15865-0_17

56. Thalheim, B.: Syntax, semantics and pragmatics of conceptual modelling. In: Bouma, G., Ittoo, A., Métais, E., Wortmann, H. (eds.) NLDB 2012. LNCS, vol. 7337, pp. 1–10. Springer, Heidelberg (2012). https://doi.org/10.1007/978-3-642-31178-9_1

57. Tohidian, I.: Examining linguistic relativity hypothesis as one of the main views on the relationship between language and thought. J. Psycholinguist. Res. **38**(1), 65–74 (2009)

58. Tulinayo, P.F., Hoppenbrouwers, S.J.B.A.S., Proper, H.A.E.: Integrating system dynamics with object-role modeling. In: Stirna, J., Persson, A. (eds.) PoEM 2008. LNBIP, vol. 15, pp. 77–85. Springer, Heidelberg (2008). https://doi.org/10.1007/978-3-540-89218-2_6

59. Tulinayo, F.P., van Bommel, P., Proper, H.A.: Enhancing the system dynamics modeling proces with a domain modeling method. Int. J. Coop. Inf. Syst. **22**(02), 1350011 (2013). https://doi.org/10.1142/S0218843013500111

60. Wilmont, I., Barendsen, E., Hoppenbrouwers, S.J.B.A., Hengeveld, S.: Abstract reasoning in collaborative modeling. In: Hoppenbrouwers, S.J.B.A., Rouwette, E.A.J.A., Rittgen, P. (eds.) Proceedings of the 45th Hawaiian International Conference on the System Sciences, HICSS-45; Collaborative Systems track, Collaborative Modeling minitrack. IEEE Explore, Los Alamitos (2012)

Author Index

Printed in the United States
By Bookmasters